"The hardships, challenges, and traged[...]
will inspire you to see how God does r[...]
who is fully committed to God and is willing to take risks. [...]
to discover Ekvall's courage, creativity, and resourcefulness and to see
how God used Ekvall to accomplish God's larger plan."

—**MIKE SOHM**, former director, Compassion and Mercy Associates

"It was a privilege for me to accompany David Jones into Tibet as he did
the research for this book. Seeing the mountains and terrain of the countryside brought a greater admiration for this third culture kid, Robert
Ekvall, who worked in this hostile environment. Jones has done a superb
job in researching hard-to-find resources to now make this story available to the mission world."

—**RON BROWN**, missions mobilizer

"*Brave Son of Tibet* reads like part missionary biography, part action-
adventure novel. Nothing boring here. David Jones refreshingly shows us
a real human behind the ministry hero. We're reminded that all Christian
lives include faith and doubt, devotion and detour, loss and pain, and yet
hope. God's ways—in us and through us—are mysterious, but he uses
them for his good purposes."

—**TIM CROUCH**, vice president, Alliance Missions

"*Brave Son of Tibet* narrates the fascinating life of Robert Ekvall, an MK
(child of missionaries) who became a successful missionary in China and
Tibet. Ekvall went on to serve as an intelligence officer in the US Army
and then as a university professor. David Jones has woven this MK's di-
verse life into an engaging narrative, which reads like a novel."

—**DAVID ANDRIANOFF**, retired missionary

"David Jones peels back the skin to expose a raw history hitherto untold
in such an integrated fashion. Drawing from original writings, he pieces
together an unforgettable depiction of life in far western China and Tibet
from the late-nineteenth to the mid-twentieth centuries. The depiction of
the intrepid—their lives, deaths, successes, and failures—are the stuff of
which today's superheroes only dare dream to equal."

—**GRACE JORDAN**, retired school teacher

Brave Son of Tibet

Brave Son of Tibet

The Many Lives of Robert B. Ekvall

DAVID P. JONES

Foreword by Stanley John

RESOURCE *Publications* · Eugene, Oregon

BRAVE SON OF TIBET
The Many Lives of Robert B. Ekvall

Resource Publications
An Imprint of Wipf and Stock Publishers
199 W. 8th Ave., Suite 3
Eugene, OR 97401

www.wipfandstock.com

PAPERBACK ISBN: 978-1-6667-6903-6
HARDCOVER ISBN: 978-1-6667-6904-3
EBOOK ISBN: 978-1-6667-6905-0

04/03/23

Unless otherwise indicated, all Scripture quotations are taken from The Authorized (King James) Version. Rights in the Authorized Version in the United Kingdom are vested in the Crown. Reproduced by permission of the Crown's patentee, Cambridge University Press

Cover Illustration: photograph by William D. Carlsen, permission by Robert Carlsen

Cover Design: Thomas W. Jones

Author Photo: Sean O'Connor

Dedicated to the memory of Robert B. Ekvall, a man whose amazing life, forgotten for decades, needs to be remembered again.

Robert B. Ekvall, 1939.

In addition, I dedicate this book to two men who helped champion the preservation of Robert Ekvall's amazing life story. Both of them, Ray Smith of Wheaton, Illinois, and John Weiss of Cutchogue, Long Island, New York, are "blood relatives." John is a grand-nephew and Ray is a first cousin-once-removed of the protagonist of *Brave Son of Tibet*. Their longtime encouragement helped push this project over the goal line, and I am grateful for their support.

Contents

List of Illustrations and Maps

Glossary of Place Names and Abbreviations

Burma (Myanmar)

Chengdu (Chengtu)

Chone (Choni, Jonê, Zhuoni)

Chongqing (Chongking, Chungking)

Dalat (in French Indo-China, Vietnam)

Denga (Diebu, Tewo)

Dragsgumna (Zagana, Stonebox Valley

Drangwa Valley (Robber Valley)—midway between Lhamo and Dragsgamna

French Indochina (Vietnam)

Golok (Golak, Golag)

Haiphong (port city of Vietnam)

Hami (Kumul)

Hanoi (capital of Vietnam)

Hehtsuh (Hezuo)

Hochow (Hezhou)

Kanchow (Zhangye)

Kansu (Gansu)

Koko Nor (Qinghai Lake, Blue Lake)

Kunming (Yunnan-fu)

Labrang, Siaho (Xiahe)

Lanchow (Lanzhou)

Lhamo (Taktshang Lhamo, Langmusi)

Lupa, (Lupa-si, Luba, Ka Che Xiang)

Minchow (Minhsien)

Nanjing (Nanking)

Ngawa (Ngaba, Aba)

OMA (Office of Military Attaché)

Paoan (Baoan)

Pao-shan (Paoshan, Paoshan)

Peking (Beijing)

Rongwo (Tongren)

Saigon (Ho Chi Minh City)

Shensi (Shaanxi)

Xinjiang (Sinkiang)

Sining (Xining)

Sichuan (Szechwan, Szechuan)

Suchow (Suzhou)

Sungpan (Songpan)

Ta-li, Tali (Dali)

Tangar, Dangar (Huangyuan)

Tachienlu, Dartsedo (Kanding)

Taktshang Lhamo (Langmusi)

Taochow Old City (Lintan)

Tienshui (T'ien-shui, Tianshui)

Tihwa (Urumchi)

Titao (Lintao)

Tun-huang (Dunhuang)

Turfan (Turpan)

Urmchi (Urumqi)

U-Tsang (Tibet, Xīzàng)

Xining (Sining)

Zagana, (Dragsgamna, Drags-gumna, Stonebox Valley)

Foreword

EVERYONE LOVES FAIRY TALES. We love them because we identify in some way with the characters of the story and wish for their story to be true for us also. We celebrate the themes of these stories: good wins over evil, the underdog pulls through, the long arc of justice is served, and they live happily ever after. The stories differ but the themes and narrative plot become predictable.

Can this be true of mission biographies? We love them for the stories of sacrifice, faithfulness, obedience to divine calling, wholehearted abandonment, utmost sacrifice, anguish and pain, the adventure and engagement with a new people, and devotion to a vision that we all hold dear: of the lost coming to know Christ.

The first half of Robert Ekvall's story promises every bit of the fairytale mission biography that we have come to expect. It captures the life of a man born to missionaries, who also received a calling to follow in the same footsteps of his parents as a missionary to China with a focus on northwest China and into Tibet. It follows the story of one who meets his future bride while studying for ministry at a Christian college. And captures the dynamics of missionary endeavor in the middle of the twentieth century through the Christian and Missionary Alliance.

Mission biographies provides rich narrative for analyzing key themes of twentieth century missions. One may especially trace the role of western mission interaction with regions undergoing transformation emerging into nation states and self-governance in the wider context of colonialism and rising post-colonialism. The role of missionaries as emissaries of the church and messengers of the gospel can easily become confused with the nations they represent and the cultures they bring with them. Also valuable for analysis is the emphasis given to topics related to exploration of new regions, travel, language acquisition, and establishing

a base for future ministry on the one hand, and evangelization, disciple-
ship, prayer, Bible translation, recruiting new workers and partnership
with indigenous leadership in the work of mission on the other hand.
Biographies tend to emphasize some of these themes more than others.
In an age of viewing missions as "going" or "sending" it is easy to fall cul-
prit to emphasize the travel and exploration themes, and not sufficiently
address the work of nurturing faith and building capacity of local faith
leaders. The inverse is also true that emphasis can be placed on transmis-
sion of faith without adequate emphasis on the challenge of language acquisition and transportation and clothing in hitherto untraveled regions.

Biographies also offer the opportunity to peer through the window
into personal interactions between the missionaries and the local people,
with special attention to how they are represented. The role of indigenous
workers in mission and their representation in the narrative and the im-
plicit superiority of the western missionaries are worthy of questioning.
The role of women and their place in the story warrants our attention as
description of the climate and expectation of twentieth century missions.

The dangers of pioneer mission work and the role of missionary
as explorers feature yet another theme. Horseback, yak-back, four-wheel
drive jeeps, and ships provided the common way of transportation. Yet
in the deep jungles and far away remote villages, away from healthcare
and with exposure to various illnesses, the foreign missionaries faced
perilous diseases with no medical care often their lives ending tragically.
The pain of loss of loved ones can't be expressed in mere figures as battle
losses. They leave caverns of anguish and grief, doubts, and questions,
often with little to no opportunity for wounded hearts to heal. The work
of member-care in recent years with attention to mental health counsel-
ing and spiritual formation rose to fill the gap of caring for the souls of
wounded international workers.

However, there is a second half to this mission biography which
does not follow the pattern of the fairy tales and the narrative plots that
we have come to expect. Is it possible for missionaries to lose faith? Stated
differently: is it possible for people who share faith to have no faith? What
is the role of tragedy in shaping doubt? What is the nature of unprocessed
grief and pain?

Loss of faith presents unique problems for Christian workers who
have devoted their education and vocation to being gospel workers. How
may these skills be repurposed in a non-religious context? Ekvall found
the answer in diplomacy and later in the academy bringing to his work

profound sensitivities for the local people and value for their life's aspirations. Giving voice to their culture, heeding their wisdom, addressing their concerns, and developing empathetic listening, these values became the core contribution of a missionary turned agent of the state.

Yet, superintending Ekvall's story is a reminder of the grace of God. In Wesleyan terms, prevenient grace describes the generosity of God in offering his presence and witness to hearts long before they become fully devoted disciples of Christ. It describes a guiding grace, an active hand of God upon lives nudging them toward his kindness, preparing them to be receptive to his love, and pointing them toward his redemptive purposes. That grace reminds us that mission work is no fairy-tale and missionaries are not heroes, but fully human beings experiencing the depth of sorrow and joy, loss and achievement, love and pain, and excitement and doubt. Yet leading them through it all is the faithful and kind generous grace of God who nudges each of us into his love and redemptive purposes for our lives.

Stanley John, PhD
Associate Professor of Intercultural Studies
Associate Dean for Global Initiatives
Alliance Theological Seminary, Alliance University

Preface

BRAVE SON OF TIBET: *The Many Lives of Robert B. Ekvall,* came about from an unexpected path taken several years ago after finishing a new biography of A. B. Simpson, *A. B.: The Improbable Founder of a Global Movement.* In my library, I discovered five old books huddled together on one of the shelve, all about Tibet. As a break from writing, I read them over the Christmas holidays. This deep dive eventually took me to Western China and the Gansu-Sichuan Provincial border region and three books about Tibet.

As I delved into the history of Christian missions in that region, I repeatedly came across the name and exploits of Robert B. Ekvall of the "Kansu-Tibetan Border Mission of The Christian and Missionary Alliance (KTBM)." I knew that he had written the words to Nyack College's (now Alliance University) school song, "Mount of Prayer and Blessing," and that he had worked among the Tibetan nomads of the border area. The more I read about his amazing life, the more I wondered why so little had been written about this forgotten "illustrious nobody."

As I began to dig into Ekvall's scattered biographical information, I discovered much previously unpublished material by him and others, covering distinct periods of his life. Yet, no single record had ever attempted to cover the full arc of his eighty-five years. Consequently, I decided to attempt remedying this gap in evangelical missions historiology, which turned out to be a challenging project lasting more than two years.

From the turn of the 19th century to the waning years of the Cold War, Robert B. Ekvall lived a remarkably full life worthy of its telling and our remembering. His story is one of call and commitment, courage, adventure, heroism, intrigue, sacrifice, suffering, tragedy and sorrow. Shattered faith and years of spiritual wandering gave place in his final years to restoration and peace with God and reconnection with his spiritual

family. This account does not fit neatly into the genre of heroic missionary hagiography, but is a story that amply displays the grace and grip of
God on the life of one of his called ones.

Acknowledgements

BOOK WRITING REQUIRES HOURS of research and reading before a word goes on the first page. This book would not have been written without the encouragement and aid of Mr. Ray Smith of Wheaton, IL. Ray and I have been "virtual friends" from some time in 2019 when I began work on *Only Thibet*, the first of a quartet of Tibet titles produced since then. Ray is a first-cousin-once-removed of Robert B. Ekvall and a fathomless fount of Ekvall family lore. Documents, photos, newspaper clippings, emails and a plethora of other material found their way from his files to my computer or mailbox. For his constant support and resources of information, I offer many thanks, and also John Weiss of Cutochogue, Long Island, New York.

The first time I saw the evocative photo of a horseman crossing an iconic Tibetan bridge, I thought, "That would make a great cover shot." What was meant to be came to be, and I thank Robert Carlsen, son of William D. Carlsen, one of the post-WW2 C&MA recruits to the Kansu-Tibetan Border Mission, who took the picture. Other Carlsen photos also appear in *Brave Son of Tibet*.

To avoid confusion, please note that there is another Carlson in the book, with an *o* and not an *e*. I extend thanks to Eric and Ted Carlson, sons of Robert Carlson, one of Ekvall's last visitors before passing in 1983, and grandsons of Edwin Carlson, Bob's closest friend on the mission field. They shared many of their Dad's photos, some of which appear in this book. I am also very grateful to the Carlsons for preserving their father's unpublished manuscript, *Breakthrough: The Story of Bob and Betty Ekvall*, a major source of information for this book.

Once again, this volume is a family affair, since my first proof reader and inquisitor of tortured text is my wife, Judy Jones. Many thanks, Dear, and please keep your eyesight. My oldest son, Thomas Jones, did the layout for the book cover and also produced the map that opens the book and one in Chapter 10. Many thanks Son.

I am also indebted to the "readers" for their patient work of plowing through the "rough draft" before the bumpy places had been polished into proper prose. Many thanks to all of you: Dr. Ronald Brown, Rev. Mike Sohm and Ms. Grace Jordan, with a special word of thanks to Mr. David Andrianoff and Mr. John Bray, who took it upon themselves to be copy-editors and whose work vastly improved the final product. God bless you and may your kind increase. Also, many thanks to Dr. Stanley Jordan of the Alliance Theological Seminary—Alliance University, who was so kind as to also write the Foreword. To all of you, may God bless you.

Introduction

AFTER EMBARKING ON WRITING this book, I quickly learned that it would not be an easy road. Many people have made "career changes" in their lifetime, but honestly, this man's life stretches the imagination. And what's more remarkable, it's all true! In the eighty-five years that Robert Ekvall walked this world, he married three times, followed three major career paths with several side trails tacked on during his active years. His was a long life, well-lived.

Organizing "The Many lives of Robert Ekvall" proved a daunting task. In chronological order: (1) He served on the West China-Gansu border as a missionary educator, linguist, evangelist, anthropologist-ethnologist, translator, researcher and writer for nineteen years. (2) Then, due to a massive tectonic shift in his life course, in World War II, he became a Captain in the U.S. Army, a combatant with "Merrill's Marauders," language liaison, and then Major in the US Army as an intelligence officer (read "spy"), military attaché and diplomatic interpreter, before retiring as a Lieutenant Colonel, after almost fourteen years of military-diplomatic service with the US Army. (3)Entering his sixth decade of life, he ventured into the rarified air of academia at the University of Washington-Seattle as a "been-there-done-that" Tibetologist, Tibetan language and culture instructor, mentor to Tibetan refugees, as well as a research associate and prolific writer of scholarly articles, academic and popular books on Tibet for sixteen years before retirement at seventy-four. He lived an active life in the Cascade Mountains of Washington until ill health forced him to a retirement home in Seattle and his passing in 1983 at the age of eighty-five.

While researching Ekvall's life, I discovered an interview with Robert Shuster of the Billy Graham Center Archives at Wheaton College with the following dialogue:

EKVALL: When somebody tries to get . . . when somebody tries to tell me that they want me to write an autobiography, *I say it's an impossibility.*

SHUSTER: Too big a task.

EKVALL: *Too complicated a task.*

"Complicated" accurately describes the process of tracking down books, unpublished manuscripts, magazine articles, taped interviews, letters, emails, and telephone calls, investing much time reading and wrestling the many sources into a cogent narrative of this complex story of God's amazing grace and His faithful grip on a life crushed by Job-like loss.

Missionary biographies often have a touch of "hagiography," dramatic accounts that seek to inspire the reader's admiration in light of the challenges confronted by the gospel messenger. This volume, full of adventure and true heroism, has many such experiences. Yet, the Ekvall story has some "Solomon" in it, i. e., one who knew God closely, yet later wandered away before renewing intimacy with his Lord late in life. *Brave Son of Tibet* follows a man serving God when he suffered successive death-blows which shook his faith, to the point of his "taking leave of God" for years. While never denying the faith, his trust in God strained to the point of breaking—but it did not.

In 1975, Nyack College (Alliance University) honored Ekvall, presenting him with the Alumnus of the Year award. Speaking to students and faculty gathered for the occasion, Ekvall wryly suggested a title for the autobiography he never wrote—*Better than He Deserved.* I believe that *Brave Son of Tibet: The Many Lives of Robert B. Ekvall* deserved to have been written years before, but for whatever reason, it was not. Perhaps those who knew him were "embarrassed" by some of the twists and turns in Ekvall's life. We often disapprove of behavior that does not fit our sense of evangelical propriety. However, none of us, no matter how blessed our lives might be, can claim any credit for whatever good God has accomplished through our lives. This volume tells the story of one who received an ample supply of that undeserved favor that we all desperately require for this life, and the next.

I sincerely hope that this book resurrects the memory of a man whose life should not be forgotten, not only for the amazing careers that he lea, but also for God's grip of grace on his life.

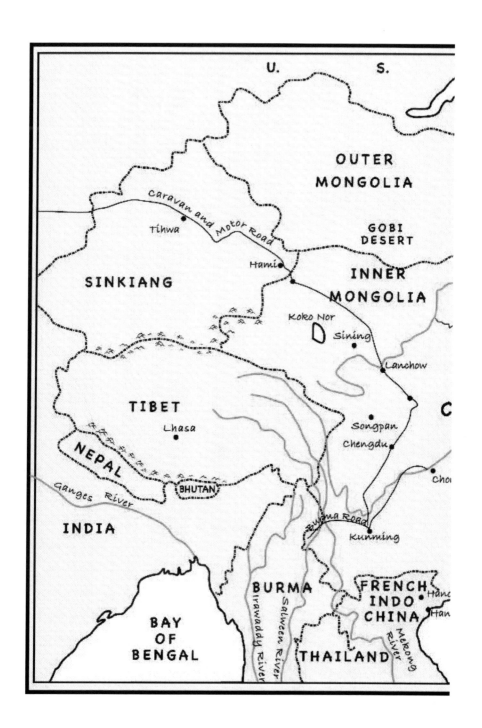

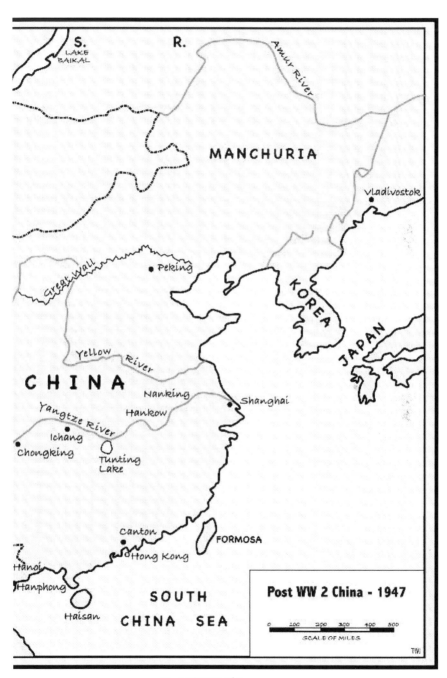

Post WW II China - 1947.

Chapter 1

How Do You Say?

T HE BREATHLESS BAND OF dark-haired youngsters crept nearer the wheat-blond, boy like iron filings to a magnet as he read from Daniel Defoe's *Robinson Crusoe*. Their almond eyes grew wide as the thin missionary kid (MK) interpreted Defoe's story for them. Chapter by chapter, young Bobby Ekvall wracked his two-track brain for equivalent Chinese words to transport his Chinese pals to Robinson's desert island and the harrowing tale of castaways, cannibals, captives and mutineers.

Ekvall later described his first attempt as an interpreter: "I remember, somewhat vaguely, my first experience in the search for semantic equivalents as I explained Robinson Crusoe, page by page and scene by scene, to my Chinese playmates, after which we staged, with the help of imagination and a packing case, a shipwreck in the [mission] back yard."[1] On another occasion, Bob reminisced about his life-long role as an interpreter: "And I knew that was going to be it, I supposed, when I was only a boy sitting with my Chinese playmates attempting to tell them in Chinese the story of 'Huckleberry Finn.' Can you imagine an American boy of five or six sitting around in the dirt of West China and explaining 'Huckleberry Finn' to a group of Chinese boys?"[2]

1

Helen and Bob Ekvall, circa 1907–8.

    Bob's parents, David and Helen Gailbraith Ekvall, who first met at the Missionary Training Institute (MTI), had moved from *Minchow (Minhsien)* to *Titao (Lintao),* a Chinese town farther east in Gansu Province. "Stone Bridge," the name of the street they lived on, was where Bob began to develop his amazing abilities as an interpreter. He described making friends with the boy next door, *Luh Shi San,* whose name means "Sixty-three," grandson of the kindly deaf lady who made treats for the boys. Young Bob's name was *Ngai Ming Shi,* or just *Ming Shi* (famous scholar) for short. His newfound neighbor pal had the "sweetest smile in all the city . . . ; it brought the big dimples into his cheeks and made his eyes twinkle most invitingly." The pale-faced MK, longed for a friend, and they soon became pals, the ringleaders of their neighborhood "gang" of barefoot youngsters racing around the muddy streets, acting out the story of *The Last of the Mohicans,* or just chasing kites on the nearby fields.

Bob Simply Flicked a Mental Switch

Born on the Sino-Tibetan borderland of multiple tribes and tongues, he was the son of David Ekvall, a Swedish immigrant and Helen Gailbraith from Syracuse, New York. Bilingual from earliest childhood, Bob Ekvall learned Chinese as his second mother tongue, picking up numerous dialects as he grew. He later described it as simply flicking a mental switch from one language to the other, like a train shifting from one track to another, only much faster. That bilingual background laid a solid foundation for a fruitful lifetime of searching on the spot for the perfect equivalent in English or Chinese. He grew up in "that happy bilingual state of semantic innocence" where the young interpreter does not consciously think about what he is doing. He simply spoke Chinese when appropriate and English when the case called for it.

Robert Brainerd Ekvall, born February 18, 1898, was delivered by Canadian missionary, Dr. Susie Rijnhart, in Minchow, Kansu Province, three-days travel on horseback southeast of the Tao-chow mission headquarters. There, his cousin, Margaret Simpson, daughter of W. W. Simpson and wife, Otilia, had just been brought into the world by Dr. Rijnhart's skilled hands.[3] A few months later after returning to their station at *Tangar (Dangar)*, far to the northwest, the Rijnharts looked forward to their long-planned journey into the heart of *Tibet (Xizàng)*. Dr. Susie and her husband, Petrus, set out on their ill-fated effort to reach Lhasa with their baby boy, Charlie. Both father and son died in the attempt, and Susie arrived months later near death at *Tachienlu (Dartsedo, Kanding)*, hundreds of miles to the southeast on the *Sichuan (Szechuan)* Province border in November 1898.

The revolt of Chinese nationalism against unjust treaties imposed by European powers erupted into the infamous "Boxer Rebellion" in 1899. It forced the Ekvalls and their Christian and Missionary Alliance (C&MA) counterparts to flee the wave of rage that killed hundreds of American and European missionaries and thousands of Chinese civilians. David Ekvall evacuated his family on a primitive single-sail *junk* that transported salt down a tributary of the Yangtse River to Chunking and then to Shanghai and boarded a ship for North America. After two years back in New Hampshire, they returned to China and back to Minchow.

Raised in the rough town of Minchow, his parents home-schooled Bob. His Swedish-born father, David, read to him daily from the classics, Norse and Greek mythology, drilled him in Latin and a smattering of

Swedish. His mother taught him to read and concluded each class with tea and cookies. Heavy doses of world history and English poets rounded out his literary education, turning Bob's into an avid reader.

Eventually, as the C&MA mission grew and other MKs came on the scene, a small school was opened in the frontier town of *Taochow Old City (Lintan)*, where Bob studied for two years. Alliance missionaries, W. W. Simpson and Grace Agar, both experienced in elementary education, divided teaching duties. Simpson's two older daughters, Margaret and Louise, and their younger brother, William Ekvall Simpson, were among the students. This delighted Bob since he and first cousin, "Will," were pals and sat near each other in the one-room school. Will's Mother, Otilia, was David Ekvall's younger sister.

In 1906, the mission assigned the Ekvalls to open a new station in Titao, about eighty miles northwest of Taochow, beyond a range of mountains separating them. Two years later, David Ekvall opened the Titao Bible School. While the Tibetan people proved unresponsive to the gospel, many Chinese in the region gave up their hybrid mix of Confucianism and Taoism and wholeheartedly accepted the message of salvation in Jesus Christ as Savior and Lord. As a result, God began calling some to serve who lacked training. These young workers eventually began preaching points and planting churches and the Ekvalls had oversight for the budding churches in the region.

Bob's father, David, had a flair for writing, with many of his articles printed in *The Alliance Weekly* magazine. In 1906, he wrote a collection of "sketches" about life in Western China published by The Alliance Press of New York. Asking patience from literary critics, he wrote: "Much of the material has been arranged on horseback . . . Some has been hastily jotted down during the silent hours of the night, by the aid of native illumination."[4] The book, *OUTPOSTS or Tibetan Border Sketches*, gives a rough historical review of Ekvall's arrival in Minhsien, east of the Tibetan border, in 1895 with his brother Martin, their first years and their later move to Titao. In eighteen short chapters, Ekvall described Gansu, towns visited, the opium scourge, stories of evangelistic efforts, the gradual growth of the church, Chinese and Tibetan culture and religious beliefs. The last two chapters, finally mention the Ekvall family and young "Robert."

In Chapter 18, "A Unique Pastoral Visit," David Ekvall recounts taking his family on a one hundred and sixty mile round-trip "pastoral visit" on horseback lasting eight days. In it, he wryly described the accommodations afforded travelers at the "roadside inns." They slept on elevated hollow brick platforms, *kangs,* heated by flammable refuse and cushioned by quilts brought by the traveler. For no extra charge, the kang came with uninvited company, the ubiquitous and unrelenting fleas.

The chilly March Sunday morning before the Ekvalls set out on their long journey, ten-year old Bob was baptized in the frigid Tao River. With that public commitment to faith in Christ, he joined three others as the first baptized Christians in Titao. Setting out, David and Helen had to ride slowly since Bob's donkey could only trot as fast as its short legs allowed. Bob proudly carried his 22 caliber rifle as did all male missionaries on the border, more as a visual deterrent for bandits than an offensive weapon.

On the first night, the family and their mounts all slept in the "inn's" open courtyard. Arriving late on the third day, they came to a fertile valley in the heavily Muslim Howchow district where one Christian family of farmers lived among the followers of the Prophet. Many, having never seen "foreign devils" from across the ocean, had strange ideas. Young Bob, upon dismounting, fell to the ground, immediately getting up while trying to hide his embarrassment. One of the villagers exclaimed: "I told you so." They had been discussing whether foreigners had knee joints or not; one villager insisted that a foreigner once fallen to the ground would be unable to get up without help. Bob's rapid response to his fall quickly disabused their naïve notion.

On that prolonged pastoral visit, Bob learned a new dialect, a valuable talent which turned into a lifelong avocation. As his father wrote: "The acquisition and frequent use of a few of their localisms will very much facilitate intercourse with those ignorant villagers, whose world has been so circumscribed. These childhood experiences would stand Bob in good stead in later life. The many unique dialects became part of his lifelong language learning.

Will and Bob, first cousins, grew up living in towns about eighty miles apart; Will in Taochow and Bob in Titao. Daily they played with their Chinese buddies and saw Tibetans from time to time, either the wild and wooly nomad tribesmen from the mountains to the south or the more peaceful farmers that lived in the foothills across the Tao River. Every year, the Simpson and Ekvall families met at the annual Kansu Tibetan Border Mission Conference where the adults discussed ministry issues as well as being fed spiritually. Meanwhile, the cousins and other MKs had ample time for children's meetings and playing together.[5]

Bob was two years eight months older than Will, who was quieter and more introverted. As his older sister, Margaret remarked: "Will . . . lived from babyhood on to teenager state on the Tao-Chow Mission Station. Missionaries who remember him during those years agree that he was an unusually silent child who kept his thoughts to himself to a remarkable degree . . . ."[6]

Robert Was a Most Resourceful and Happy Individual

Margaret's description of Bob differs greatly:

> We would be inclined to pity the child for his lonely state but Robert was a most resourceful and happy individual. Lacking playmates of his own race, he played with Chinese children and does not remember a time when he could not speak their language . . . . In his father David, he found an enthusiastic guide to the joys of scholarship as well as to the outdoor sports that American boys loved.[7]

Despite the rigors of West China's spartan lifestyle, poor communication with the outside world and the slow progress of their efforts, the missionary families on the border trusted God to empower them for their mission as in the days of the early church. On April 6, 1906 in Los Angeles, California, it seemed that the much-prayed-for "new Pentecost" had come in a powerful revival marked by healings, salvation, Spirit infilling and gifts of the Spirit. This awakening fell upon the humble Azusa Street Mission led by African-American preacher, William Seymour.

Quickly, word of the revival traveled across North America. A. B. Simpson, founder of the C&MA, headquartered in New York, read of the movement in the newspapers.

He, along with other evangelical leaders, welcomed the news from the West Coast. However, in less than a year, Simpson and these same leaders observed an unhealthy emphasis on the spiritual gifts accompanying the Spirit-baptism experience. In particular, the gift of "other tongues," as found in Acts 2, became the major focus. Simpson and many others had long prayed for a powerful move of the Spirit to empower the church to fulfill the Great Commission and bring about the return of Christ. This troubling imbalance of one particular gift rather than the gift Giver created a major schism among evangelicals the world over.

Meanwhile, back on the borderland, the hardness of the Tibetan soul soil had driven the Kansu Tibetan Border Mission (KTBM) team to pray for supernatural "power from on high" to reach this unresponsive people. Many prayed for "Pentecost" and just one year later, in April 1908, breakthrough seemed to have occurred at the Minchow conference. Several outstanding conversions and answers to prayer were reported. One member of David Ekvall's Titao church publicly burned a book on necromancy; secret sins were confessed; reconciliation took place and many were healed. More than four hundred townsfolk packed the gospel hall with another four hundred at the windows trying to hear. Follow up meetings were planned for Taochow and Chone (Jonê); years of tears and persistent prayer had softened hard hearts.

Yet, a spurious manifestation of tongues at the same Minchow conference brought confusion to those gathered, halting God's blessing for almost two days until a false spirit had been identified and driven out of one of the local Christians. Then, the meetings proceeded with more conversions and healings. This first encounter with the newly-minted Pentecostal phenomenon stirred the mission to seek more of God, keeping a clear-eyed lookout for false fire while pursuing "genuine gold."

In hindsight, this experience at Minchow proved a watershed event. The mission staff unanimously accepted all of the gifts of the Holy Spirit as biblical and valid for the church, as did Simpson and the Alliance. No "Cessassionists" were numbered among the KTBM. Yet, the "evidence doctrine" of tongues became the edge of a wedge that eventually split the mission.

Bob, a bright and observant ten year-old, doubtless saw the growing rift. His uncle, W. W. Simpson, became the voice of the "tongues camp" while his father, David, came to be one of its most vocal opponents. Gradually over the next few years, the mission alternated between times of spiritual refreshing and strained relationships as W. W. Simpson asserted the necessity of the "sign gift," despite not yet having spoken in tongues.

Threats of physical danger followed the 1911 overthrow of the Qing Empire and the establishment of the Republic of China, Sickness and deaths of staff members and the ensuing strain on those remaining overwhelmed the mission staff and drove them to seek God. At last, on May 5, 1912, W. W. Simpson "received the baptism in the Spirit with tongues. Simpson's wife and children, William Christie's wife Jessie and ten year-old son, Milton, Mrs. David Ekvall, and, over the next several months, about a hundred people from the mission soon also received spirit baptism with tongues."[8]

Bobby Ekvall and Cousins, circa 1910.

David Ekvall wrote in the March 23, 1912 *Alliance Weekly*, of "The Present Conditions of Foreigners in Kansu," noting that seventeen foreigners had been killed by mobs in another province as a result of the overthrow of the corrupt Qing Empire. Those living on the Kansu border region were isolated, thus receiving no mail for months. Fortunately, the China Inland Mission treasurer provided emergency funds to tide the KTBM team over until their normal monthly allowances arrived by mail. Despite these difficulties, God blessed and the work went on. Revival had been experienced in several areas. In February, two students of the Titao Bible School from the first graduating class of six, received the Spirit and spoke in tongues. David Ekvall, believing the manifestation spurious, rebuked them. One replied that he should not resist the Spirit of truth. With even his parents apparently divided regarding tongues, Robert likely sensed the fracture in his family's unity in those challenging days.

Death Seemed to Stalk the Mission

Nineteen twelve proved to be a particularly painful year for the KTBM workers, with, in rapid order, the death of Elizabeth Ekvall, daughter of Martin and Emma Ekvall (Bob and Will's first cousin), from scarlet fever. A few days later, five-year old Mary Simpson, Will's little sister, died from the same dreaded fever. W. W. Simpson also contracted typhus and barely survived. Death seemed to stalk the mission.

Less than a month after the first students graduated from Titao Bible School in April, Bob's dad, David Ekvall, founder and principal teacher, died on May 18 from typhoid fever contracted from Chinese Muslim soldiers fleeing fighting in Central China. David went out to share the gospel with the tired troops camping near Titao. Despite the brevity of his visit, the deadly "camp fever," typhus, took David's life three days later. Helen, Robert and little Alice, due to distance and poor communications, grieved alone for three days before the nearest missionaries could arrive to help and comfort them.

Subsequently, Mrs. Ekvall and her children went to Chone on the Tibetan border to live with the William Christies. The July KTBM conference held in Minchow was attended by just six adult missionaries and their children. The tragic deaths of David Ekvall, age forty-two, and the two mission children, weighed heavily on the group. Six of their colleagues had already left for furlough, leaving those remaining stunned but clinging to God's promises. Yet, at that moment in their weakness, God met those gathered in a powerful way by the presence of His Holy Spirit:

> While the missionaries were gathered at Luba Si in loneliness, yet conscious in a unique way of the presence of God, blessing came to the local Tibetan and half-Tibetan community. The sick were healed, demons were cast out, and the Tibetan homes cleaned of every vestige of idolatry. Salvation flowed into the village of Luba. Idols were burned, idol scrolls were destroyed and the rubbish of charms and hoary shrines tossed into the Tao River which carried away the wreckage and then became the waters of baptism for those who publicly confessed their Lord. Humanly speaking, at the most unlikely of times, salvation crossed the borders.[9]

Encouraged in heart and comforted by their missionary family, Helen, Bob, age fourteen and four-year old Alice, left in mid-August traveling to Shanghai. There, they boarded ship and returned to a land that Bob had last seen at age four and barely remembered.

Chapter 2

Learning America

AFTER HELEN AND HER children arrived on the West Coast late in early fall 1912, they traveled by train across a land with vastly different scenery than what they had just seen in their journey across China. In about five days, they reached the East Coast and visited the C&MA "headquarters" in New York City before spending time with Helen's sister in Binghamton, New York and the Ekvall family in New Hampshire.

After years of life among the Chinese and border Tibetans in the dry and dusty hard-scrabble land of West China, the forests and gentle mountains of Northeastern USA comforted Helen as Bob and Alice adjusted to a new land and a much different way of life than life in Western China.

In February 1913, Bob enrolled in Wilson Academy in Nyack, New York and began his studies having just turned fifteen years old. Wilson Academy, founded by A. B. Simpson in 1906, offered quality Christian high school education. The Simpson's home was located on the lower slope of the Nyack "hillside," not far from the Wilson Academy. The students often saw the aging president of the C&MA walking up the hill from the Nyack train station to his home or climbing the long stairs up to the Administration building, later called Simpson Hall, for his evening classes at the Missionary Training Institute.

Bob described his entrance to the teen culture of the day. "I had my first contact, you might say, with the youth of America. I probably would have become a recluse and with very good grades and completely out of the swing because, to begin with, my vocabulary [was] the vocabulary of an educated adult, but fortunately I was crazy about athletics and that put me right into the swing of American students."[10] A few of Bob's MK comrades also studied at Wilson during his time there, "the ones that wore glasses and studied in corners and had fantastic grades . . . ." Because of Bob's athletic prowess, his gregarious personality and his parent's dedicated home schooling while on the field, he was spared the isolation and pain that many missionary kids face upon return to their parent's homeland. He soon became fluent in the "American dialect" spoken by his academy classmates.

Alice, Helen and Bob Ekvall, 1912.

Bob entered a high school begun for children of missionaries, pastors and Christians to have a superior academic experience without the withering effects of "godless" secular education. For this serious blond MK, who "talked like an adult," learning America challenged him as he tried to find his place in the classrooms and boy's dorm. His pals in school, the MacArthur boys, were sons of "Daddy MacArthur," long-time friend and colleague of A. B. Simpson. One son, Charles, later became a famous Broadway playwright and husband of the "First Lady of American Theatre," Helen Hayes. The other, John, became a successful businessman in insurance and Florida real estate, making him one of the early mega-millionaires of 20th century America and founder of the MacArthur Foundation.

Bob did very well at Wilson, quickly learning how to play basketball and tennis. His outgoing personality and excellent educational grounding from his parents and the Taochow school helped him excel. During the boring summer months following their second year at Wilson, Charles and Bob decided to swim the Tapaan Zee, a 3¾ mile wide stretch of the Hudson River. First, Charles swam from Nyack to Tarrytown, becoming the youngest man to swim the river. Next day, Bob did the same from Tarrytown to Nyack and set a new record. Charles's feat made the newspapers, but Bob's didn't because World War I broke out on the same day, July 28, 1914, and grabbed all the headlines.

Bob Finished with High Grades in June 1916

During his senior year, one of Bob's classmates from Florida, asked Bob to go along with him since both loved playing tennis. Walter Turnbull, the school director and one of Bob's teachers, seeing how Bob excelled in his studies, permitted Bob to go with his friend for an extended vacation, from January 1 to April 1. Turnbull told Bob to take his textbooks to keep up with his classwork and prepare for the rigid New York Board of Regents final exam required of all graduates. So, Bob went south with his friend, played plenty of tennis, studied hard and passed his Regents with flying colors. After three years at Wilson Academy, Bob finished with high grades in June 1916, a gangly six feet tall, all gristle and stringy muscle. Due to financial restrictions and a decreasing student body brought on by the ongoing war in Europe, the Academy closed in 1917 and was turned into married student's housing for the MTI.

Despite Professor Turnbull's urging Bob to enter the Missionary Training Institute and take the two-year course, then return to West China at the tender age of eighteen, Bob had other plans. Like his father, David, who received a call to go to Tibet after hearing Simpson preach about the dearth of the gospel there, Bob also had decided that he would return to the Kansu Tibetan border as a missionary. However, he chose to go to Wheaton College first for two reasons. One was practical; his mother, Helen, had moved there and served as a "house mother" for Wheaton's students. While Wheaton was not "home" for Bob, his mother and younger sister, Alice, were there, and he had seen little of them while at Wilson Academy.

He knew Wheaton stood out among Christian colleges in the United States as a place of scholarship and serious study coupled with a strong evangelical reputation. By this time, fundamentalism in North America had grown; and the Alliance, like many other groups, looked upon higher education with reservations. They had seen European liberal theology contaminate major American Protestant denominations, once orthodox in theology. That infection began in their seminaries and colleges. While The C&MA never identified officially with the fundamentalist movement, a number of sympathizers existed within the Alliance. As a result, in 1914, Dr. Charles Blanchard, second president of Wheaton College, personal friend of A. B. Simpson and honorary Vice President of the C&MA, proposed to the Alliance Board of Managers that Wheaton be recognized as the approved school for MTI students from the Alliance who desired to go on for higher education. This the board approved and the arrangement continued for decades.

Bob Ekvall, upper right, at Wilson Academy, 1915.

Bob decided to attend Wheaton first, and then get his Alliance "finishing" at Nyack. He felt that he needed to learn how to learn, how to then find and access resources and, thus, organize the knowledge to make it useful. These considerations led him to finalize his decision to attend Wheaton, then back to the MTI and off to West China, a little older and wiser.

Like the majority of students in pre-student loan days, he worked his way through college. He completed his four-year B. A. in English in three years, taking off two semesters to work, before graduating with honors in 1920. Despite a heavy academic schedule, he lettered in basketball, football and track. In addition he joined a literary society, sang in the Glee Club and took up boxing and wrestling. He even managed to date classmate Betty Fischer, a quiet brunette and granddaughter of Wheaton's founder. Apparently the gentle coed caught the eye of the energetic athlete-scholar, and a life-long love relationship developed. His long career as a writer began in college where he learned to write well under the exacting English Department. He went on to win prizes for short stories in college competitions. Likely, today, he would be labeled an "overachiever."

Bob Was Due to Ship Out to France

The summer before his junior year, Bob worked in Florida. Earlier in the year, April 1917, the United States entered World War I as an ally with the British and French against Germany and the Central Powers (Austria-Hungary, The Ottoman Empire and Bulgaria). At that time, the U.S. Army numbered a mere 100,000, one twentieth the size of Germany's army. Consequently, mass enlistment began, and colleges became training centers for a much-needed officer's corps. Bob returned to Wheaton at the end of the summer and joined the Army, entering officer's training school at Fort Sheridan just north of Chicago. Arriving after the course had started, Bob did not receive an officer's commission but left Fort Sheridan as a "Top Sergeant." He returned to Wheaton to help run the Student Training Corp unit with more than forty students under two lieutenants. "To accommodate them, the gymnasium was converted into barracks; and soon the College Campus was much like a camp."[11] During that semester, he helped train students for the war effort. When the Armistice came about, effectively ending hostilities on November 11,

1918, Bob was due to ship out to France within a few weeks to serve with a horse artillery unit. Thus, he was able to complete his final year after serving "two short months" in the Army.[12]

Bob Ekvall—Wheaton ROTC, 1917.

Following graduation in 1920, Ekvall got a job at a nearby Western Electric Company factory as an administrative trainee. In order to earn extra cash for marriage and return to Nyack to complete his missionary training, Bob did free-lance writing doing book reviews for the *Chicago Daily News*. Bob's boss at Western Electric noticed his name on one of the reviews. Realizing that he had a valuable asset in his office, he asked Bob to create a mock-up for a company house organ and was given two weeks off to create two sample issues. The resulting product so impressed his boss that he offered Bob the job as editor of the periodical with a small staff, an office, a good salary and a steady job.

The tempting opportunity was hard to turn down since he and Betty would soon marry and could use the funds. Yet, he politely refused, explaining that they both were enrolled at the Missionary Training Institute for a year before leaving for China. Fortunately, the attractive young couple had caught the attention of the new president of the C&MA, Rev. Paul Rader, pastor of the nearby Moody Church in Chicago. A dynamic, take-charge leader, Rader helped smooth the way for Bob and Betty to enter Nyack.

They married on October 6, 1921. On the same day, after their reception, they boarded a cross-country train for New York and the Missionary Training Institute on the slopes of South Nyack, just two years after A. B. Simpson's death in the fall of 1919. They were about a month late for the fall semester but quickly caught up with their senior classmates. Bob and Betty settled into life at the MTI, walking in the woods up to Balance Rock overlooking the beautiful Hudson River that Bob had swum just a few years previously.

As part of Rader's arrangement to help Bob and Betty with their expenses at Nyack, Bob was made athletic director. He played and coached basketball and wrestling during his year at Nyack, with the result that his strenuous activities as coach and player wore him down from a lean 169 lbs. to a reed-thin 146 lbs.!

Included in their tailor-made program of study, Bob and Betty took several Bible courses, Church history and finished the required curriculum readying them for China. Bob later reminisced in an interview with the VP for Public Affairs at Nyack, Rev. John Taylor, that he recognized, once on the field, that he had not studied enough theology. However, the C&MA "Headquarters" in New York City approved their deployment after one year at the MTI. With the agreement of the KTBM missionaries, the Board assigned Bob to direct the Titao Bible School founded by his father. Since he spoke Chinese, and was known and loved as the only son of David Ekvall, the decision seemed obvious to all. Thus, before leaving America, the Ekvall's future was sure.

One of the Music Department profs, having seen some of Bob's poetry posted on a bulletin board, had encouraged him to try his hand at writing a school song for the MTI. The result was the poem, *Mount of Prayer and Blessing,* set to Elgar's *Pomp and Circumstance,* which became one of Nyack's prized traditions, sung at graduations and other special occasions. At the end of the year of study, the senior class elected Bob, a fifth-year transfer, as class president. He ended up in the graduation ceremony as one of the student speakers.

A year and a half after graduating from Wheaton, Bob's qualities as a natural leader with a privileged intellect and amazing physical endurance were put on full display. His peers and those his senior perceived that this young man and his quiet wife promised much as they set off for Western China.

On December 7, 1922, after a time of saying their "goodbyes" to family and friends in Wheaton, the young couple began a cross-country train trip. In Omaha, Nebraska, they stopped and were made members of the Omaha Gospel Tabernacle and farewelled in grand style. The pastor, Rev. Robert "R. R." Brown, a dynamic leader, had met young Robert Ekvall and realized that he and his wife represented a new generation committed to reaching Tibet, the forbidden land that had caught Simpson's attention a generation before. For that reason, he had invited them to visit. The Omaha Gospel "Tab" would prove to be a faithful support church during their years on the field.

Bob and Betty Ekvall, circa 1922.

Mr. and Mrs. Robert Ekvall Stopped, Enroute to the Coast

As reported in *The Alliance Weekly*, January 20, 1923:

> Two very interesting missionary farewell services were held in
> Omaha recently. The first, for Rev. and Mrs. Martin Ekvall [Rob-
> ert Ekvall's uncle, older brother of his deceased father David]
> and their children who spent a day enroute to China. Greetings
> were held in the Y. M. C. A. [and] Y. W. C. A. and the Calvary
> and First Swedish Baptist churches. Two days ago, Mr. and Mrs.
> Robert Ekvall stopped, enroute to the coast. This splendid young
> couple is going out to the field supported by and representing the
> Omaha branch. A very impressive service was held in our own
> tabernacle at which they were made members of the branch and
> publicly dedicated to the Lord by the committee. It was the first
> service of its kind many of our people had ever seen. On Satur-
> day night an informal farewell reception was held at the home
> of Mr. and Mrs. W. W. Bradley, after which a large company of
> young people accompanied the Ekvalls to the station where they
> sang good-byes and gave them a warm sympathetic farewell.
> Deep and lasting blessing came from those services.

Chapter 3

Steps on the Way

FOLLOWING THEIR HEART-FELT SENDOFF from new-found friends at the Omaha Gospel Tabernacle, the Ekvalls boarded the train at the Union Station in downtown Omaha, sat back and enjoyed the remainder of their train trek across America. They traversed the rolling plains to Denver, over the Rockies to Salt Lake City, then passing through Reno and Sacramento down to San Francisco where they boarded their ship for China. Bob was returning home; but Betty found it all new, exciting and more than a little challenging. The two weeks voyage gave them a much-needed rest before the long journey across China.

Upon arrival at Shanghai's busy port, Bob supervised the retrieval of their bags and boxes. When the dockworker carelessly manhandled the baggage Bob burst out in fluent Chinese, clearly telling the worker to be more careful. After ten years away from China, his second language surfaced quickly, with his brain automatically flipping the switch from English to Chinese. The next day, Bob gave his testimony at a local church and put to rest any concern about being able to manage the trip from the coast to the Tibetan border.

The "Honorable" Son Had Brought Back a Young Wife

The grueling trip from the coast to the Kansu border by boat and carts took more than two months. Betty drank in the newness of it all, thankful that her China-born husband, had things under control. Finally, arriving in Titao, mission headquarters of the C&MA mission in April 1923, they received a royal welcome from local believers. The "honorable" son of their beloved Pastor and Teacher, David Ekvall, had brought back a young wife, the dark-eyed, lovely brunette, Betty. The newcomers quickly settled into their roles with the Kansu-Tibetan Border Mission, focusing on ministry to the Chinese. As Bob described it:

> We lived in homey comfort in a little house behind the Bible School compound, for soon after our arrival we were able to set up our own *menage* [household]. Our days were full of work and achievement: Betty soon began to match me in familiarity with the strangely meaningful ideographs, and with gentle smile and low level voice, made her contact with the Chinese women of the church and the guests that came to see the 'new daughter-in-law' in the family of the elder pastor Ekvall, a characterization that gave her a standing quite out of the ordinary for a newcomer . . .[13]

On June 5, just two months after their arrival, Bob was asked to travel east one hundred *li* (about 33 miles) to help returning KTBM missionary, Jens Rommen and wife, Katherine, travel the last miles to Titao. Rommen, one of the most accomplished workers on the KTBM staff, had returned to the field despite poor health, to continue a new effort to access the hard-to-reach Tibetans. About a week after their arrival in Titao, Rommens, fluent in Chinese and Tibetan, succumbed to his illness and died. William Christie, veteran field chairman, had looked forward to his return, expecting Jens to take over as the new field leader. This sad event gave the Ekvalls a premonition of the battle before them. Jens Rommen's wife, Katherine, served with her little daughter, completing her term of service before furlough several years later.

Bob and Betty Ekvall had arrived at a key moment in the mission's history. In 1919, after A. B. Simpson's death, the new C&MA president, Rev. Paul Rader of Chicago, brought a renewed sense of urgency to the Alliance. He called for more male candidates to match the number of single-women serving hard-to-reach peoples in hard places. Shortly before Bob and Betty's arrival in 1923, the KTBM mission had three new male recruits on the field: M. G. Griebenow, Stan Harrison and Charles Koenigswald. Their fiancées soon followed with the agreement that they could marry after two years on the field and successful completion of language study. That mission policy encouraged the new recruits to study hard and learn fast. The new candidates focused primarily on reaching

Tibetans. When Bob came back to China with Betty, he returned as "a son of the field" with high expectations and a pre-determined career path in Chinese ministry.

Within a few weeks of arrival in Titao, the mission installed Bob, just twenty-five years old, as director of the Titao Bible School. At the same time, he began to study the complex Chinese ideographic writing system, which he had not learned as a boy. He also worked on developing a more appropriate adult vocabulary. While maintaining the colloquial language of the people for everyday use, he studied to acquire proper academic Chinese as befitting the Principal of the Bible School founded by his father more than a decade earlier.

Bob took on a full class load: church history, theology, calisthenics and Chinese martial arts, as well as teaching English once a week at a nearby government high school. He continued his language study and passed four difficult language exams over the next two years. To practice his growing fluency, Bob preached in outlying villages on Sundays. He also served as the youngest member of the Field Executive Committee. Bob's intellectual and linguistic gifts, high energy level and built-in-knowledge base gave him exceptional opportunities for one his age.

Born and raised in China, Bob's perspective on mission policies and practices contrasted with the viewpoint of his Ex Com colleagues. Bob did not agree with the ideas of the church leaders and Bible School faculty just because of his fluency in the language.

> As a member of the [KTBM] Executive Committee, I had a part in evaluating proposals and requests from the leaders of the indigenous church. Those suggestions might at times seem strange, or even slightly outrageous, to my fellow missionaries; but to me they would appear to be quite reasonable and made good Chinese sense in a Chinese context. I was, it is true, occasionally twitted—in all good fellowship—with being half Chinese and 'thinking yellow.'[14]

Bob's role as a "half Chinese" missionary and Bible School director required him to straddle the two cultures, an often uncomfortable stance. It embarrassed Bob to act as Principal of the Bible school. The Vice-Principal, Paul Keo, a middle-aged Christian scholar who had once cared for David Ekvall's horses and took Bob swimming as a boy, showed himself as a superior teacher and a much more capable administrator who clearly merited the position. Paul accepted the mission's decision, but it did not sit well with Bob, recognizing the cautious paternalism of his missionary colleagues. Bob knew that this kind of thinking's days were numbered. The release of leadership to nationals in the growing Chinese church needed to be done, and the "three-self" indigenous principles implemented.

Bob Was the Natural Choice

Bob expected to spend the rest of his missionary career walking in the footsteps of his father, David Ekvall, and seen by his Chinese brethren as "one of them," not over them. The three new Tibet-field recruits would carry the gospel across the border, taking Jens Rommen's place. Bob and Betty would labor on in Titao. Still, something tugged at their heart, that is, the seemingly impossible challenge of reaching Tibetans with the gospel, the original purpose of the Kansu-Tibetan Border Mission. Lack of results for more than two decades had given preference to the "Chinese work," due to their surprisingly ready response. This improbable pull on Bob and Betty's hearts led to "unthinkable" thoughts. Bob was the natural choice for the "Chinese work, and the C&MA headquarters in New York and field Ex Com had already made the decision. Yet . . . but . . . maybe God had other ideas.

The 1923 Annual Conference of the KTBM missionaries took place at the border town of *Chone*, located on the Tao River and home of the Prince, *Lobzang Tendzin Namguel Trinle Dorge* (1899- 1937), a despotic hereditary chief over forty-eight clans. The mission had purchased a large "haunted house," considered so because someone had been murdered in it. Field chairman William Christie had purchased it from the owners for a good price since no Tibetan would live in a "cursed" residence. Thus, the mission house in Chone hosted the conference with every room and cubby hole occupied by the growing mission staff.

Betty had won Bob's heart at Wheaton because of her zest for life and love of adventure, despite being raised in a genteel home. She loved horse-back riding and outdoors activities like camping and hiking. As a result, the "youngsters" decided to ride to the mission conference, from Titao to Chone, about eighty miles as the crow flies. However, crows in that mountainous region rarely fly in a straight line. Their overland trek took them over the rugged Min Shan mountains. Setting out with two horses and a helper with a baggage mule, they camped out each night. To save time and cross over the border into Tibetan country, they took a short cut. On the third day, following a zig-zag trail up a steeply-wooded slope, they rode along a path on the ridge line before cautiously descending to a shallow bog-filled valley that tried the mule's footwork and energy. Looking for a place to stop, they spied the red and white checked *Charkhi* monastery perched halfway up the hill overlooking the sheltered valley.

While close to Taochow and hoping to get there before dark, Ekvall's party had to stop because the heavily-loaded mule could not go farther. They freed the animals to pasture before setting up their little tent. They planned to prepare a simple meal, then another night in their little tent before setting out the next morning. However, as soon as they stopped in the marshy valley, a line of novice monks in their dirty wine-colored robes came tumbling down the grassy hill chattering away in Tibetan, which meant nothing to the travelers. Mutual confusion reigned.

Then another monk, a few years older, walked over and spoke in halting Chinese. "You can't stay here . . . too dangerous . . . lots of thieves at night. You come up . . . be my guest and I will be your . . . ," he searched for a word, finally coming up with "master." This introduced the Ekvalls to the "host/guest" arrangement that made travel and relationship with Tibetan nomads possible in a land lacking inns and roadside eateries.

In a few minutes, many hands made light work of their baggage, and Bob and Betty found themselves taken to the young monk's cloister where they were given tea and *tsampa* before being taken to guest quarters. At the evening meal, Bob and Betty learned more about tsampa, a Tibetan staple made of roasted barley flour mixed with Chinese brick tea, yak butter and salt. They were shown how to mix a sizeable slab of butter into their wooden bowl of tea. This they drank while blowing the floating butter to one side. After a few bowls of tea, their host added the barley flour, mixed by hand to the consistency of modeling clay. Gravel-like sun-dried cheese was sprinkled into the bowl and mixed with the barley-ball. Tsampa was a staple of Tibetan life.

With little knowledge of Tibetan etiquette and unable to communicate, Bob presented a few Tibetan gospel tracts wrapped in a white silk "felicity scarf," a *khata*, both a calling card and proper covering for offering a gift to a Tibetan host. The few silver dollars slipped in the modest present brought a smile of appreciation to the monk's face. Later, the sonorous sound of monks chanting their nightly mantras serenaded them to sleep. The double-bass drone of the older monks overpowered the boyish voices of the novices. The morning wake-up call echoed the monotonous repetition of *Om Mani Padme Um,* the murmured mantra repeated countless times across Tibet at thousands of temples and monasteries, every day.

The next morning, after more tea and tsampa, Bob tried out his first Tibetan phrase, *thu-je-che,* or "thank you," to the monk's approving smiles as they waved goodbye to the strange but friendly foreigners. Bob and Betty rode off slowly since the mule, not just stubborn, was still worn out from yesterday's slog through the bog. Arriving at the peak of the last pass before descending back into Chinese territory, they reined in their horses, and as Bob wrote later:

> As we waited for the still laggardly mule and owner, we could take in the snow-crested rocky wall of the Min Shan range—eighty miles away and stretched across more than ninety degrees of the horizon. 'No missionary has ever gone to the other side of those cliffs,' I explained, 'and the land beyond—for hundreds of miles—villages, encampments and monasteries—[are] all Tibetan.'[15]

The arrival of the Ekvalls at the Taochow mission station, on horseback no less, amazed their less adventurous colleagues. A few days later, they rode the rest of the way to the Alliance station in Chone for the annual Mission Conference. The eight days of conference provided time for spiritual refreshment and renewal, as well as opportunity for the newly-arrived missionaries to meet the veterans. Mealtimes and regular tea and tsampa breaks offered relaxed settings for story telling, burden sharing and plans for reaching the long-prayed-for Tibetan people.

While at the Chone conference, Bob learned that earlier in the summer, Al Fesmire, M. G. Griebenow, Charles Koenigswald and Stan Harrison had crossed "to the other side of those cliffs"—the never-passed frontier Bob had mentioned on the last day of their trip. These four men with national helpers, had undertaken a month-long survey trip across the ethnographic fronter into "Tibet," traveling light, moving fast, and tracing "a great arc through hitherto unknown country. Their reports named tribes, villages, encampments and monasteries; told of hostility and unexpected friendliness, of arrogance and suspicion on the part of chiefs and high lamas; and everywhere rumours of robbers—but no sightings."[16]

One of the most encouraging reports at the conference concerned the KTBM missionary team stations in *Labrang (Xiahe), Paoan (Baoan), Hetsuh (Hezuo),* and *Chone.* Paoan had been opened years before and forcibly closed due to violent, hostile opposition by nomads spurred on by monks from a nearby monastery. Now, the Charles Koenigswalds stationed at Paoan, had just begun an out-station in the previously hostile monastery town of *Rongwo (Tongren)* just ten miles southwest of their station. Clearly, the "push" by President Paul Rader had resulted in real advance on the border, the first seen in decades. Amazingly, the conference reported:

> "These forward steps into Tibetan country have been made possible by Mohammedan troops who have subdued the Tibetans of this region. The Lord uses even the wrath of men to praise Him."[17]

The subjection of the Tibetan people had always been a strategic goal of the Chinese government. They recruited the Hui Muslim troops loyal to General Ma Qi, the warlord clan leader in northeast Amdo (Qinghai and Kansu). After bloody clashes with the brave but unorganized Tibetan fighters, the Muslim soldiers established a military garrison in Labrang, a large monastery, and brought an uneasy sense of law and order. This, in turn, permitted missionaries such as M. G. and Blanche Griebenow, and Will Simpson of the Assemblies of God mission, to establish stations in the monastery town.

Twenty Full-Blooded Tibetans Professing Faith in Christ

The Alliance Weekly later reported "there are twenty full-blooded Tibetans professing faith in Christ in Taochow and Lupa Sze," with three of them preparing to minister to their own people. The Tibetan gatekeeper of the Taochow station, formerly a chief in a nearby village, had spent hours with Jens Rommen in debate and conversation. His life as an idolater and heavy drinker, bound up in worthless worship, had left him lost and hopeless. Eventually he yielded to the Spirit, confessed his sins, received forgiveness and was gloriously born into Christ's kingdom. Delivered of alcohol and idolatry, the next three years saw him in charge of the guest room at the Taochow station where Tibetans coming to town could find a place to stay and hear the gospel. Both he and his son had been baptized and had begun witnessing to their tribal friends.

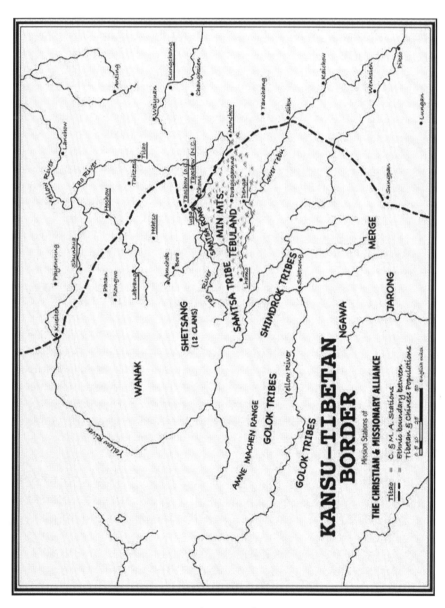

Kansu-Tibetan Border Map

Bob and Betty listened to the encouraging conference reports with "detached interest," since the die had been cast, and their future lay in Titao and the Chinese work. Yet, they thought about that first-time missionary venture which had just crossed the Min Shan and seen firsthand what lay beyond. A vein in Bob's adventurous heart throbbed as he and Betty rode back to "their good life" in Titao: Good because they had experienced God blessing their ministry. Their little home and future, in God's hands, seemed sure.

Unexpectedly, at the end of the Bible School year, during the winter break, the Ekvalls were asked to accompany a newly-arrived couple slated to work in Labrang. There, the new couple would meet with M. G. and Blanche Griebenow, meet Tibetans firsthand in the monastery town, and prepare for their apprenticeship, language study and life in this adjacent village. With more than 3,000 monks and many "lamas, i.e., reincarnated buddhas," Labrang was about to receive reinforcements.

Bob and Betty, delighted by the assignment which meant another trip cross country on horseback, took the couple on the three-day ride to the Griebenows. After arrival, Bob, tall and blond with piercing blue eyes and Betty, brunette, dark eyed, sallied forth into the streets. Surrounded by curious crowds, they took in the sights and sounds of Labrang, with its many temples, chanting halls and white cloisters where the monks lived. They explored the wild and wooly "edge town" outside the *gompa's* (Tibetan Buddhist monastery or temple) limits where M. G. and Blanche Griebenow lived in a tiny roof-top "apartment." In the streets, hundreds of sheep were slaughtered daily, dozens of stores sold the essentials of life, and savory smells emanated from the many none-too-clean food stalls which served delicious food, Tibetan, Muslim and Chinese. The young "foreign devils" enjoyed the experience, as they waded through the crowd with many pointing at Bob's "yellow" hair and blue eyes. He later learned that some of the demons of the Tibetan Buddhist's sixteen "hells" looked similar to Bob, except that their demons had blue hair and yellow eyes.

What Kind of Christians Will Tibetans Become?

Bob and Betty had arrived in Labrang in time to see the *Monlam* "wishing-prayer ceremony" of *Losar*, the New Year, celebrated at the new moon in February, first month of the Tibetan calendar. The dance-drama ritual ran all day.

> Until sundown, we watched the richly garbed masked dancers,
> impersonating gods and demons, and moving to the rhythm set
> by drums, trumpets, and cymbals, until a confused climax, and
> shouts of relief from the spectators.[18]

This ritual dramatized the conflict of good and evil, curses and blessings, disaster and well being. Bob thought, as he watched the thousands of monks and onlookers: "Only messengers—maybe I should be one of them—witnessing in halting speech and stammering tongue could bring the truth to set them free." They watched ragged, dusty pilgrims circumambulating (circling) the monastery, most walking with *mani* beads in one hand while swinging their prayer wheels around with the other. Others painfully circled the holy place like human inch-worms, by repeated full-length prostrations, taking hours to make one full circuit. All this to earn karmic merit, to gain relief from their evil acts and, hopefully, to reincarnate to a better life than their present one. The Ekvalls, silent under the heaviness of what they saw and sensed, could only think, *"with all that intensity of longing and effort, what kind of Christians will Tibetans become?"*[19]

While at Labrang, Bob went to the Muslim garrison to report their arrival to the commander. In his office, Ekvall met a twelve-year-old staff member called "The Little General" by everyone. One day in the not-too-distant future, Bob would meet this little "officer," *Ma Zhongying*, in less pleasant circumstances.

Labrang Monastery, 1947.

Returning to the Griebenow's cramped and drafty temporary quarters in the grimy market town, the mealtime was surprisingly quiet. The normal pleasant table talk had given way to an uneasy silence until the new recruits announced that they had "second thoughts" and had changed their minds. They wanted to return to Titao to prepare to work among the Chinese or Muslims, but not remain here in Labrang. While surprised at the news, Bob assured them that he would take them back to Titao with their outfit, leaving the next day.

That same night, Bob went out to investigate one of the horses, with a sore from the rough ride that needed attention. Betty went with him to the darkened stable to hold a candle. Almost simultaneously, they both said, "If only we could have had a chance like theirs to make a choice!" The couple with second thoughts, unnamed in KTBM records, returned to Titao with the Ekvalls. But the unthinkable increasingly proved impossible not to consider. A plan rose to the surface in Bob's mind.

A few weeks after returning to Titao and the Bible School, the field Ex Com met. Bob, out of the blue, asked for permission to bring a Tibetan monk to Titao "to help us with the language." That unexpected request spurred instant consternation followed by full-on opposition. Bob had plenty of work at the school and other duties; he could not "waste time" learning Tibetan. What was the point? He was the Bible School director, fully integrated in the Chinese work. No, that idea was out of the question. However, Bob, explained that he "had no intention of studying, though Betty might.

He wanted to try and experiment in a new way of learning a language. The best definition he could give was 'From sound to meaning instead of the old way of meaning to sound.'"[20] He explained to the skeptical Ex-Com that near the end of the 19th century, a French linguist, L. Sauveur, had recommended that students begin intensive verbal interaction in a target language, learning directly from a native speaker, gradually progressing from sound to sense of meaning. Sauveur had opened a language school in Boston in the late 1860's and the method became known as the "Natural or Direct Method."

While Bob had no intention of "studying" Tibetan, he definitely wanted to "learn" it. His language-learning theory had come from his own bilingual upbringing, where he learned to speak English and Chinese as any other child, by hearing, gradually understanding and then mimicking what older folks said. Also, just six years previous, while in the Officer Training Corps at Wheaton College, he had been instructed by "an enthusiastic, innovative teacher" in a crash course in French taught by one of the army instructors, in preparation for shipping out to France as a horse artillery soldiers. Grudgingly approving Bob's crazy idea, the committee agreed to give Bob "his Tibetan."

When "their monk," *Akku Rinpoche*, who had taught other missionaries, arrived to teach Bob and Betty, he was mystified at the idea of not using books and dictionaries to teach the difficult Tibetan syllabary. Bob explained, that they just wanted the monk to talk about everything and anything, whatever struck his fancy or whatever they asked him to pontificate on, whenever they met. While not convinced, the monk agreed, and this novel process went on for many weeks until, gradually, the sounds began to make sense as they became associated with objects and ideas identified as he talked. They listened and took notes. Words, phrases, even short sentences began coming from their mouths. The monk, grudgingly, admitted that their "sound" was very good despite the slow, unconventional method. Convinced that the couple had a good idea for language learning, he decided to set up his own "total language immersion" experience.

Akku Rinpoche suggested that during the 1924–1925 winter break, they accompany him to his village beyond the border and remain there for a month with relatives while he spent the weeks in spiritual retreat at a nearby monastery. So, Bob and Betty rode from Titao to Taochow; and from there with Akku, out to a remote farm hamlet in "ethnographic Tibet," far from Chinese influence. Their stuffed bags carried appropriate gifts, including khata scarves and other "goodies" pressed on them by their bemused missionary colleagues. The Ekvalls would live with Akku's family members, eat their food and communicate for thirty days, only in Tibetan.

The dawn-to-dusk ride with an extra baggage horse took them to the village and an open-arms welcome. They were shown their little one-room "apartment" on the flat roof of the relative's house. They had brought a month's worth of black tea, tsampa, butter, cheese, dried frozen turnips, and mutton. Grain for their horses, and plenty of dried yak-dung fuel for their big iron cooking pot completed their gear. They settled in and quickly learned the trick of blowing their "cow-chip fire into bluish flame and glowing red embers." They had free access to the big living-room-kitchen on the ground floor where they sometimes shared a meal with the family. At other times, they ate alone, digging into their store of cocoa for a cup of hot chocolate and hard bread.

Their daily routine saw them sitting outside on their "penthouse perch" in the sun, drinking tea and talking to their neighbors. Their monk mentor had given them names; Bob was called *Sherab Tsondru* (persistent wisdom) and Betty named *Dorje Mtso* (invincible sea). Visitors came by daily and Bob and Betty visited their homes, drinking copious quantities of tea and tsampa; which, over time, became one of their favorite foods. When the villagers understood that the "foreigners" desired to learn Tibetan, they stopped by and talked, and talked. "The sounds of the 'sound-to-meaning' formula becoming more and more individualized with repetitions and aided by gesture, tone, accompanying action, situational context and the logical continuity of narrative, became meaning in instinctual, spontaneous responsive speech."[21]

Two of the men living in the town knew how to read, and they decided to teach Bob and Betty. Using gospel tracts given out to the townsfolk, they arranged the Sanskrit symbols in correct order and began chanting the sounds of the "syllabary" (symbols of syllables rather than letters totaling 30 characters, each a consonant matching a single syllable).[22] With their help, Bob and Betty soon, much to their delight, began reading and understanding.

> At mid-point in their stay, they had an unexpected but welcome guest. Bob's first cousin, Will Simpson, a missionary with the Assemblies of God, had heard rumors of foreigners living in a nearby Tibetan village, and curiosity sent him on a two-day ride to investigate. To his delight he found his cousin and wife! For Bob and Betty too, it was both a delight, but also encouragement. At last, they had met someone who heartily endorsed their mid-winter folly as being the only way to access Tibetan lives and establish mutual confidence.[23]

In a Nameless Remote Tibetan Farm Village, the Two Cousins Met

Bob and Will had not seen each other for years, not since Helen Ekvall left the field with Bob and little sister, Alice, after David Ekvall's death in 1912. This separation happened because Will's father, W. W. Simpson, had become an ardent "evidence doctrine" Pentecostal and had withdrawn from the C&MA mission. Now, in a nameless remote Tibetan farm village, the two cousins met, much to their mutual delight, as adults and missionaries of missions with opposing doctrinal views. Will's Dad and family left China in 1915, returning three years later with the Assemblies of God mission. Will became an A.G. missionary a few years later and eventually moved to the Labrang "edge town" in late 1920.

Bob described him as "My cousin, Will Simpson, the uniquely Tibetan of all Gospel messengers to the Tibetans by reason of experience, travel and language virtuosity."[24] In *Gateway to Tibet*, the history of the Kansu-Tibetan Border Mission, Bob spoke in glowing terms about his cousin:

> In pushing into Tibetan country, by learning the routine and technique of caravan travel and finding the key of friendship with which to unlock the door of opportunity among the farther tribes, he was a trail-blazer . . . .
>
> Every year his yak caravan started out from Labrang to lose contact with the outside world for months and to push ever farther among the untouched, unreached, and even unknown tribes of northeast Tibet. And each time he came back not only were there fewer white spots on the maps, but less of uncertainty and more of detailed knowledge of the great task that was yet ahead for all of the Tibetan missionaries.[25]

Bob and Betty's linguistic progress through the "sound-to-meaning" method amazed Will, and he heartily endorsed their "mid-winter folly." He, the committed bachelor, honestly questioned whether it was appropriate for Betty to live in such spartan conditions. Will had earlier expressed serious misgivings as to whether "white women could stand—or should be asked to stand—such living."[26] However, after seeing Betty on the trail with Bob or later living in a remote a monastery town days away from "civilization," subsisting on Tibetan food, doing domestic chores with the village women, caring for the horses and "riding like a Tibetan—with no fear," Will changed his mind, though he remained a confirmed bachelor.

Over time, Will taught Bob and other Alliance missionaries the niceties of Tibetan culture and taboos, pitfalls to avoid and skills to develop. Through informal sharing as well as example with the nomads, Will gladly shared his knowledge and experience with any and all who had come to the border share the "Yeshu salvation way."

Will told of tribes near and far, *Golok (Golag), Ngura, Shimdrok (Zhingdrok), Soktsong (Suokezang Si)* and, *Ngawa (Ngaba, Aba)* far to the south, close to the border of Sichuan. "They could all be reached, despite official and governmental restrictions, if good friends were found, and one operated within the Tibetan host/sponsor—guest/client relationship."[27] Will had a simple outlook on the challenges in the evangelization of the tribes: Carefully follow the guest/client relationship, take sensible precautions on the trail, choose campsites wisely, and travel secure in God's protection, refusing to panic in all circumstances, always believing that breakthroughs would come in God's time. Though Will was young, his counsel proved wise and worthwhile.

The final day of Will's visit and the Ekvall's month-long Tibetan tutelage turned out to be a marathon of feasting in six different homes, with sumptuous meals of tea, tsampa, meat dumplings, boiled mutton and pork, fried bread, and yogurt. Then the local monastery where Akku Rinpoche had stayed invited them for another banquet! When the day's festivities came to a close, the overfed missionaries retired to their rooftop aerie to sleep off the day's hearty fare. The next morning saw Will ride off bright and early for Labrang while the Ekvalls, accompanied by their monk mentor, haltingly spoke Tibetan farewells to their new-found family and friends. Bob and Betty had tried and proven that the host/sponsor relationship worked, and this practice formed the basis for future travel and ministry among the nomads of Amdo. That same evening, after a hard day in the saddle, they rode into Taochow tanned, smoked, buttered and grimy from an afternoon windstorm, but, otherwise, unharmed and happy to climb into the tin tub for a warm, soapy bath.

Four days later, they got back to Titao in time for the March spring semester. Bob resumed teaching while Betty, happily in her third month of pregnancy, went back to Chinese study, since she still had to pass the mission language exam. Bob taught eight class-hours weekly and also preached in the Chinese church's evangelistic meetings. At the same time, it had become something of an open secret that the "inconceivable increasingly looked more like the inevitable." Ironically, just when Bob's command of Chinese had made him an accomplished orator in the eyes of the locals, free of any "barbarian" accent, and his trove of Chinese maxims and knowledge of culture and customs amply justified the mission's original intent for him to work among the Chinese, major change was in the air.

Bob and Betty had increasingly sensed God leading them into Tibetan ministry. Bob was willing to exchange his mastery of Mandarin for a novice's knowledge of a half-learned language poorly spoken with a beginner's accent. Bob had watched the struggles of the three new KTBM candidate couples trying to get their tongues wrapped around the tough

Tibetan tongue. Now he contemplated abandoning his ease of speaking Chinese for the frustration of halting speech. He had been called "half Chinese" who "thought yellow." He would have to forsake that identity since Tibetans had no love for the Chinese. What had come unconsciously to a child born in two cultures and languages would be laid aside as he and Betty sought to identify with a new people and culture while acquiring fluency in a difficult language. Would they ever hear a nomad would admiringly exclaim, "Half-Tibetan you!"

The next Executive Committee meeting was not easy. The chairman, Rev. Thomas Mosely, future president of Nyack's MTI (Nyack College), openly opposed the change of their assignment. However, Bob met the logical objections of the senior committee members by describing their recent experience on their "mid-winter folly" at Akku Rinpoche's village as confirmation of God's direction for their lives. As reported by Ekvall: "We humbly, seriously and formally requested that we be considered candidates for Tibetan work."[28] The committee made no decision nor "officially" voiced refusal. The agenda item was "held over for later consideration."

Soon after, on August 29, 1925, a fair-haired infant, David William Ekvall, arrived at the China Inland Mission Hospital in *Lanzhou* (*Lanchow*), Kansu's capital city. By riding all that next night, Bob arrived in Titao in time to take up his duties as secretary of the Ex Com. He later reported:

> The first motion passed and entered on the minutes, was to the effect, that as the Fesmires were soon leaving on furlough, Betty and I were to be appointed to Taochow Old City: I was to supervise and guide the church, and we, to study Tibetan. I was also to remain Principal of the Bible School, and when school was in session, I was to make a quick trip every six weeks to check on the running of the school.[29]

It Was a Small Price to Pay For Our Freedom

To Bob's way of thinking, this halfway decision regarding the Bible School smacked of paternalism. However, Assistant Director, Paul Keo, graciously accepted the arrangement, which proved within a year or so to be totally unnecessary. As Bob later remarked with a touch of sarcasm: "It was a small price to pay for our freedom."

Chapter 4

A Different Future

THE PRAYER-WISH UTTERED BY Bob and Betty in the darkened Labrang stable received an answer a few months later. God confirmed their "unthinkable idea" and convinced the reluctant ExCom to reallocate them from the Chinese work to ministry among the Tibetans. This required their moving to a new mission station. Bob described their novel travel *a la Tibete* as newly-assigned missionaries to that field in October 1925:

> David, our little son, was just six weeks old when he made the trip from Titao to Taochow Old City on horseback: cradled, Tibetan fashion, in the pouch formed when a Tibetan cloak was bloused up and tightly girdled around my hips; supported by the crook of my right arm; and he rocked by the rhythm of a horse on the trail. Of course there were frequent halts—in the temporary shelter of an inn; under a tree whose branches yet let some rain drops through; in the sunshine on a mountain meadow; half shielded at the base of a leaning cliff at the summit of the 11,000 ft. Lien Hua pass, where a passing storm sprinkled us with snow—so Betty could nurse her child and change diapers. Then again back into the warmth of his nest so very close to me.[30]

Leaving Titao in mid-October 1925, the Ekvalls rode to their new station in Taochow. The five-day cross-country ride retraced the trail taken when riding horseback to the August 1923 mission conference. Betty and Baby David stayed with colleagues Ed and Carol Carlson at the Chone station, and Bob rode back to Taochow to meet the mule train carrying their belongings. He spent the next several days unpacking and setting up house on the mission compound. Then, he rode back to Chone and brought Betty and David to their new home just a few miles from the Tao River and their new life among the Tibetans. With little David "grunting delight" at being back in Dad's warm fur robe and lulled to sleep by the horse's rolling gait, the miles were covered with a minimum of fuss. Upon arrival, they "rode into an incredulous and startled welcome in the mission compound of Taochow Old City. No missionaries on the field had ever put an entire family on horseback for travelling in that manner before."[31] This trip was the "first of many firsts" for Bob and Betty Ekvall and son David. Travel by horseback proved to be much more efficient for lady missionaries than being carried in a litter by men or mules.

Soon after arrival, they met with Akku Rinpoche, their Tibetan "talker," now in his teacher role. Bob and Akku both agreed that it was time for some real "book learning." Therefore, they began formal language study armed with the Tibetan New Testament, grammars and dictionaries prepared years before by Moravian missionaries. In preparation for future work among Tibetans in their black, yak-wool tents, they "bent their legs and wills to sitting with [Akku] on felts and rugs on the floor, as we had our lessons, and even as we studied in anticipation of life in a chairless society: grounded in the quasi 'lotus position'; and learning to be comfortable, without awkwardness, where one must be limber enough to rise from the ground and walk—not hobble on legs asleep—to his horse or wherever else he is going."[32]

After the "senior missionary couple," the Al Fesmires, left on furlough, Bob became the head of the Taochow station, which included pastoring the Chinese church. While Bob had been "put in charge," he was not comfortable taking over leadership of an established church of thirty years already led by Mr. Chu, a capable preacher/colporteur. While assigned to learn Tibetan, the ExCom expected Bob to supervise a man many years older, more experienced and the recognized leader of the congregation. Consequently, Bob made it clear at his first meeting with Mr. Chu and the church committee that he and Betty were in Taochow to learn Tibetan, and he was not going to "take over" a church already well led by a respected pastor. This unexpected reply flustered Mr. Chu (not yet called "pastor" officially), who normally took his cues from the missionary in charge of the station.

Bob had studied indigenous church principles and stated clearly that Mr. Chu, with his church committee, were in charge. The Ekvalls would attend the church and support them, but not supervise. Bob saw himself as the link between the mission and local church, a servant sent to help, but no more. This unexpected response stunned Mr. Chu and his committee; but within a few minutes, they began to talk among themselves. "Much talk followed, and plans began to emerge. Pastor Chu, hesitantly but clearly beginning to be more at ease with his new title and responsibility, began to lead. The praying, before the circle broke up, was strangely different than before."[33]

One of the members at that unforgettable first meeting with Pastor Chu was *Su Ta*, a local businessman of some means who traded with Tebbu tribal communities beyond the forbidding Min Shan range. He had attended the meeting as an unofficial observer, listening hard and saying little. Following the meeting, he waited around to talk with Bob about outreach to Tibetans, tentatively offering to help from his experience. A few days later, he returned to speak with Bob about the Tibetans who lived near the *Lupa (Lupa-si, Luba)* mission station just a few miles from Taochow, on the far bank of the Tao River. "That would be a good place for Bob and Betty to start, was his suggestion." Bob replied in an unexpected way, suggesting that these "half Tibetans" farmers and tradesmen, actually embodied the natural mission field of the Chinese church led by Pastor Chu. Many of the Taochow church members spoke Tibetan; and after three decades, it seemed high time for the Chinese congregation to become a missionary church. Some of the Tibetan-speaking members lived close to Tibetans without access to the gospel. "What more effective witness it would be if Tibetan-speaking Chinese would go each Sunday to the villages and help those 'half Tibetans' worship in Tibetan for all their neighbors to hear—thus proclaiming and spreading the gospel."[34] Su Ta wryly agreed that Bob's unexpected idea deserved further thought.

He Shook His Head in Dismay and Protested

When Bob revealed his plans for an exploratory trip southwest of the Min Shan massif to visit the *Dragsgumna* tribe and *Lhamo (Langmusi)*, the dual-monastery town, and perhaps even as far south as *Ngawa*, Su Ta was startled. "He shook his head in dismay and protested that, in all that region there was no Chinese rule for protection; our passports would be useless; there were 'thieves and robbers everywhere; and some areas were 'wildly savage'—e.g. the *Drangwa* tribe halfway between Dragsgumna and Lhamo."[35] After much discussion, he cautiously made two practical suggestions: (1) His business dealings with Tibetans required many good "host/sponsor" relationships in Dragsgumna. The next time any of those friends came to Taochow, Su Ta would introduce them to Bob as potential sponsors down country. (2) Also in Taochow's Muslim area, the "New Sect Trade Headquarters" was the focal point for all exchange between Muslim traders and Tibetans. He suggested that Bob get to know the Muslims who had a great deal of practical expertise and hands-on knowhow. Both suggestions proved valuable in the future.

Bob and Betty continued studying Tibetan, and he visited the New Sect market area occasionally, developing useful relationships with many, including a trader, *Musa,* who became a close friend with a wealth of good advice. Despite Su Ta's misgivings regarding Bob's plans to venture far into Tibetan territory, he clearly had partnered with Bob's intent to go beyond Min Shan's dog-toothed peaks.

Soon fall turned to early winter, when the Tibetans nomads came to Taochow in great numbers to barter their year's production of wool, lamb skins, cheese, butter, yak tails, deer antlers, and musk for barley, salt and sugar, tools, cloth and myriad items found in the town's shops. Bob's visits to the Muslim market gave him opportunity to observe Tibetans up close as the New Sect traders did business with them. These observations helped prepare him for future travel beyond the Min Shan and Tebbuland. Bob noticed that his blond hair and blue eyes always caused the same reaction when meeting Tibetans for the first time. He invited the tribesmen to visit the mission station for tea and tsampa in the visitor's guest room. During conversation with a guest, Bob discovered that his yellow hair and blue eyes reminded them of the demons in the sixteen Tibetan hells who had blue hair and yellow eyes.

The Ekvalls warmly received all Tibetans who came to the mission house. For those who could read, generally monks, they offered gospel tracts that explained the "Jesus religion writings." "Religion" and "writings", the monks understood well; but "Yeshu/Jesus" was a new name. As Bob wrote later, "The 'writings' I proffered, Tibetan-letters typeset and attractively sharp and clear as compared to wood-cut printing, had their own acceptability. A small minority politely refused them. Among the others, some would begin to fumble for their beads and mutter Tibetan prayers; reverently lifting the paper to touch their foreheads in the hope that blessing would come from 'religious writings'—the word 'Jesus' and all its meaning all unknown."[36]

Mind Shan's "Dog-Toothed Peaks," 2019.

A few months later in December 1925, much to their delight, Bob and Betty met a new missionary couple just arrived in town. Torsten and Elna Halldorf, Pentecostal missionaries sent out by the Smyrna Church of Gothenburg, Sweden, had come to study Tibetan for a year before moving to their assigned mission station many *li* (one-third mile) to the northwest. Through earlier correspondence with Will Simpson, they had decided to come and work among the Tibetans with the Assemblies of God mission under Will's leadership. Their eventual goal was the monastery town of *Rongwo*, not far from *Paoan*, where Alliance missionaries, Richard and Helen Koenigswald already lived and worked. In fact, Dick was supervising the construction of a large new Alliance mission station in Rongwo, where they planned to move upon completion. Will Simpson had opened an "outstation" in Rongwo in a very humble dwelling. The Halldorfs hoped to improve their home after finishing language study.

During the annual Tibetan nomad's trading visit, Bob and Betty welcomed another visitor met two years before on their cross-country trek from Titao to Chone for the 1923 mission conference. The friendly monk who had invited them to stay at the nearby Charkhi monastery had come to town before going on business to Titao. Staying at the mission guest house, he explored the local commerce for trade goods. Now able to practice the guest-client relationship established two years before, the Ekvalls hosted him for several days. Bob saw an opportunity to deepen their relationship as well as getting extra help with his Tibetan studies. Hence, the two of them planned to travel together to Titao; they agreed that they "would only speak Tibetan to each other." This stipulation met with the monks approval. Since it was time for one of Bob's regular visits to the Titao Bible School, he would combine business with pleasure.

Consequently, they set off early and reached Charkhi later that day. On the way, they stopped at the monk's village, where he took orders for silk and brocade, fine paper, spices and sundry items. At the evening meal, they agreed to leave at the first rooster wake-up call. In Charkhi monastery, they kept roosters as alarm clocks, but no hens allowed! The next morning, the insomniac rooster crowed very "early" and the two were on the frosty trail just after 2 a.m.

I Went on to Preach My First Sermon in Tibetan

Under a cold, clear midnight blue sky bedecked with blazing points of light, the riders and mounts, breath steaming as they trotted, talked of stars, constellations and other celestial subjects. The monk began an excursus into abstruse astrology which soon lost Bob somewhere beyond the Milky Way. However, the monk's monologue finally focused on "big stars" that point to important times and events.

> That is true," came Bob's rapid reply. He then took the floor and "went on to preach my first sermon in Tibetan—encapsulated, and spoken with a stammering tongue, in broken sentences with halting phrases, and stumbling words—about the great star: shining to make sheep herders know where Jesus the true savior was born; moving to lead three kings so they could offer gifts and believe. Somehow it was understood, for my companion asked no more questions merely exclaiming 'Amazing, truly truly amazing.'[37]

By dint of riding long and steady, they arrived in Titao by breakfast the next day. As the monk began his round of haggling shopping, Bob arrived at the Bible School and a warm welcome. These Chinese brothers and sisters had known Bob, some, since his childhood. The ties of relationship strengthened as he visited the school, observing its operation, the classrooms and teachers. Everything seemed very well run. In fact, it appeared that a subtle change had come over the place. "The routines and progress of the Bible School had flowed smoothly—maybe even more smoothly—than ever before. The sense of anxious need that somehow I retain control by frequent trips of inspection had virtually disappeared."[38] As Bob had suspected, the well-meaning paternalism of the mission proved unnecessary. Despite his trip having been delayed by several days, Assistant Director Paul Keo made no comment. He merely suggested that Bob's next visit be put off till mid-spring, to which Bob heartily agreed. It had become abundantly obvious to Bob that Paul would become the "Director" *de facto* and *de jure*, sooner than later.

Sunday turned out to be the last day of their visit. By that time, the monk had completed his purchases and packed them for their return trip. As was his custom when in Titao, Bob preached at the Chinese church. Not burdened by the tongue-tying Tibetan language, he spoke at will and well. His chosen topic focused on "the essential core of the Gospel message and the ordered—by Jesus Himself—breadth of its proclamation; then narrowing down the breadth, and a number of 'alls', to a close focus across the nearby border on the people whom the Chinese casually identify as 'barbarians.'"[39]

Concluding his sermon, Bob, addressed the congregation of friends and long-time members who had known him as a boy; some had even seen him baptized with the first three Chinese converts years before. Now, he pleaded with them to become a "missionary church," the same challenge that he had given to the Taochow church a few months before. The "Ai Family," [the Chinese name given to his father] were Titao's missionaries. Bob and Betty represented this congregation founded by his father many years ago with evangelistic zeal. Now, the day had come when someone from their midst should go across the border to the Tibetans. Bob stated his intent to be the first one, but many more from his home church needed to follow.

Bob's monk friend from Charkhi listened attentively. While his spoken Chinese was serviceable only for basic communication, his comprehension was good. He understood the message, all of it. After the service closed and the benediction pronounced, he came forward, wine-colored robe and all, and with typical Tibetan dramatic flair, he spoke, in Tibetan: "*'She-rab-dzon-dri*, [Bob's Tibetan name] you know Chinese will not come to the Tibetans to talk the Jesus religion. When they come, Chinese want to trade; Chinese want wealth.' It was said very slowly—impressively sonorous—so I would be sure to understand." Ekvall, not wanting to let the moment die replied, slowly and carefully, since his spoken Tibetan fell far short of the monk's eloquence: "Maybe yes, maybe no—not quite certain."[40] The monk, grinning, replied that Bob spoke the Jesus religion very well in Chinese. Most of the Chinese congregation looked on un-comprehending, while the few conversant in Tibetan wondered.

Their return trip took more time since the monk's loaded pack horse went slowly. Although Bob's tortured Tibetan wearied the monk at times, the agreement held, and their mounts heard the two speaking the language of the *Bodpa* [Tibetan people]. After leaving his bonze friend at Charkhi gompa, Ekvall continued on alone over the trail till, at last, he could look down on the Tao plain and spy the town where William Christie and W. W. Simpson had first arrived in 1895 to open the Kansu Tibetan Border Mission of the C&MA.

Baby David Received Lots of Attention

Upon Bob's return to Taochow, Betty told him the news of the past several days. As soon as he left for Titao, the gateman, despite Bob's orders, had barred the entrance. Immediately, Betty went out and ordered him to open it and make welcome all Tibetans who came for a visit. And come they did, men and women, to drink tea, receive gospel tracts and hear Betty play the pump organ. Their son, David, the major attraction, had his Dad's straw-blond hair. Since Tibetan nomad families had a very low birth rate, they deeply loved children and Little David received attention and compliments, with his baby-blue eyes. Betty also received her share of compliments due to her chestnut brown hair and dark eyes, which complimented her olive complexion. The Tibetan ladies thought Betty should grow her hair long and plait it into one hundred and eight braids like a proper Tibetan wife; then she could decorate it with coral, amber, turquoise and silver according to their fashion. She commented to her smiling husband that it was going to be costly for him to have a "Tibetan wife."

Obviously, Betty had been able to talk freely with both women and the men. Bob was delighted to see how well Betty had done in his absence and felt that she fit in well with Tibetan culture. Interestingly, one of the major differences between the Chinese and Tibetan cultures was that Chinese women were very diffident, rarely willing to talk with a strange man, and loath to express themselves in a group. Tibetan women were polar opposites, comfortable in mixed company, fearless expressing themselves and full of hearty humor. Betty, though quiet by personality, related well with young and old, male and female.

Since it was the dead of winter, Bob decided to get made-to-order fur outfits for the family. At 9,000 feet, Taochow's long nights and short daylight promised frigid weather. So, he paid a local Tibetan tailor to hand-make their fleece-lined outfits complete with furry hat, warm boots and bulky sheepskin robes belted at the waist, thus making a roomy pouch for storing their wooden teacups and other articles they might need on the journey.

Along with their regular Tibetan classes, they helped at the local Chinese church on Sunday, Betty playing the pump organ. The strange chords and reedy sound attracted passersbys like bees to honey. Bob shared preaching duties with the pastor. Tibetan believers rode in twelve miles each Sunday to attend. To encourage them to share their faith, Bob led a Tibetan service following the Chinese meeting where he and Betty taught hymns and gospel songs, read Scripture, prayed and gave opportunity for them to give testimony to their families and friends in their language. The merchant monk from Charkhi timed his visits so he could attend the Tibetan service, and he gladly read the New Testament passages when asked. On some occasion, they held the Tibetan services in the believer's homes in their village, while other Sundays saw them ride out to the old Lupa outstation where the local "half-Tibetans" heard the Word in their tongue.

That same winter, the Ekvalls, this time with baby David, revisited Akku Rinpoche's home village, where they had stayed for a month the previous year. The homecoming of sorts saw the whole town come out to see the beautiful little boy, murmuring "oh, compassion," as they gazed on his fair skin, blond hair and sky-blue eyes. Since Muslim and Chinese traders never traveled with their wives and children, the presence of David with his parents proved very beneficial as they visited the nomads. The attraction of a honey-blond boy with big blue eyes made him popular.

The townsfolk laughed as they recalled Bob and Betty's first fumbling efforts at Tibetan, now pleased and surprised at their fluency. Traveling as a family endeared Ekvalls not only to these villagers, just a day's journey from Taochow, but also with the fierce Tebbu and thieving Drangwa in years to come. As they traveled far and wide among the tribes south of the Min Shan carrying the message of God's son, *Yeshu,* who came to redeem sinners and take them into His family, little David's presence with his parents uniquely touched the otherwise hard-hearted nomads. The Ekvall "family was also an example of the family life that Jesus blessed, but which the religion of the Tibetans barely tolerated as of inferior worth."[41]

During the next few months Tibetan traders came again to Taochow with their yearly production from their flocks and herds to sell or barter. Bob gained valuable information from the manager of the New Sect traders, regarding lay-of-the-land data, tribal traits, and characteristics of the monastery towns where they hoped to find good host-sponsors. He gleaned information on camp placement, trail safety and which trade goods were in demand among other details. Since neither Tibetans nor Muslim traders used compass or clock, Bob had to ask about the sun's angle, time of year and other pointed questions to determine direction, time and season.

Bob, Betty and David Ekvall, 1925.

When the informants gave distances in "stages" (a day's travel), Bob asked why trips took so long, three weeks or more to go to *Ngawa*, less than 300 miles southwest of Taochow as the crow flies. They informed him that the hardy Tibetan pony, twice as fast as the sturdy yak, could not stand up to the temperature extremes and harsh conditions faced on the weeks-long trips over the mountain and plains full of treacherous bogs. The counsel he received from both Muslim traders and Tibetan tribesmen encouraged him to acquire a seasoned team of yak and *mdzo* (yak/common-cow hybrid), since the latter were more manageable, carried heavier loads, held up better and gave superior milk and cream. No KTBM missionary had ever used yak before, but Will Simpson agreed with the counsel, already having begun to use the slower but more dependable short-legged, sure-footed animals on his long treks across the steppes. The suggestion would have to wait with the needed funds unavailable at that time.

Unreached Regions Begged for Someone

The Muslim manager in Taochow introduced Bob to likely candidates for the host/guest relationship from towns that he planned on visiting on his next trip. *Taktshang Lhamo*, nestled in the mountains at 12,000 feet, topped the list of places to visit. With a rushing stream slicing the valley into opposing slopes, each side housed a monastery, the south side in Sichuan Province and the northside is Kansu. To Bob's mind, *Lhamo (Langmusi)*, "Tiger's Den," seemed an ideal location for an advanced interior mission station. The *Gurdu* and *Sechu* lamaseries both belonged to the same Gelugpa Tibetan Buddhist sect; yet they were unfriendly rivals and often battled, leaving scars and long-lasting grudges.

Farther to the south and west lay *Ngawa*, home of the centuries-old hereditary Mei Kingdom, ruled by a powerful queen and prince consort husband, who controlled dozens of villages and tribes for miles around with a population in the tens of thousands. And still farther south lay *Sungpan (Songpan)*, once a China Inland Mission station in the late 1800s, then abandoned for decades due to brutal treatment of the last missionary family to live there. These unreached regions begged for someone to take the message of Christ to them.

Su Ta, the Chinese trader in the Taochow church, helped Bob acquire hard-to-find gear: tents, saddles, packing bags, iron hobbles with locks for their horses, and many other items needed for the upcoming trip. As other Alliance colleagues became aware of their plans, excitement grew in the mission. More than thirty years after Christie and Simpson had first arrived in Taochow intending to take the gospel to Tibetan no-mads beyond the border, this spirited young couple, was about to embark on a far-flung survey trip that would test their mettle.

Every other month, Alliance colleagues, Ed and Carol Carlson, about fifteen miles away in Chone, visited Bob and Betty with their little Bobby, about David's age. On alternating months, the Ekvalls rode to Chone. These visits drew them together for prayer, fellowship, and shar-ing experiences. The Carlson's assignment, like Ekvall's, had them study-ing Tibetan while assisting the local Chinese church started years before by William Christie. In addition, the Ekvalls were fortunate to have their Swedish friends, Torsten and Elna Halldorf, living right in Taochow, also applying themselves diligently to language study. Torsten, last to arrive on the field, endeavored to master Tibetan and Chinese at the same time, as well as perfecting his precarious English! He prayed long and hard that God would enable him, to the point of Bob believing that he had asked "for a gift of tongues that would meet his special need and set him free [from language study]."[42]

As they visited together, the Ekvalls shared their travel plans for the spring. It soon became apparent that the Halldorfs loved the idea of a trip south of the mountains, but didn't express what they felt. "Sensing their eagerness we finally broached the matter and soon, to Betty's special satisfaction, agreement was reached on making the venture a joint one."[43] Along with the young Swedes went their Chinese servant, *Ting Ko*, who had trekked widely all over Tibet and knew the ins and outs of travel. Energetic, optimistic and hardworking, he became a valued companion and teacher for the tyro travelers.

The advice given to Bob by his friends, Muslim, Chinese and Ti-betan, regarding travel, added up to one basic rule: Never announce when you are leaving, your route, or your final destination. Such infor-mation commanded a good price on the local rumor market since thieves paid well for it, foreseeing a good return on their investment from those robbed on the road. Consequently, as unobtrusively as possible, the mis-sionaries and helpers slipped out of Taochow's western gate at sunrise in late May, 1926. The local Chinese official didn't know of their leaving, and apparently didn't want to know. Thus, they got on their way unobserved, by-passing Lupa, since they were well known there.

Despite their precautions, a Christian in a nearby village saw them and asked them to stop for tea. He asked where they were going; and since the brother was trustworthy, they said, *"Dragsgumna."* He immediately shook his head, indicating that it was too dangerous, on the other side of the Min Shan. Tebbu tribesmen who had tried to destroy Lupa mission station years ago still lived there. Years before, hundreds of armed tribesmen had attacked the high-walled former Buddhist monastery. Led by William Christie, the handful of missionaries, firing rifles borrowed from the local Chinese military post, managed to scare off the attackers with steady gunfire from strategic positions all around the compound. That memorable feat gave the missionaries great "face" among the local "half-Tibetans," when they learned of the successful defense of Lupa.[44] His final words to "go slowly" and take care, commending them to the grace of Jesus, encouraged the tyro travelers.

The route chosen by Bob lay arrow- straight through the heart of Tebbuland. The Chinese brother wished them well and told them to go slowly and carefully, knowing that the grace of Jesus the Savior would accompany and protect. He promised prayer and murmured, "Come back soon."

Horses Walk Up the Hill and Man Walks Down

For the next three days, the novice travelers, accompanied by Ting Ko and Ekvall's Tibetan teacher, Akku Rinpoche, rode carefully up and down steep hills rising ever higher toward the ridgeline of the Min Shan range. Despite their inexperience and ineptitude, they were learning to set up camp, light yak-dung fires, and fix their food, tea and tsampa. After the long climb up each mountain, upon reaching the crest, Akku would throw a rock on the rough cairn of "mani stones" and shout, "The gods win!" At the top, the riders dismounted, tightened the saddles, adjusted the loads and began walking down the other side. This time-honored act was a point of honor. Horses walk up the hill carrying the rider, and humans walk down the other side. All the while, little David nestled in his dad's heavy fur robe, or was passed over to Betty's loving care.

By the end of the third day and well beyond the Min Shan watershed dividing the Yellow River to the north and the Yangtze to the south, they came to a narrow canyon which entered the Dragsgumna (Rock Box) valley where five little hamlets nestled near their fields with a small red and white monastery clinging against one of the cliff walls. Their barley fields sloped gradually up toward the surrounding rock walls. And according to plans made beforehand, their "host" for the night was a friend of Akku Rinpoche, a white-haired monk, *Akku Dontro*, who hurried out to greet the travelers with two younger monks who showed them where to place their tents. They helped set up camp and stayed nearby to guard things while Bob and his travel companions went to the monastery. The local villagers had rarely, if ever, seen anyone from "beyond the ocean," and especially, people so pale with such blue eyes and yellow hair. All the way up the hill toward the gompa, people pointed, laughed and commented good naturedly. Then, spying little David in his mother's arms: "Look—look—a foreign baby—ah compassion."

In Akku Dontro's cloister room, they exchanged silk khata scarves covering their gifts and then were served a lavish meal with bowls of meat stew, tea, tsampa, yoghurt and cheese. Seated on cushions before low tables, the meal and conversation soon turned to one of the gifts given to Akku Dontro, who picked up the Gospel of Mark. He reached into a nearby cupboard and pulled out a carefully wrapped Gospel of Mark, identical with the one just given, except that it obviously had been well read and worn by much handling. Their host monk, smiling, indicated that he had received a copy of Mark's gospel when in Taochow sometime before: "turning the pages of his own copy he added, 'Ah, the beautiful printed letters—but hard to understand and the meanings are different—very, very different.'"[45]

Torsten, overwrought by seeing the monk with the Gospel of Mark in his hand and choked with emotion, plunged into his first sermon in tongue-tied Tibetan, trailing off into a babble of Chinese and English, tapering off into a heartfelt prayer in Swedish. Not one to miss the moment, Bob began a more coherent attempt at explaining the message in Tibetan, struggling to make himself understood, when, Akku Rinpoche, still fingering his mani beads, apologetically broke in:

"She-rab-dzon-dre's custom of speaking is about the Jesus religion; and the book is the birth story of Jesus who is faith's salvation of that religion." Following that explanation, he went on for several minutes to explain some of Mark's Gospel. At the close of his impromptu "sermonette," there was a low murmur of appreciation from the throats of the monks who listened intently. Bob, smiling, spread his palms and exclaimed: "Great thanks—truly truly great thanks."[46] As sometimes happens in God's wondrous world, an unexpected messenger will declare

His message, like Balaam's donkey or the demonic who remonstrated by word and deed the seven sons of Sceva. Bob's Tibetan Buddhist teacher had preached the Christian gospel!

Back at their camp before sundown, the Ekvall-Halldorf party received many visitors, including *Ah Tang,* the local friend of Su Ta, the Christian merchant back in Taochow. He invited Bob and his friends for tea the next morning at his home. Thus, after a restful night in the stone-box valley, their host led them to his roomy two-story house of mud and stone, the largest in the five hamlets, with beautiful woodwork inside. Ah Tang's wife served them hearty portions while giving them an unfriendly stone face. In answer to their question as to why Bob wanted to move on to Lhamo, and perhaps even Ngawa, he explained by pointing to the gospel tract that "salvation's good news about Yeshu" was for all Tibetans, monks, merchants, farmers and nomads. Their hostess mumbled comment, "Tebbu Tibetans need no new religion," indicated her displeasure at the message and the missionary bearing it.

Akku Rinpoche's friend, Akku Dontro, arranged a guide. a trustworthy young monk from the monastery, assigning him to take them to *Jangtsa*, just a short distance from Lhamo. There, they would be handed off to a nomad brave who would take them to the two-monastery town of the "Tiger's Den." For two days, the missionaries visited Dragsgumna and talked among themselves at what they were experiencing. The day of their departure, only known to Akku Dontro and their monk guide, dawned dark under a steady downpour that lasted all day and far into the night. With all of their camping gear and packs soaked and heavy, the horses strained under their loads. Finally, they crested the rim of rock surrounding them, and the sun came out and misery turned to joy, affording them abundant grazing for the horses, clear spring water for noon-day tea and a chance to dry out their equipment. Moving on later after lunch, they pressed on till the monk took them to a secluded side valley and told them to collect only dry wood so that their fire would produce little smoke. They were in robber country; every precaution would be taken.

Their Guide Growled, "Robbers!"

The next day, with the order to eat and drink well at their early meal, they would not stop for lunch since they were coming up on the dreaded *Drangwa* country. In the valley far below their trail, they could see fields and villages and hoped to be unnoticed by the unfriendly tribes people. Despite a few curses and rock-throwing, they made it to their next stop, *Jangtsa*, finally turning into the valley of the same name with its hot spring, where locals, male and female, bathed *au naturel*. Although the warm, clean spring water looked enticing, the grimy missionary team turned down the invitation. After an uncomfortable night's lodging in the corner of one of the villager's ground-floor rooms where the animals also bedded down, they rose at daybreak and soon were on their way under a cloudless sky. Their new escort, proud of his rifle and mount, led them single-file through the mountains all day till they came to a wide and open plain. At that point, he bunched the riders together and increased the pace. Coming around a hillside bend, eight riders, all armed, hauled back on their reins and looked over Ekvall's party. Their guide growled, "Robbers!" Bob reached for his rifle as did the Tibetan brave. "Go slowly, slowly. Don't run and don't try to turn back." The warning reminded Bob of Will Simpson's words: "Secure in God's protection, never panic under any and all circumstances."[47]

"Show the guns," ordered their guide, who then rode forward toward the raiders with Bob alongside. They kept between the robbers and the rest of Ekvall's party. Bob's Savage .250 bolt-action had a decided advantage over the thieves single-shot powder-loaders. Although the showdown, eight to two in number, favored the robbers, the guide's Russian rifle, also a repeater with a full clip, evened the score. Separated by about one hundred yards of deep grass, they had come to a standoff in the mountains of eastern Tibet. The thieves tried to get the escort to abandon the foreigners. They didn't want him; they wanted the easy outlander prey. Angry at being tempted, the Jangtsa guide made it clear that Bob and his partners were "his guests," and that raised the level of the offense contemplated. To attack a fellow Tibetan's guests was not just bad form, but a break in custom that would make them outcasts among their own people. The young brave sat solid in the saddle, shifted his rifle and waited with Bob. At last, "Let's go," shouted the leader of the thieves and they galloped off laughing.

Riding back hard toward the party, Bob and the guide found them all well although the prayer-enhancing experience had been fearfully disconcerting. Thus, they wasted no time riding hard a "bow-string straight course on into a maze of shallow valleys and steep slopes, climbing to a pass from which the full panorama of Taktshang Lhamo (Tiger's Den Goddess) with its two monasteries Gurdu and Sechu—each one having its satellite hamlets and trading-post spread before us."[48] Safely delivering his missionary charge to the threshold of the monastery where they were to stay for the night, their guide rode off with a half-smile and muttered to Bob, something about "son untamed," high praise from one brave to another. Tibetans only gave such accolades as "brave son untamed" to one who demonstrated true "Tibetaness," i.e., one who exhibited traits of courage, bravery and risk-taking.

Bob later described this strange and somewhat exhilarating experience: "Throughout the incident, I was savoring for the first time that strange—sometimes addictive—flavor of stark danger that can both paralyze and stimulate: it was something very personal and secret."[49] That calm in the face of calamity and his confidence in the God who had put him there arose unexpectedly but not unwelcomed. Courage under fire for the "son untamed" became a growing constant throughout the rest of his life.

After receiving a parting thumbs-up from his new-found guide friend and an open invitation to visit any time he passed through Jangtsa, Bob led his party toward the Gurdu monastery. Knowing no one in the monastery which sprawled across the hillside with its temples and cloisters, having no letter of introduction and no sponsor inside, Ekvall felt like the proverbial "gate crasher." He hoped that somehow someone would notice them, perhaps the blond baby in his mother's arms might do it. Their wine-red-robed monk, Akku Rinpoche, did give them a degree of respectability but no guarantee of a positive reception. In fact, their apparent advantage immediately disappeared as he rode off after announcing his going to visit a monk friend at the rival Sechu monastery nestled on the hillside looking over the creek dividing the valley. So, fording the boisterous stream, they rode up to the gate of the Great House of the Gurdu Lama, the *tulku* (living Buddha) whose ultimate approval would be necessary if Ekvalls were ever to gain permission to live in Lhamo. "Monks, pilgrims—momentarily deflected from their rites of worship—and traders began to gather: curious, watching, waiting, and non-committal."[50]

Knowing that the Lama would never deign to talk to *piling* (foreigners), Bob asked a monk leaning in the doorway if the *nerwa* (monastery steward), a kind of business manager, happened to be available. The monk ducked inside and the missionary party waited. A few minutes later, a stocky figure appeared and took charge, taking in the strange scene before him at a glance. With his best efforts in Tibetan, Bob, palms held outward, explained their presence to the monk and asked where they might make camp. The nerwa directed monks in attendance to take them outside the gate, to a level spot near the creek. Erecting the Ekvall party's tents in short order, the young monks brought dried-yak chips for fuel. About the same time, the local agent of the New Sect Muslims in Taochow, who Bob had met previously, came and offered to go with Bob and Torsten to the steward's residence for tea. Since they were in a "man's world," Betty, Elna and the baby, stayed with the tents; their horses were taken to the monastery fenced-in field.

Soon the nerwa strode into the room where Bob, the Muslim local agent and Torsten sat waiting. Burly and bossy, he barely took note of the gift carefully wrapped in a silken "scarf of felicity." Automatically, he reached over and pulled a similar scarf from a rack nearby and presented it to Bob. Then followed tea and tsampa along with platters of steaming mutton. The nerwa, *Akku Gomchok,* seated on a raised cushion, indicating his high rank, smiled while holding his tea bowl. Bob sipped his butter tea and waited for him to begin the conversation.

Where Did You Come From? Why Did You Come?

"Any trouble on the way?", the steward asked with a knowing smile. Bob, recognizing that the proper response was not truth but time-worn Tibetan tradition, answered: "We have arrived safe and in peace at the Gurdu Great House." Doubtlessly, Akku Gomchok knew all that happened in his region; so Bob did not bring up the fearful faceoff with the eight mounted bandits who only retreated when they saw the combined firepower of the Jangtsa guide and Bob's rifles. With routine protocol out of the way, the steward asked directly: "Who are you? Where did you come from? Why did you come to Lhamo? What and whence did we want to go?"[51]

In a moment, the nerwa transitioned from protocol to plain talk. As best able with his limited Tibetan tongue, Bob replied, giving a simple statement of their beliefs and mission as messengers of the Good News of Jesus and His Saviorhood for all people everywhere, including Tibetans. When explaining who he and his colleague, Torsten, were, the steward found it fascinating that these foreigners came in different sizes, colors, languages and countries of origin. Then, circling back to the original question as to why Bob and his party had come to this far off place, the nerwa asked for more specifics. Accordingly, Ekvall added that besides visiting the tribespeople in the region, he mentioned, *en passant* , that he and Betty hoped to be able to live in Lhamo among the Tibetans "so that we can speak the Jesus religion," a subtle feeler inserted into the conversation and clearly understood by the boss monk.

Taktshang Lhamo—Gurdu Monastery (Tiger's Den Goddess), 2019.

Sensing that the nerwa wanted more, Bob referred to the bright yellow booklet, *The Gospel of John*, part of the khata-wrapped gift package. Akku Gomchok pulled it out and began reading intently, flipping pages and frowning in concentration: "It is very, very different. Differences of all kinds exist everywhere in this book of religion. The beautiful letters are Tibetan but the meaning is foreign and very strange. I'll read much more when I have time."[52]

Once again, all business, the nerwa laid down the ground rules: In the Ekvall camp, they could talk the Jesus religion with whomever came by and could freely give out their gospel booklets. However, the monastery grounds were off limits for Jesus talk and literature. They could remain as long as they wanted and would be supplied with fuel by the monastery. Camping nearby, their safety was guaranteed, but Akku Gomchok advised them to keep their equipment in the center of their tents as a precaution again temptation. Their horses could graze with the monastery's herds, and the Ekvalls and Halldorfs could walk all over Gurdu territory, i.e., the monastery property, the nearby trading post and hamlets where the locals lived. The rival Sechu gompa on the other side of the valley remained unmentioned.

At that, the steward noted that monks did not have wives, and the Muslim traders never brought their women with them. To him, it was another indication of the differences between Tibetans and these folk from afar. He then commanded: "Go and tell the foreign women to come and also drink tea. They too are guests of the Gurdu Great House—and bring the child—ah compassion on it." Soon, Elna Halldorf, nordic-fair next to dark-eyed, dark-haired Betty caused more puzzlement on the steward's face. But he quickly seated them and served them with a graciousness that had not previously displayed. He bantered with Betty that she must be half Tibetan with her brunette hair, dark eyes and complexion several shades closer to Tibetan tan than the fair Swedes, Bob, Torsten and Elna.

For the next five days, the gospel messengers camped by the stream close by the gate of the Gurdu Lama's Great House. The outlanders provided entertainment day and night for locals who peered into their tents while they rested, gazing on them as they fixed their meals around the fire. While not overly courteous, their boisterous half-friendly manner gave the missionaries opportunity to try out their timid Tibetan. Many eagerly received the gospels and tried to sort out the meaning of the beautiful letters while a few of the monks coldly refused them or simply threw them down and trampled on them. Their literature stock was fast being depleted, with many more received than rejected. On balance, they looked back and felt that those first days in Lhamo had laid a foundation of guarded good will which boded well for the future.

After questioning dozens of tribesmen, Bob concluded that Taktshang Lhamo with its two monasteries, their trading posts and nearby hamlets, served as the religious and commercial hub for tribes living within a radius of two-days ride in all directions. From the nomadic herders, he learned that eight trails radiated out from Lhamo like spokes toward the points in the compass, all passing through a belt of "robbing grounds" which required travelers to be on guard, openly displaying weapons and showing no fear. Any sign of weakness invariably prompted an attack. Their recent experience with bandits confirmed the information.

Before leaving for their next destination, the Mei Kingdom of Ngawa, far to the southwest, a surprising invitation came from the *Jang Nak Lama* of the Sechu monastery on the far slope of the valley. Ekvall gladly received the invitation directed to "all the foreigners" for tea. The visit proved to be very cordial, in light of the fact that Bob's party had been given permission to camp by the steward of the rival Gurdu Monastery. While not wanting to get involved in the rivalry between the two lamaseries, a wish from the Lama was a command. The missionaries discovered that he had an old copy of the Gospel of Mark, much read and worn. Years before, he had visited Taochow, had been well received by the Alliance missionaries and had stayed in their guest quarters for several days.[53] He was impressed by the fact that colleagues of his hosts of years before were now camping just across the creek from his "great house." Noting that the foreigners had come with a baby, "ah compassion," he laughed as he ventured that "Maybe they will live in Taktshang Lhamo."[54] While only banter, that unanticipated comment proved prophetic.

Scarcely back in their camp from the visit to Sechu's lama, a monk from Gurdu Great House asked Bob to come alone to visit the nerwa, Akku Gomchok, for tea. Following the exchange of khatas, he asked what the Jang Nak lama of Sechu had to say. Bob told him that the lama had offered to help Bob travel south to Ngawa by recommending a host-sponsor, *Dzopa Duggursjip*. Gomchok agreed that Duggursjip was a "son untamed . . . with a straight mouth and a good heart" and gave the thumbs up sign of approval. A few days later, about to set out on the next step of their trip, the steward, Akku Gomchok, came and sent them word that the ferryman on the Black River, which they had to cross, would be informed of the Ekvall party's arrival and would take good care of the foreigners. Once again sensing God's hand of blessing on them, the missionaries and guide left Lhamo on one of the well-traveled trails.

Their immediate destination was the camp of the *Samtsa* tribe and Duggarsjip of the "straight mouth and good heart." After several hours of travel over hills and down into valley heads, they came to a high pass giving them a view of hundreds of square miles of more hills, wide valleys and great weathered mountains, with not a tree in sight. This was the famous *Samtsa Drok* (high pasturage) of countless miles of grasslands. In the distance at the foot of high mountains lay the winter quarters of the Samtsa nomad herders. Many hours later as the sun kissed the lower lip of the horizon, they arrived at the camp to be received by their host, who protected them from the fierce Tibetan mastiffs purposely trained as camp defenders.

The reception by their Samtsa host gave promise of a good future relationship. "Duggarsjip himself—fat as a laughing Buddha and dignified without in the least trying to be—was friendly in a casual way and restfully laconic."[55] While not the head of his tribe, he definitely figured as one of the leaders of Samtsa, a valuable friend and host sponsor. His unique household, made up of his first wife, "of the big tent," and his second, younger wife, "of the little tent," caused the two wives to warmly welcome and feed the missionaries, vying for their husband's approval.

Akku Rinpoche, their language coach and constant companion, left the party to spend some time at the Shetsang Monastery. His reassuring presence and tacit endorsement of the strange foreigners deep in Tibetan territory would be missed. However, they soon discovered that the rotund husband of two wives could more than make up for their teacher's absence. For the next three days, they stayed at Duggarsjip's camp before moving farther south. The unhurried visit afforded ample time to explain the reason for their extensive travel while sharing their faith and handing out Gospels to their host's wives. Duggar also took Bob to visit the Samtsa chief, who controlled eight hundred tents and thirteen villages.

Why Are You Traveling in Tibetan Country?

Following the routine greetings and khata exchange, the chief asked the reason for the visit. "Are you a foreign merchant or a foreign official and why are you traveling in Tibetan country?" Ekvall explained that he was neither a merchant nor an official but "a speaker of religion and [would] tell of the Jesus religion which is the way of salvation for all men." While the chief showed disinterest in "monk talk" and arguing about religion, he did appreciate the gospel tract, "ah beautiful lettering—it will explain the Jesus religion. We need not talk about it."[56]

Bob's new host sponsor and friend, Duggursjip, took the floor and began to persuasively plead Bob's case about the advantages gained by the Samtsa to have an influential friend like *Sherab Tsondru*, with his many contacts in Taochow where the Samtsa went yearly on their trading expedition. Ekvall, already an honored guest of the Gurdu Great House in Lhamo and good friends with the Jan Nag Lama of Sechu monastery, represented a valuable asset who should be made a guest-sponsor of the Samtsa tribe. The "smiling Buddha's" sound reasoning won over the chief and Bob and Betty became part of the tribe.

As they savored tea and other treats, the chief asked to see Bob's rifle, a Savage .250 lever action hunting rifle that held five shells. It's appearance and mechanics differed greatly from the local single-shot powder loaders or the assortment of foreign military rifles like the British Enfield, and various Japanese and Russian models found throughout Tibet's interior.

Dzopa Duggursjip, Samtsa Tribe.

Following his approving inspection of Ekvall's firearm, the chief extended a meticulously qualified open invitation to visit, or even stay among, the Samtsa, under the care and responsibility of Dzopa Duggarsjip. While the chief recognized the advantage that "yellow hair" might accrue to his tribe, he firmly placed all responsibility on Duggar's broad shoulders, who seemed glad to accept it. The next morning, the "two brothers" went out to watch over Duggar's large flock from a mountain perch. Setting up their three-stone fireplace and placing a small kettle on the fire for the inevitable tea to follow, Duggarsjip began to quiz Bob about the world beyond Tibet's borders. He wanted to know if the "great sea" that Bob had crossed was salt or fresh. He wanted to know not just the "what," but also the "where and why" of phenomena heard of, yet not seen locally. Bob showed his small engineer's compass, a barometer and his binoculars to Duggar, explaining the purpose and how they worked. At the same time, Duggar explained aspects of Tibetan life and culture.

That day spent together made the two men "kettle partners" who made their tea and tsampa from the same copper kettle over the open fire. Late in the afternoon, at Duggar's prompting, Bob stalked a gazelle, taking it with one shot, without use of a forked gun rest. Using Bob's binoculars, Duggar watched the foreigner silently slither through the high grass, draw a bead on the animal about one hundred yards distant, which leaped high and fell in a heap with one well-placed heart shot. They butchered and divided the carcass, Bob taking the head and skin. Arriving back in their fire, they ate the heart and liver. Overall, this was an important day for Bob, who learned much, yet found no opening to share the gospel. "All religions are good: yours for you and mine for me; but they truly are different. I don't need yours and you don't need mine. There is nothing more to be said."[57]

Returning to camp after a fascinating day together, a messenger from the Shetsang monastery awaited them with a message from Akku Rinpoche, Ekvall's language teacher and adviser. "The message was short but brutal, totally wrecking our plans: the friendly caravan would not be taking us safely to Ngawa; the lama at Soktsong did not care much for foreigners and he controlled the ferry at the White River Crossing . . . ."[58]

According to custom, the messenger repeated the entire message, making sure we understood. He offered no additional information; Akku Rinpoche had spoken. Serious discussion ensued among the Ekvalls and Halldorfs regarding the startling news. Much had been accomplished: the safe journey from Taochow to Lhamo, good relations established with both monasteries and a warm reception by the Samtsa tribe. Perhaps this should be enough. Their servants were ready to return to "civilized country" and the Halldorfs tended toward being satisfied while Bob and Betty felt more prayer and time was needed before deciding.

While Duggursjip did not understand the conversation going on among the two couples, he easily perceived the disappointment on their faces. Consequently, he offered to host the missionaries for the next weeks at the Samtsa summer campsite up in the mountains. When the suggestion evinced a hesitant response and seeing Ekvall's reluctance, he "posed the prime question, asking why we so wanted to go on to Ngawa?" Bob's reply regarding their message and witness to Yeshu's gospel was brushed off. "Tibetans have their own religion and there are thousands of monks at Ngawa." Asking what hope they had in being received in Ngawa by the royal Mei family, Bob showed the letter written by Akku Gomchok of the Gurdu Great House introducing the missionaries. Duggursjip read the letter and realized that such a missive would not be brushed off lightly.

"Ja Ja . . . God's Will . . . We Must Go On."

With his typical sarcasm, Duggar declared: "If Boat Boy Akku Gom-chok—son untamed by rebel who plays wild games—thinks he can send you to the Mei Royalty in Ngawa, then I can send you to my friend the Tang Kor Lama who controls the monastery of Soktsong. You really want to go? Then no need to listen to a message from an aged Akku—just go". He promised to provide a guide for the trek to Ngawa and a letter of introduction to the lama of Soktsong, who would act as their host/sponsor. After the gist of his offer made in Tibetan had been explained to the Halldorfs, they heartily agreed: "Ja ja . . . God's will . . . we must go on."[59] The Lord's hand of guidance once again opened the way.

A few days later, the missionary party left before dawn; their guide urged haste due to the long ride ahead and his need to get back to help move the tribe's camp up to the high summer pastures. Their days ran long with very short noon breaks. The guide constantly rode back and forth to ensure that no one followed to set up an ambush. Climbing the flank of a 13,500 foot mountain, they arrived at a pass which looked out over the "great southern plain" specked with encampments. The guide pointed to the horizon of high mountain ridges, 22,000 to 24,000 feet high about two hundred miles in the distance. He explained that Ngawa lay on "this side" of the mountains while the fierce Golok tribes camped on the "other side." At this moment, Ekvall recognized the frightening challenge posed by vast distances to travel, rivers to cross, unknown tribes to pass, and wide-open plains with no natural protection. However, despite the whispered warnings of dangers ahead, quiet came to Bob's heart: "We were infinitely close to the creator God and had instant contact with the love of the Saviour in whose name we were committed to spreading a witness across and throughout all those distances."[60]

With that thought, they descended the steep slope and crossed a shallow valley toward a circle of black tents of the *Bu* camp. Their arrival, nightfall, proved to be a bad hour to come on an unknown encampment. The herds, returning to the safety of camp with bleating ewes looking for lambs, cows lowing to be milked and a mass of animals milling about and mastiffs booming out their barks, produced a scene of turmoil. In the midst of it, the guide found their host who led them through the melee to a campsite where they could camp near his black yak wool tent with its spider-like support poles.

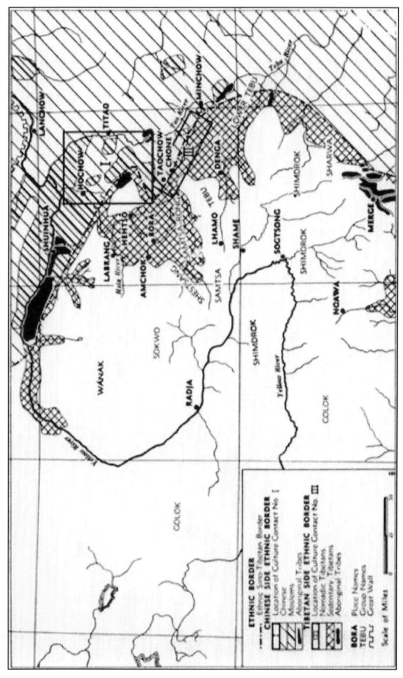

Gansu-Tibetan Border Ethnic Map, 1939.

Their Bu tribe sponsor, *Rinchen*, though grim-faced with formidable features and the nickname "Slab Face," gave the travelers a hearty welcome. Because of his friendship with Duggarsjip, he went far beyond the protocolar reception normally done. After receiving the khata-wrapped gifts and gospels, "He seized on the tract as opportunity to show how—as an ex-monk—he could read and asked for 'other writings.'" As they sat around Rinchen's fire and feasted on boiled meat, tsampa and cheese, followed by fresh yogurt desert, little David became the star of the show, crawling around the fire and going to whomever put their arms out. In a short time, the travelers became acquainted, and Rinchen would become another of Bob's longtime friends who would receive his hospitality in the future.[61]

As night fell, its "blackness of black" with no moon or stars and deep cloud cover guaranteed invisibility for thieves who lived to steal from tribes near and far. The Bu tribe's security system bedded men down around the rim of the encampment with mastiffs patrolling, baying their bell-toned bark creating a constant roar. The men shouted back and forth, fired their rifles on occasion and hurled curses against any unseen thieves lurking about. Despite the nocturnal pandemonium, the tired travelers managed to get several hours of sleep. Rising well before dawn to down their tea and tsampa before hitting the trail, they pushed hard all morning, arriving at the ferry crossing of the Black River before noon.

The horses towed the square wooden scow across the river. Some swam the stream while the four strongest steeds, led to the bow, received a few curses and strokes of the whip. Whereby the horses, their tails, grabbed by the boatmen, swam powerfully, pulling Ekvalls, Halldorfs, their helpers and equipment safely to the other side. Despite the efforts of the boatmen to detain the travelers for "tea," they pressed on promising to enjoy their hospitality on the return from Ngawa. While there Bob discovered that "Boat Boy" Akku Gomchok of Gurdu Monastery, related to the boatmen, had worked with them as a teenager.

Once across the Black River, they traveled hard for hours, finally arriving at the *Shami* tribe's encampment, and once more, they struggled, searching among the hundreds of tents, for their host-sponsor. Since the Shami had just arrived at this site, their host received them with proper care, although impersonal and obviously torn between his domestic duties and his role "of the great friend-friend, host-guest and guest-host web of societal interaction that helps bond Tibetan society and makes travel possible."[62] Bob had offered him hospitality in Taochow Old City when the Shami came to trade for grain the previous year. Since the Ekvall party had to leave the next morning, their host insisted that they stay with him on their return north to Lhamo.

Before the starlight dimmed announcing dawn, the travelers left for Soktsong, riding through storms of wind, rain, sleet and gusts of hail. Riding across the barren plains provided no protection from the elements. Eventually, drawing near to Soktsong and its monastery, the guide galloped ahead to take his message to the *Tang Kor Lama,* the resident lama and ruler. When the party arrived, their guide and the monastery steward awaited. He announced that the lama was about to tour of the tribal camps but would see them before leaving. The group waited with some trepidation since it was known that the lama did not like "foreigners" in his region.

Why Do You Travel Among Us the Tibetans?

In a short time, the formidable Tang Kor Lama of Soktsong, younger than expected, arrived and eyed them carefully. His cool courtesy bordered on curtness. While exchanging the customary khata-wrapped gifts and drinking tea, he made it clear that their presence there owed itself to the relationship that the living lama had with Bob's new friend, Duggarsjip. The steward would care for them and help them move on to Ngawa. Relieved, Bob replied, "Great thanks." The lama mused ironically about Old Duggar, "son untamed but full of wisdom—knows I do not care for foreigners and he send me four—and a baby—for no reason!" Then, the inevitable arrived with his blunt query, "Why do you travel among us the Tibetans? Why don't you stay in Taochow Old City where I know you have a comfortable home?"[63]

Bob's stock answer elicited a grunt, whether in agreement or disagreement, he couldn't tell. "I am a messenger with a witness to the Tibetans about the Yeshu religion that is salvation's way, and because of that I must travel and live among Tibetans—Taochow Old City is Chinese, not Tibetan." The lama then picked up the brightly-covered Gospel of John and began to read with increasing interest. Suddenly, he closed it and handed it back, stating with no hesitation that "This is not for us the Tibetans." Then rather strangely, he went on, "We too think the Word is important. Speech-speaking is one part of the triad of personal being, but the Word in the book of beautiful letters is everything and of great strength. How strange." Seeing him fascinated by the first chapter of John regarding "the Word," Bob urged him to keep the booklet. "The monks of this monastery are under order to never have or read one of these writings and how could I keep one?" Then he clearly ordered us to not give any of the "writings" to the monks or other guests of the monastery while they stayed in Soktsong. "Right?" he asked. "Right," was Bob's reply.[64] With no further ado, he was off on his tour of the Shami camps.

As a consequence of the lama's lukewarm welcome, the Ekvalls and Halldorfs with their cook and helpers camped on a rather uncomfortable sloping ground in a hollow swept by the storms with little fuel provided by the steward. While not living in great comfort, they shared their "kettle" with others camping nearby, including a monk and two laymen with thirty yak-loads of grain for Ngawa. Daily, curiosity seekers visited the foreigner's camp. While not able to give literature to the monks, nothing had been said about answering questions. Hence, the monks furtively queried about the content and meaning of the colorful booklets. No rules were broken since nothing had been given but witness went forth and seed planted.

Quickly, a kettle partnership" developed with the monk and his laymen. Both parties had mutual needs and capabilities. The yak were useless for pulling a loaded ferry across the river. Their short legs and barrel bodies barely kept them afloat, much less providing swimming power to pull the barge-like ferry. Ekvall's party had twelve horses which could help transport the grain across the river. In return, the monk and laymen would guide them to Ngawa. Thus, the partnership formed and "one hand helps the other."

Soktsong, the town and monastery, with its ferry sat at the "elbow of the Yellow River" where the mighty stream made a hard left turn, curving northwest, then looping back eastward past Lanzhou, capital of Gansu, before sluggishly traversing China's 3,500 miles through nine provinces and finally arriving at the Bohai Sea on China's east coast. The river, fed from mountains to the west, required a skilled crew of boatmen to maneuver the barge-like vessel with a single steering oar on the stern. Somehow, one of the crew carelessly let the oar slip its fastening, and it began floating downstream. The sudden shouts of consternation quickly showed that the "boat boys" did not know how to swim, as was the case with most Tibetans. The loss of the oar would cause days of delay to find lumber to make another in the treeless region.

Bob, who had already crossed the river with Betty, their equipment and some of the horses, saw the developing tragedy and shouted, "I'll get it." Quickly he pulled off his warm robe and dove into the river. Despite being a warm sunny day, Ekvall described the water as "liquid ice," which spurred his effort to take the errant blade back to the barge. He swam to the bank where Betty stood with a big towel for her freezing husband. The open-mouthed boatsmen echoed a trail of thanks and grateful words of obligation. At the end of the day, after all of the lama's thirty loads of grain had been transported to the far bank with the aid of the Ekvall party's horses, the ferry men gave Bob some of their finest cheese. Since Tibetan "cheese" is actually sundried, crumbled cottage cheese, the finest grain used to make the tea-tsampa combination, this gift represented the gratitude and admiration of the rough-tough river men. As they drank tea and rolled the balls of tsampa, they joked how the foreigner resembled an otter in the water. That quick-thinking act by Ekvall guaranteed that he and his parties would always be preferential clients at that river crossing.

For the next several days, the two "kettle partner" teams crawled across the grasslands at the pace of loaded yak, about two miles per hour! Starting at dawn, they stopped at noon so the beasts could graze during the afternoon. Their slow tempo permitted the riders to make little side trips to search for greens, wild onions, chives, dandelion and caraway shoots for their evening stew. Game was scarce but demoiselle cranes, always nearby, provided meat for supper. The long afternoons gave opportunity for Ekvall and Halldorf to visit the monk's camp and share literature with his men who read well, anxious for reading material. After a quick read, they entered into discussion about the beautifully printed tracts and the meaning of the Yeshu religion. Heeding the Soktsong lama's orders, they gave back the "writings," but the message had been read, explained and more seed planted.

This routine went on for three days, when the monk announced that he would not be going directly to Ngawa valley, Ekvall's goal. However, he promised to point out the side trail to follow which would take them to the Mei royal family's summer encampment. There, they could meet the queen and her consort husband, the king, a Golak chief's son from beyond the mountains. Ekvall explained the significance of the Mei Kingdom:

> "Briefly summarized the Mei Royalty and its style of rule were in the tradition of the 'kings of religion—the fierce ones' who ruled the Tibetan empire of the seventh and eighth centuries: supportive of the Buddhist religion and all its observances; interested in

the education of their subjects; ruling sternly and suppressing violence; and fostering long-range and local trade. The territory of the kingdom was centered in a segment of the great Ngawa valley so large that a man on a very fleet horse would have to ride for five days to measure its length, and this was bordered on both sides by extensive high pasturage."[65]

The well-organized Mei government under the royal family could have ten thousand armed horsemen come to their aid within three days of a call to arms.

At last, the caravan began to leave the plains and gradually ascended a "maze of low hills and shallow valleys" that led to high pasture lands. The night before the two groups went their separate ways, they camped together. Strong wind and heavy rains lulled them to sleep that dark and cloudy night. Upon rising, they discovered that one of Halldorf's horses, not equipped with iron hobble locks, had been stolen. This disconcerting experience caused Bob to realize that travel this deep on Tibetan territory required constant "skyline vigilance" and situational awareness. The loss of the horse, while disturbing, did not cripple their travel. Readjusting the loads, they traveled on to the point where the monk and his caravan went on their way. The missionary party followed the indicated trail leading to the royal summer camp. Sure enough, the directions proved accurate and they soon came upon yak and herdsmen who gave precise directions to the royal encampment.

At last, after weeks on the trail, they had arrived at the summer camp of the Mei Kingdom royal family. The royal tent, "several times as large as an average tent—was adorned with a gilded peak and guarded by six, exactly matched, purebred Tsang mastiffs sounding their uniquely fog-horn-tone voices as they patrolled the area."[66] The manager of the encampment met them, and being told of the letter of introduction from Akku Gomchok of Gurdu monastery, he noncommitingly noted the khata-wrapped packet of unknown contents. Explaining that the royal couple had returned to their palace in Ngawa, he coolly directed them to a place to pitch their tents. So close to their goal, yet not quite there, they pitched their tents and prayerfully made their next plans.

Chapter 5

Seed Sowing on Stoney Ground

Due to the depletion of supplies during the weeks of travel on the trail, Ekvall decided that the trip to the royal palace had to be bare bones. Leaving behind the six weakest horses, two helpers and most of their remaining supplies at the royal encampment, they stuffed their saddlebags for a quick four-day trip. One day going in, two days at Ngawa and another day back to the camp to collect the other horses, helpers and supplies to return to Lhamo.

Their evening meal was meager, but they arrived at their goal and were safely protected by royal guards and patrolling Tibetan mastiffs whose baritone barks made their presence known. No thieves would be stealing any horses tonight.

Next morning, a herdsman guided them toward the royal palace. They began a steep climb to the mountain pass, then into the vast Mei Kingdom valley. At the highest point, Bob's altimeter marked 14,500 feet, which explained the light-headedness felt by the travelers as they hungrily inhaled the oxygen-depleted air. Both men and beasts struggled up the ascent. "The giant glacier-snow mountain loomed expectedly close and awesome as it reached high into the sky."[67] At the foot of the mountain, the guide led them to a secluded cove full of lush grass and a sparkling spring. There, he told them to wait for "two kettles of tea to boil" so that they animals could graze to their full and fill up with plenty of water since the palace grounds had poor pasturage.

Once in the valley, the palace stood out like an adobe brick fort three stories tall, located in the mouth of a side valley facing south. Nearing the palace, the manager greeted the tired travelers and asked for their letter of presentation. About a half hour later, he reappeared stating that the king and queen, "in the performance of worship," would see them on the morrow. He led the party to a campsite, despite the fact that they had not brought a tent with their light baggage; fortunately, he furnished a tent. At last, they had arrived, coolly but courteously. Safe in the care of the palace authorities, they looked forward to seeing the queen and king. They ended the day with pancakes and the last of their sugar, then, a welcome night of undisturbed sleep under the star-filled sky.

The next morning after tea and tsampa, while awaiting the royal summons, Bob's binoculars revealed yak caravans crossing the valley, a close-up of a monk teaching a circle of children, distant farm houses scattered among the fields and clusters of buildings housing the Mei government. At last, word came for the "four foreigners—with the baby" to enter the fort-like palace to meet the rulers of Ngawa. "At one level, in a chapel richly decorated and filled with shrines, idols, idol scrolls, offering of incense and lighted butter lamps, a single monk [sat] . . . muttering the sutras and turning a prayer wheel."[68]

Entering the royal reception room on the top floor, they found the king and queen seated on elevated cushions at the far side of the room. The foreigners were led to pads facing them behind low tables piled with food. Bob presented their khata-wrapped gifts of Chinese gold-lettered brocade, a pack of raisins from Central Asia, and a bound copy of the New Testament. The steward took the gifts to the royal table and returned with a richly-textured white scarf. Then, in silence, the king and queen looked them over while the visitors sat uncomfortably.

At last the queen, the one in charge, held the letter brought from the Gurdu monastery great house, remarking that the seal and signature looked like the real thing. She went on: "In that letter it was indeed said that you were not traders yet had foreign wisdom, and wanted to visit the Mei Royalty and the kingdom of Ngawa. Why did you want to visit us?"[69] Conscious of his limited use of his limited language, Bob answered as clearly and simply as possible. He said the merchants in Taochow Old City had described Ngawa as a "most important place" where the fierce yet wise Mei Royalty ruled. The fortunate people of this kingdom were "obedient, able to read" and the whole land orderly and at peace."[70] With that, a back and forth conversation ensued. Betty sat quietly next to him holding David while Torsten and Elna remained silent, trying to understand the local dialect, distinct from what they learned from Akku Rinpoche.

Cutting the small talk, the queen, while wryly complimenting Bob's tentative Tibetan, asked. "Tell me truly why you travel in Tibetan country when you could live at ease in the land of China?"[71] This same question, repeated many times already on this overland odyssey, had led Bob to develop a concise response: "Because we—speakers of religion—must travel and witness the truth of the Yeshu religion to Tibetans so they might have faith and know salvation's way." He went on to explain that the New Testament presented will make clear what Ekvall's hesitant Tibetan could not. Since everyone in Ngawa reads, "the book will make it all clear."

Picking up the New Testament with its beautiful type face, clean print and fine paper, she admired the book, as do all Tibetans, who revere the printed words on their wood-plate scriptures. All printed word has value for communication and veneration. The queen turned the pages reading "many names no meaning." Slowly thumbing her way through the book, she arrived at the sentence prayer that closed the Revelation.

"Very strange, she commented, "all about Yeshu, his power, his love and his doctrine. We too wait for the one who will come—*Sham-ba-la* (hail loving one)."[72] And with that, she changed the subject and spoke as a hostess, while queen of her domain.

She assured Bob of the safety of Mei Royalty's guests while in Ngawa and among all the tribes in its borders. Then, the king wanted to know about horses, dogs and guns while the queen talked with Betty, who she was sure was half-Tibetan. "Is the baby boy or girl; do you have 'mouth taboos' (eating restrictions) like the Muslims?"[73] Like so many others fascinated with the outside world, they wanted to know how far away beyond the great ocean lay their homeland. After a while, the talking petered out and it was time to take their leave. Relieved and rejoicing, the visitors left and went back down the stairs to the ground floor where the old monk still murmured his sutras as the butter lamps flickered. While not coming right out, it sounded like the royal couple might visit their camp. Three palace servants followed bearing a quarter of mutton, a large tray of fine cheese and a plate of fresh butter, welcome additions to their meager larder.

Returning to camp, after the royal visit, monks, laypeople, youths and adults quickly appeared, eager to read the brightly-colored gospel booklets before returning them. They asked myriads of questions about the great ocean and "western magic," i.e., binoculars, compass, altimeter and barometer. During that pleasant afternoon, two contacts significantly impacted the party's immediate and long-term future with the people of

Ngawa. One, a monk, asked to speak only to Bob. Outside the camp, sitting opposite him, he stated that he hated the monastery and wanted to enter into agreement with Ekvall to "work together with you with foreign magic and the power of your new religion."[74] He promised much trouble for the monasteries; Bob immediately smelled a rat and responded that, as a speaker of the Yeshu religion, he had not come to sow strife among the Mei people. He only came to bring the message of Salvation's way and suggested that the monk carefully reread the gospel tract in his hands. With that, the conference ended and they returned to camp.

The other contact, a barefoot teenager, in a neat but ordinary sheepskin cloak, came into the foreigner's encampment. With little fanfare, he entered their tent and began playing with David, now crawling from arm to arm. When asked his name, he replied, "*Hsiang Chung*, Mei Royalty son." While his reply did not impress little David, the Ekvalls realized they had made a valuable acquaintance. The boy asked to see the "western magic," and later borrowed Bob's binoculars so that he could look over his future kingdom from the palace roof. He returned that evening with a serving woman bearing a plate of *zho*, the delicious custard-like yogurt that serves as a *pièce de rèsistance* for a Tibetan meal. The young Mei prince stayed for their evening meal and the sharing of hymns and prayer. While beginning inauspiciously, the day ended on a high note of praise.

"Get Going and Get Out!"

Next morning, their camp area lay deserted, like when they arrived. No friendly faces, no curious questions, nobody asking to see the fair-haired little boy, "Ah, compassion!" Nothing. Then, around noon, the local agent for the Taochow traders arrived in a panic. Terrified, he said that the monasteries demanded that the Mei royals let them attack the Yeshu talkers to kill or drive them out. The royals refused but offered an alternative: Immediate expulsion from Ngawa, "get going and get out!" Between a rock and a hard place, death at the monk's hands or danger on the journey, the missionaries awaited the final verdict of the battle of wills.

Once the business agent disappeared, left to themselves and the Lord, they prayed for wisdom. Following his instincts, Bob told their Chinese helper to get the horses from the pasture and have them on hand. Also, understanding "face," Bob knew the nomads would interpret a hasty retreat as a sign of fear, thus encouraging violence from the monks. The best strategy seemed to be a visit to the palace to inform, in polite terms, that the press of time required the Yeshu speakers to leave at daybreak. After more discussion and prayer, Bob took a silk scarf and approached the royal palace with *Ding Ko*, their Tibetan-speaking Chinese helper.

As they approached the palace, gathering black clouds suddenly unleashed a fierce salvo of ping-pong-size balls of hail. Racing to avoid injury, the blond missionary and his dark-haired helper ran to the doorway of the reception room and waited, since a dash across the open courtyard meant serious injury. When the furious storm slacked a bit, Bob ran to the palace door and Ding Ko held the horse's reins. Although the storm's roar was somewhat muted in the palace, the ground-floor chapel was jammed with monks chanting sutras and mantras, long-haired sorcerers shouting incantations, all the while accompanied by drums, cymbals and horns, a true cacophony of fear and fury. The king walked back and forth, wringing his hands and shouting at the window: "There has never been such a storm; all the crops will be destroyed; men and sheep might be killed. *Om Mani Padme Um.*"[75] The palace was in pandemonium!

The Mei queen, a bit more composed, but clearly upset, asked Bob: "Can you with your religion and foreign magic create this kind of storm?" "No," he replied. "Can you then cause this kind of storm to stop?" "No. But we who have faith can always pray to our all-powerful God."[76] As the intensity of the hail storm soon weakened, Bob explained the purpose for the hasty visit, presented the silk khata scarf and proffered apologies for having to leave the next morning. In his farewell, he mentioned his hoping to return again sometime with wife and son. Relieved that the storm had eased up, the queen bluntly stated, "If you were a merchant, there would be no difficulty." Then, after a long pause and whispered discussion with her husband, she spoke: "Do not make a special journey to visit. The road is long and dangerous. You met robbers and lost a horse Another time might be worse. But if you are going somewhere else and pass by, certainly you are guests, and under the protection of the Mei Royalty." Then picking up the New Testament as though a booby-trapped book bomb, she told Bob to take it since it had "great magic and power" but dangerous to those who had no faith. Her last word to Betty was to take care of her blond son, "ah compassion."[77]

By the time Bob and Ding Ko returned to camp, the tent, though battered by the storm, had survived the hail and promised a dry night's sleep. The hobbled horses, had not stampeded or suffered injury despite bruises caused by the hail stones. They started a smoky fire from the damp wood and dined royally since another quarter of mutton had been given, with more delicious yoghurt zho. The door to Ngawa though not wide open was still ajar.

Years later, an elderly Bob Ekvall wrote in his unpublished manuscript, *Tibetan Breakthrough*:

> A full fifty years later, as I focus on recall and write these pages, I have been rereading the book of Job in the New English Bible version. When the Lord Jehovah, speaking out of the tempest, challenges, and overwhelms Job with questions about the mysteries of all creation, one of those question is about the mystery of hail:
>
>> Have you visited the storehouse of the snow
>> or even the arsenal where the hail is stored,
>> Which I have kept ready for the day of calamity
>> And the hour of battle?[78]

Almost fifty years later, Ekvall recognized that on the last day of visit in Ngawa, God-sent hail from His "arsenal in the air" had saved them from death at the hands of enraged monks. Despite their forced withdrawal, He kept the door open and the tired travelers gave glory and honor to their King who cares for His own.

The next day, heavy rain pelted the lonely camp, and just one royal servant came to take the tent back to the palace and—palms turned upward in the sign of peace—murmured: "Slowly, go slowly." Facing heavy winds and a long wet ride back to the royal encampment and the rest of their party, they departed, "not at all slowly."[79]

Regardless of the heavy weather and high winds, they were going home, not into the unknown and revisiting former camp sites over traveled trails. Even the driving snowstorm seemed less grim since the rest of their travel team and camp awaited them. Arriving at the royal campsite, they found the six worn-out horses restored and their companions in good spirits. Ekvall and company had just sat down to eat when they received a summons from the royal tent manager for "tea," complete with meat, dumplings, sausage, fried bread and zho. He apparently knew about the monks' death threats, the sudden hailstorm and the miraculous ending. Someone must have ridden hard to inform him before they arrived. The manager assured them all that they had no reason to fear the next leg of their journey to Soktsong and the ferry crossing since they now were guest-clients of the Mei Royalty. He promised that they would soon find a "cheap old horse" to replace the one stolen from their camp, and true to his word, a local herder came the next day with a little disheveled-grey, mongrel horse. While not a prize specimen of horseflesh, it was relatively well-muscled, not limping and cheap enough to still leave a few silver dollars in their dwindling reserves. Thus, with their whole party back together, Ekvall et al set off for Lhamo. The manager advised them to be careful on the return trip since they would traverse barren "robber land."

Shami Tribesmen Had Spotted an Armed Band

Many days beyond their estimated return to Taochow, they set off with barely enough rice and tsampa for skimpy evening meals even with Bob shooting wild game to help fortify the meals for eight hungry adults and a ravenous little boy after a long day of travel. The bogs, ponds and winding streams slowed them down, requiring three days to reach the ferry crossing. There, the ferrymen enthusiastically greeted them, still grateful for Bob's plunge into the ice-cold river to retrieve their precious steering oar. Once across the river, they traveled under a day-long downpour, before finding the Shami tribe encampment and the tent of their host-sponsor. Mercifully, given dry fuel, they quickly built a fire to make their evening "stew". The Shami tribesmen warned Bob that they had spotted an armed band of ten men, "not from these parts," likely bandits. So with that unwelcome news, they bedded down for a night of fitful sleep despite the howling mastiffs scouting the area and the braves posted around the camp.

Pushing off the next morning with their host's advice to "go slowly, slowly" (be careful), they left the Shami with their herds and entered a maze of low hills. Throughout the day, Bob kept his party off the main trail to avoid horsemen that he saw in the distance with his binoculars. Coming down to the Black River plain, he saw the nomad's black tents at the river crossing. Sending his party ahead, Bob scanned the landscape behind and beyond and saw nothing. Later, scanning the nearby foothills, Bob spotted the riders in the distance moving at a "traveler's steady gait." Keeping himself between the riders and the rest of his party, Bob, with binoculars, had the advantage and kept them in his sights as his party drew near the Black River ferry crossing. Eventually, the horsemen stopped, as though in consultation, before heading toward Bob and his party who were closer to the river. The horsemen, clearly armed, changed direction and started forward at a steady trot.

Since they were still distant, Bob caught up with the rest of his team, and they laid their plans. They tightened the packhorse's loads led by two of their helpers. The shotguns were put into the hands of Torsten Halldorf and another helper. While having only a few shells, they looked dangerous with their weaponry ostentatiously carried by the would-be warriors. Bob would fire the first shot before the others. Their goal was to reach the river and the safety of the ferrymen. They would maintain a steady pace with no headlong rush for the river, since panic would break their ranks. With his "troop" organized and moving, Bob dropped back to his role as rear guard and decoy. He would stay between the "bad guys" and his little band of travelers. The riders, numbering ten armed horsemen, began to stalk Bob from a parallel course, edging ever closer. Bob held his Savage rifle in his right hand like a handgun. By this time, the bandits could see that he was not Tibetan or Chinese, and came up to threaten him, demanding one hundred ounces of silver as ransom. At his refusal, one of the rider's came from behind and tried to grab for Bob's rifle. A hard pull on the reins and a kick in the stirrups caused the horse to leap sideways. Then, Bob swung his rifle to bear on the marauder who quickly fled the field of combat and returned to his companions. They shouted, "On the other side of the river it will be easy." And they rode straight down the trail to the ferry and crossed.

After crossing the river, the ten bandits waited for Bob's party to cross. The ferrymen refused to take them across with danger on the other side, and Bob agreed. When two of the thieves went to the far edge of the river and aimed their long-barreled powder-loaders at the party, Bob lay in the grass on the near side of the river with his rifle and aimed at them. Since his position was higher than theirs, he had the shooter's advantage. It appeared that they had another "Tibetan standoff," this time at the edge of the Black River rather than on an unnamed mountain slope. Taking the ferrymen's advice to "drink tea and wait," Bob and his fellow travelers boiled a couple kettles of tea while awaiting the thieves next move. "The sun was high and hot and time became very long."[80]

Recognizing that Ekvall's strategic location and weapons checkmated their numerical strength, the two bandits joined their comrades and rode away on the Lhamo trail, going in the same direction that Ekvall and his group would follow the next day. Eventually, looking through Bob's binoculars, the ferryman agreed that the thieves were well on their way up the mountain and no longer a danger. He then ferried the Ekvall party across the river and they continued on to the nearby *Bu* tribe's encampment. There, Bob found his friend and client-sponsor, Rinchen, with another night of safety assured.

Within just a few hours, the Tibetan telegraph informed the nomads of the robber incident and who had won the standoff. So Rinchen bragged on the success of his guest-clients and even gave credit to "the power of our religion." Once again, God's promised presence had protected His own. With a group of Tibetans pilgrims about to leave for Lhamo the next day, Bob and his group slept well knowing that, on the morrow, they would have "strength in numbers." The barking dogs and shouting guards firing off the occasional gun made for sweet sleep music. As the missionaries sang and prayed before bedding down, they praised their "Great Jehovah—Guide and Refuge in a barren land."

Their next day's journey proved uneventful; by late afternoon, the twin monasteries and stream flowing through the valley came into view, a welcome sight. No different than a month before, Lhamo now almost seemed like "home." The familiar landscape, faces remembered from their previous visit, and loud greetings from new-found friends welcomed them back to their creek-side camp site. The monastery steward, Akku Gomchok, was away on business, but his assistant received them and arranged a guide for the next leg of the trip back home. Introducing him, the assistant steward said that Bob's party "did not need protection, just someone to show the way." Ekvall's new-found fame from the robber incident, had already caught up to him in Lhamo. After paying their escort in advance, they had one silver-dollar left, which they used to buy much needed tsampa.

It Seems as Though We Belong in Tahktsong Lhamo

That evening, they received congratulations for their safe journey from townsfolk who had previously seen them as curious-looking strangers. They received gifts of milk from the women for David, and fresh meat from the Jang Lak Lama. Townsfolk crowded their cook tent as they sang and prayed, giving away the last of their tracts and gospels. Later that night, after the crowd had departed, "Betty summed up our second arrival in a single sentence: 'It seems as though we belong in Taktshang Lhamo.'"[81]

The next morning, the Ekvall party set out on one of the eight well-traveled trails that link Lhamo to destinations near and far. While traveling across the "Drangwa robbing grounds," they saw no one, neither bandit nor herder. It took another three days going over mountains, through gorges and lovely valleys. They camped their last night near the *Chiwushe* monastery on the far side of the Tao River. On that fourth and final day, they breakfasted on scraps of food and a bottle of gruel reserved for little David's late lunch. Arriving at the river's edge, the boatman, an old friend, welcomed them back and laughed at their toll payment, scarves, thread, needles, and other items, all they had left.

Some hours later, they rode into Taochow Old City, to the surprise and delight of the mission station's gatekeeper. Torsten and Elna, hungry for news, went directly to their quarters to catch up on two months of mail. Pastor Chu shouted delightedly and told his wife to "start cooking." And after a welcome soak in the big tin bathtub, the Ekvalls sat at the Chu's table and dug into the delicious food they hadn't eaten for forty-nine days! White Chinese bread, eggs, vegetables and "all the other good things Mrs. Chu produced as though by magic." Just about that time, the other church members arrived, and later Sun Ta, Bob's Chinese travel-mentor came in. The church had heard nothing for more than a month and had been worried, holding special prayer meetings for their safe return. "They were eager to hear how God's hand had led us, and how His arm had shielded us for the 49 days we had been away."[82]

Taking stock of their long journey south of the Min Shan range, Bob and Betty understood the implications of such travel made possible by serious prayer and preparation. They had visited villages, tribal camps, monasteries and even a kingdom never before reached by other border missionaries. They now knew much more of the challenge before them, but what next?

Going over the accumulated mail of two months gave them some hints of what was to come. The expenditures for the trip had put the Ekvall's mission account "deep into the hole," yet, unexpected gifts from the Omaha Gospel Tabernacle had zeroed out their considerable debt. As a result, their account showed a small credit! Grateful words of praise came up from the lips of the Ekvalls as they settled into less-stressful mission station life and looked forward to the upcoming C&MA mission conference in Taochow Old City in August 1926.

By mid August, Alliance missionaries from all over the Kansu Tibetan Border Mission began arriving. M.G. and Blanche Griebenow from Labrang, the Ed Carlsons from Chone, Tom and Eva Mosely from Titao, as well as the recently-arrived John Carlsens and Miss Lawrence, still in language study. The Koenigswalds from the Paoan and Rongwo stations, the Al Fesmires, the Francis Dirks, the Hansens, Holtons, Ruhls, Mrs. Rommens, recently widowed, they all came from their scattered stations for a week of fellowship, spiritual refueling and deliberations regarding mission plans and policy. One of the first items for consideration was Ekvall's report of the successful exploratory venture to Ngawa. Each mission station's report was read and discussed. By the conference's conclusion, three major decisions greatly affected the Ekvalls: (1) Robert Ekvall was "relieved of any responsibility concerning the [Titao] Bible School, and Paul Keo was . . . officially recognized [as] principal of that institution". (2) Bob and Betty Ekvall were instructed to "take whatever steps that seemed feasible to strengthen our relationship with the Gurdu Great House in Taktshang Lhamo and seek to gain entrance to that place as our next station". (3) The conference instructed Bob to "begin the acquisition of a yak, or *mdzo* (yak-cow hybrid) caravan" for future travel and itineration among the nomad tribes surrounding Lhamo.[83]

Will Simpson, Bob's first cousin, living in Labrang, and Torsten and Elna Halldorf, all part of the "Pentecostal Mission" working in the same area as the C&MA, received invitations to the conference. Under the leadership of Rev. Tom Mosely, and following extensive discussion among all present, the members of the two missions decided to eliminate the duplication of workers and regions. As later reported in *The Alliance Weekly*:

> A congenial division of territory has been made between our Mission [C&MA] and the Tibetan workers of the Pentecostal Mission [Assemblies of God] which is most gratifying, as there will be no overlapping in the Tibetan work, though it has meant the giving up of Rongwu station where Mr. and Mrs. Koenigswald were located and where there are newly completed mission buildings."[84]

A fuller telling of this historic decision is found in *Cousins: Peacemakers on the Tibetan Border*, written by the author, which tells the story of Will Simpson and Bob Ekvall, first cousins and missionary kids raised on the China/Tibetan border. Their fathers, brothers-in-law, had been on opposite sides of the heated doctrinal disputes regarding tongues. While requiring neither side to compromise their theology, the 1926 Conference decision bound up wounds that had festered for more than a decade and gave time for Christ's grace to heal those hurts, bringing peace to the borderland for the evangelization of those living there.

One decision requiring wide-ranging discussion among the missionaries, veterans of long journeys over the mountains on sturdy Tibetan horses, concerned the new mode of transportation, considerably more expensive and much slower. Nevertheless, Bob reasoned:

> With a sufficiently large caravan the missionary could roam more freely and travel farther. Instead of making a dash on overloaded horses, and having to buy supplies—as we had to at Lhamo and Ngawa—at greatly inflated prices, or paying with silver or currency, he would have ample supplies of foodstuffs, trade goods, literature, etc. and would not run the added risk of carrying any great quantity of currency or silver . . . [which would] make a particularly attractive target for roving robbers.[85]

True, yak traveled more slowly, about half the speed of horses; yet, they could fend for themselves on the trail, needing no grain like horses. After much discussion, the decision to move forward with yak caravans was given the green light.

In short order, Bob bought four mdzo oxen, the first members of a caravan team for long-distance travel. Acquiring the needed gear, Bob, Betty and little David, set out for Charkhi valley and the "friendly monastery," where they practiced learning how to set up a proper camp and load and securely tie the packs on the yaks. The monks came down to visit, soon amazed at the Ekvall's progress in Tibetan, but still not satisfied with their relative illiteracy. Using the gospel tracts distributed, they drilled Bob and Betty on pronunciation and helped them understand the meaning of the tracts. The month spent there proved invaluable, with little stress and much communication with all kinds of Tibetans. Their "working vacation" ended with the first snowfall and bad news. Charles and Helen Koenigswald had been robbed on the trail, losing everything but the clothes on their backs. This forced them to march miles in fear and hunger to safety. While not hurt, the Koenigswald incident reminded the Tibetan border team of the danger of travel among the people that they worked so hard to reach with the gospel.

The August 1926 agreement led the Alliance Mission to make plans for moving southward. In February 1927, Bob Ekvall, Edwin Carlson, Francis Derk and Will Simpson traveled to Lhamo by horseback. Blizzards, deep snow and zero degree temperatures at night proved challenging. Traveling without a tent, they slept close to their fire surrounded by saddles and packs to stay warm. Their mounts huddled under heavy horse blankets. Every night, they took turns on watch until dawn, then tea and tsampa and more riding. At the end of the second day, they reached the creek in the valley between the two monasteries and found several young monks standing barefoot in the stream to warm their feet!

Led by Will Simpson, over the next four days, they asked for permission for the Ekvalls to take up residence in Lhamo. Their earlier contact, the steward, *Aku Gomchock*, no longer served Gurdu monastery. However, senior monks agreed that the "foreigner's" presence could prove advantageous, given the political unrest in China spilling over onto their region. While hopeful, the missionaries received no firm promise.

Leaving Lhamo, they followed the stream eastward down the valley to *Denga*, another potential mission station site. Just before arriving there, they were met by a messenger sent by Rev. Thomas Mosely in Titao. The courier bore a dispatch from the U. S. consul, dated February 1, 1927, ordering the evacuation of all U.S. citizens due to rising violence. In addition, Bob needed to attend an Ex Com meeting three days hence in Titao. He later wrote:

> It was indeed the ultimate emergency and, drawing on the capabilities of a truly remarkable horse—a hulking jughead buckskin with a tireless trot and a taste for meat, named Genghis Khan— and by carefully timing stops for rest and feed, I reached Titao on the day the meeting was scheduled to convene, and in time to walk in and join the others at breakfast.[86]

Earlier general evacuations had occurred several times; so, the committee moved quickly. The most pressing "new business" established the change in relationship with the growing Chinese church. The new spirit of Chinese nationalism demanded a clear distinction between "mission and church." This agreed with the C&MA's evolving indigenous church policy of self-support, self-government and self-propagation. Already, the national church had a functioning three-man executive committee in charge of church business. This important step, planned for the near future, now became the de-facto policy of the Kansu-Tibetan Border Mission.

With Genghis Khan, rested for the next leg back to Taochow, Bob traveled at top speed to care for last-minute matters before departure Then, by separate routes, horseback, mule train, ox cart and raft, thirty-three C&MA KTBM workers and children left for the coast. The impetus for the 1927 evacuation resulted from anti-foreign elements in Nationalist and Communist forces engaged in rioting, robbery, and a general uprising. Departure from the war-torn land freed the national church from accusations of dependency on the missionaries. Ekvall later wrote in *Gateway to Tibet*, "Hence it is proper to merely record that within a few months after the missionaries had left, the general executive committee of the churches asked for full status as an entirely self-supporting, self-governing and self-propagating [indigenous] church."[87]

The KTBM staff arrived in the U.S. in the spring, and by summer, they traveled to various Alliance summer camps, casting vision of the work among the Tibetans. For the next year, most participated in mission conferences all over the country. Bob even spoke at historic Old Orchard Camp in Maine, where Edwin Carlson, a young man attending, felt the call to be a missionary to Tibet. While Bob spoke at the mission conferences, Betty remained in Wheaton with David, living at her mother's home. On September 27–29, the Kansu-Tibetan border missionaries gathered in New York with the Alliance mission leaders for a special meeting chaired by William Christie, pioneer-founder of the field, now part of the New York "headquarters" team. "The conference was characterized by a very earnest spirit of oneness of vision. Recommendations were prepared dealing with the situation and looking forward to the future."[88] Those present included Rev. Thomas Mosely, Rev. William Ruhl, Rev. A. J. Hansen, Mr. Robert Ekvall, Mr. and Mrs. C. E. Carlson, Mr. and Mrs. C. R. Koenigswald, Mr. and Mrs. F. H. Derk, Mr. and Mrs. M. G. Griebenow and Rev. and Mrs. A. R. Fesmire, Miss Fesmire, and Miss C. B. MacMahon. The meeting recommended sending back those working with the Tibetans and the Muslims. This decision, made with short notice, required the missionaries to acquire, pack and ship their outfits for return to the field ASAP. They needed to be in China and in "Hankow—the take-off point for the month-long overland trip—at the earliest possible date to avoid the worst of winter weather.[89]

Chapter 6

Forward Slowly

AFTER A YEAR AND a few months furlough, Bob and Betty prepared for their return to China. Traveling cross country by train, they revisited the Omaha Gospel Tabernacle pastored by R. R. Brown, on their way to the West Coast. A substantial offering for the purchase of a well-equipped yak caravan went with them. Going on to Vancouver, Canada, they met their colleagues. Their party of five couples, the M.G. Griebenows, Robert Ekvalls, Charles Koenigswalds, Edwin Carlsons and Carter Holtons and five children, left by ship on September 6, 1928. The weeks-long voyage gave them a chance to rest before arrival in Shanghai and the long trip inland. Travel to the interior in those days was fraught with tension along the way. At one point, they had to argue with Chinese and American authorities for grudged permission to continue heading inland. They traveled in an unheated box car for five days, then many more in six mule carts in weather which had turned bitter cold. On the way, they heard rumors about Muslim rebel forces in Kansu, roundly denied by the Chinese military. At last, they arrived in *Lunghsi,* the first C&MA station in eastern Kansu. Despite having much less "seniority" on the mission staff, Bob's ability to persuade officials to give safe-conduct passes to the party made him a *de-facto* leader alongside field chairman, Al Fesmire.

The rumors about the Muslim rebel soldiers became reality about ten miles from *Lunghsi.* Unexpectedly, the missionaries found themselves caught between rebel and provincial troops. Fortunately, they managed to cover the last few miles in the lumbering mule carts and arrived safely at an inn. Everybody believed the Muslim rebels would overrun Lunghsi the next day. Bob suggested that, as foreigners, they might get a "safe pass" for their mule train. The cart drivers reluctantly lent horses to Bob and Al Fesmire for a risky scouting trip. Encountering no soldiers, they returned safely to the inn.

Early the next day Bob and Dick Koenigswald went out hoping to meet the Muslim troop's commander, the "Little General" whom Bob had met in Labrang years earlier. Right after daybreak they met Muslim scouts, who took a pistol, watch and money from them. Bob insisted that they take them to their officers. They led Bob and Dick at gunpoint to rebel headquarters and the "Major General," now a young man in his early twenties. Fortunately, he greeted them in a friendly fashion and approved giving them safe-conduct passes. Before returning to their companions, they had to witness a bloody fight. Muslim foot soldiers, wielding their swords and cry, "Allah is great; kill, kill!", charged the Chinese machine guns nests. The battle was short and brutal. The Chinese soldiers fled before the fanatical rebels, only to be cut down by rebel cavalry in a pincer move from the sides. Sent on their way by the young general's ironic words "Peacefully on your way; until we meet again," Bob and Dick arrived at the inn to the relief of their colleagues.

Chinese Roadside Inn.

They began the final leg of the trek before sunrise and saw nothing in the villages save a few scavenger dogs, and dead bodies in the fields. When they reached Lunghsi at midnight after a tense day of travel, they found the city gates bolted shut. However, having sent word ahead, the gates opened and the anxious church leaders warmly received the tired travelers. When they realized that the missionaries had not returned to take control of the Chinese church, but to work with the Tibetans and Muslims, they were even more welcoming.

"It's Up to You, Bob, . . . You've Done It Before."

Shortly after celebrating Christmas of 1928 in Lunghsi, the group divided, with Fesmires, Carlsons, and Ekvalls traveling to Taochow Old City, only to find it terrorized, with the Muslims of the city divided. Some sided with the rebel soldiers, but the New Sect Muslims took no part in the fighting. Tibetans refused to stay in the town, and the local Chinese constantly feared rumors of another attack. Then, Will Simpson, reeling from fatigue, rode into town announcing that the Little General was on his way. Refugees flooded into the mission station, believing that Bob's relationships with the Little General would keep them safe. At night-fall, prayer began in the church while Bob, Al Fesmire, and Ed Carlson worked out what to do if things got critical. Bob and Betty had already prayed and Betty's deep calm and trust in God gave him peace and courage. They waited inside the gate for whatever might come next. All of a sudden, bugles sounded and hooves clattered outside, followed by a pounding on the gate and a shouted command: "Open up!" Will Simpson's wise counsel came to mind: "Take all precautions, trust in God's care, and never panic." Al muttered, "It's up to you, Bob, to talk us to safety—you've done it before."[90] Ed gripped Bob's shoulder and opened the gate just wide enough to squeeze through; then it closed behind him.

Rifle barrels met Bob as he pushed through the gate and the lock clicked shut. Immediately, he and the angry Muslim rebels began arguing. Bob, refused to open the gate, and they threatened instant death, demanding to be let in to the compound full of fearful Chinese. Bob wasted no time with oriental niceties. He shouted back in their face threats of punishment from "the little General," his personal friend. Turning his flashlight onto his face, he asked, "Didn't you see me ride with the Little General to battle at Lung-hsi?" The shouted warning caused another voice in the darkness to cry out: "He is the bearded one who rode at Lung-hsi. Move on."[91] The rifles quickly dropped out of sight and the faceless voice spoke again, "Sir, sorry we did not recognize you. No one will bother you now." Fumes of fury, close to blazing, quickly dissipated. Bob stayed in front of the mission gate, keeping the curious away with a wave of his flashlight, and soon the streets emptied. Bob went back inside to join the prayer meeting as the gate was barred once again. Praise for the protection of Yeshu rose high that night. The fugitives from violence lit fires and cooked a very late dinner, then found somewhere to sleep. The watchman at the gate reported that the rebels left town to the sound of bugles.

Early the next morning, Bob left the compound and walked the empty streets. While barren of people, they were full of wandering cattle and sheep. Setting out to find the Little General's headquarters, Bob's goal was to "stretch" his safe-conduct pass into something a bit more extensive that would cover at least the two hundred refugees in the compound. At a roofed-over courtyard, he went in to talk with the teenage officer, when a horrific sight met his eyes:

> "At almost every post a naked figure was bound with back to the post in the zero temperature. Some were already nodding into sleep that ends in death, others, streaked with blood twisted and moaned, and one figure nearest where I waited was fully conscious, his eyes met mine pleadingly."[92]

These Tibetans, tied and tortured by the Muslim rebels, were paying for the outrage of brutalizing "the daughter of the saintly mullah and mistreating her virginity." A burly Muslim rebel raged at the atrocity before slashing the Tibetan's genitals: "Dog-headed Tibetan barbarians—animals all . . . ." Rather than kill the Tibetan brave, he smiled cruelly, "This way you die more slowly with much more pain," as he turned and walked away. Shaken by the savage scene, Bob was led into the Little General's (Ma Zhongying) headquarters. While extremely occupied with military dispatches, the smooth-faced young man greeted Bob and said they would talk again the next day and "take tea together." Bob returned to the mission and Betty sleepily greeted him. "You and the Little General get along well together."[93] And amazingly, the paradox of friendship between Ekvall and the diminutive Muslim leader, born years before on a quick visit to Labrang Monastery, proved true.

The next morning, soon after sunrise, a messenger came from the young General Ma-Zhongying asking Bob to go to his headquarters.

Tea was served, but that was not on his mind. "Do you know how to treat wounds? I have many wounded men, and they need medicine? What medicine do you have?" Bob assured him that the missionaries had plenty of medicine and some skills in dealing with wounds. Tea time quickly ended and Bob soon found himself working with Ed Carlson on first aid treatment for minor cuts as well as some major gashes and serious wounds. Although they had plenty of gauze, iodine, carbolic acid, Vaseline, and even sutures and surgical instruments, they had nothing for pain. As Bob described it, "We had no painkiller, but the sturdy Moslems had no moans, and would watch grimly as a pus-filled wound was swabbed with iodine and then sewed up."[94]

By the afternoon, the clinic closed, but Bob was escorted into a room where the daughter of the Muslim Patriarch lay, she, whose torture had enraged the Muslim fighters. "The soles of her feet and palms of her hands had been badly burned with branding irons and, though not raped, her private parts had been roughly treated with bamboo splinters." She had been chained to the floor of a stable without food or drink for two days, until rescued by Muslim soldiers. Bob treated the festering wounds on her hands and feet. As he worked to bring relief to her pain, her gray-bearded mullah father stoically watched. After cleansing and sewing her wounds, he left. On the next day, she seemed improved, but the fear of tetanus never left Ekvall's mind. On the morning of the third day, as Bob changed her bandages, the tell-tale signs of tetanus stood out. Fever, muscle rigidity and bright-red blisters at the wound site. He calmly cleaned the area and wrapped her wounds with fresh bandages and signaled to her father to follow him outside. "What is the will of Allah?" he asked. Bob told him that he had done all that he could medically, and that, notwithstanding Allah's power to heal, he could only recommend ways to reduce the pain of his daughter's last hours. He suggested obtaining opium from the Chinese and mixing it with her drink, to help relieve her pain. Grimly the old mullah replied, "It is the will of Allah. There remains only revenge."[95]

A "foreign devil" in the eyes of the average Chinese, Bob's relationship with the Muslim rebels under the Little General took on a different light. Since Christian missionaries were not "idolatrous infidels" but rather, "People of the Book," (Christian, Jew and Muslim), they were sometimes seen as co-religionaries. Ma Zhongying told Bob that the reason he and six other young Muslim officers in the Chinese army rebelled was due to how "the Chinese government looked down upon and mistrusted the Moslems . . . ."[96]

Would You Be Willing to Try to Make a Truce . . . ?

The next day, another call to tea with General Ma-Zhongying introduced a serious matter. "Would you be willing to try to make a truce between the Chone Prince and me?" He explained that he had no axe to grind with the truculent tyrant hated alike by Chinese, Muslim and his Tibetan townspeople. Bob agreed that he and Ed Carlson, who lived in Chone, would try to establish a truce to lower tensions in the region. The two missionaries went off with an escort of bodyguards for the Tibetan town about fifteen miles from Taochow Old City. Since Ed had lived in Chone for two years and had many acquaintances in town, they felt the prospects for a peaceful solution seemed favorable.

Approaching the pass that opened onto the town, armed Tibetans rode up waving bits of white cloth as they recognized Ed and Bob as friends. The bodyguards held back while the two peacemakers trotted up to a highly decorated official's tent. Ed recognized the "headman" and they greeted each other warmly. Leading the two missionaries some distance up the hillside to avoid eager ears, he listened as Ed delivered the message from the Little General to the Chone Prince, i.e., a desire for a truce and the brokering of a peace deal. Sadly, the headman shook his head. Bob later wrote: "Our mission was useless. The Prince was not in Chone." At the first alarm about the Little General's forces in Taochow, he had packed up and fled beyond the Min Mountains, literally burning the bridges behind him. Adding insult to injury, he ordered the local Chone garrison to fight to the death against the Muslim marauders. Feeling the bitterness of failure, as Bob and Ed were about to leave, the headman asked what they thought Ma Zhongying's reaction would be. Bob's expressed that this was the first time in two or more years of fighting between the Chinese and the Little General, that he had ever proposed a truce. More than that, Bob could not answer.[97]

Returning to Taochow, Bob reported the results of their failed truce-making task. "The Little General waved his hand depreciatingly. 'It isn't your fault. You did well in danger, and you found out all the facts. Go back to your mission to have a good meal and rest peacefully tonight . . . . The Chone Prince doesn't like my peace; maybe he would like my war."[98]

By nightfall, crescent-flag-led troops left Taochow with horse hooves clattering on paving stones and bugles blaring indignation at the Chone prince's arrogance. Clearly, vengeance was afoot. The Muslim forces arrived at the entrance to Chone finding no guard posted, the city defenseless and the population nowhere to be found. Only the monastery monks remained to put up a stiff fight but were crushed; their religious fortress was destroyed. The Muslim rebels pillaged and burned the town, including the Alliance mission station. With no population present to resist, the Muslim raiders "Sucked the bones of Chone clean" and left the town in ruins. They uncovered a hidden trove of the Prince's wealth in money and silver in his palace-like *Yamen* and took it, "To make the Chone Prince a beggar, . . . With your [Bob's] help I offered him peace, but he chose war."[99] Many years later, Bob would again witness the destructive instincts of General Ma Zhongying far to the northwest in Turkmenistan, today's Xinjiang.

The 1927 evacuation had left Will Simpson laboring alone on the border. All C&MA and AG workers had gone to the coast and returned to America. Will's colleagues, the Swedish couple, Torsten and Elna Halldorf, had just gotten established in Rongwo, a monastery town. After receiving orders to evacuate, Torsten somehow feared he would never get back there. However, having no choice, they returned to Sweden and remained there until their return to China in 1929. They stayed in *Peking (Beijing)* until the spring of 1930 for more language study, then set off for the Tibetan border with part of the Sven Hedin expedition. They arrived at the Lupa-si station where Fesmires had moved after the Taochow mission had been trashed. Shortly after arrival, Torsten, who felt unwell on the trip, grew very sick; after weeks of gradually weakening, he passed away from pulmonary failure on August 17, 1930. His prophetic premonition proved true. The Ekvalls, close friends of Torsten and Elna, sorely missed the passionate Swede whose love for the Tibetan people knew no bounds. Torsten's death, which occurred while Will Simpson sought medical help for his colleague and friend, left him devastated and still working alone. Such was life, and death, on the Tibetan border.[100]

After their return to the borderland in 1928, Ed and Carol Carlson went to live among the Dragsgumna villages of Stonebox Valley, 50 miles south of Taochow. They moved there in May 1929 due to the destruction of the Chone mission station where they previously had lived and worked. After about two years in the safe but isolated Stonebox valley, the Carlsons came to the conclusion that it limited access to the many unreached Tebbu tribes, who Bob called "surly morose, violent and un-predictable." They pushed farther south past the jagged peaks to *Denga*, to live in the only place opened to them, a mud and stone house with a small "penthouse." They later found out that the houseowner had rented them rooms to spite fellow villagers. In all this, the Lord's hand guided their move. At least one unforeseen benefit came from the 1928–29 Muslim Rebellion; the Tibetans now saw the "foreigners" as refugees from violence; consequently, they permitted Ekvalls to live with their fat friend, Duggur, in Samtsa Rong and the Carlsons in Tebbu land. Bob and Ed were close friends as well as "neighbors," since they were "up south" and far from their other colleagues. They often rode together visiting the nomads in their summer pasture highlands.

On one occasion, riding through a desolate region, as they ap-proached a bend in the trail, around came armed horsemen, clearly a danger to the two missionaries. The group reined in their horses at some distance as did Bob and Ed, who laid their rifles across the saddle pom-mels and waited. Unexpectedly, the Tibetan braves whirled their horses around, galloped away and disappeared in a few minutes. Ekvall and Carlson, while perplexed, praised the Lord.

"Who Was That "Shining One" With You?"

Sometime later, Bob stopped at an inn and recognized one of the braves from the encounter on the trail. Curious as to why they left in a hurry, Bob asked, "Why didn't you attack us? After a pause, the man replied, "There were more of you. We weren't afraid of you. We weren't afraid of your friend. But who was that *shining one* with you?"[101] Angels unawares.

Meanwhile, the Muslim rebels finally abandoned the border for pil-lage and rape elsewhere, and the Tibet team settled into mission quarters in *Hehtsuh* (*Linxia, Hezuo*), and Lupa. During the summer months of 1929, the five couples (Ekvalls, Carlsons, Koenigswald, Derks and Fes-mires) itinerated among Tibetan nomads in the region, distributing tracts and gospels and developing host/sponsor relationships as they traveled. Ekvalls prepared for a two month trip into the grasslands to the south-west to visit their old friend, Duggursjip among the Samtsa tents. Using the dozen-strong mdzo (yak-cow hybrid) paid for with the offering from The Omaha Gospel Tabernacle, they traveled at the leisurely pace of the Tibetans, carrying all they needed for an extended journey. David, now four, too big to be carried, had progressed, first to a little female donkey, then a small gray horse. They gained valuable experience revisiting tribes met on their first trip to Ngawa in 1926.

Later that same summer while visiting with Duggur and his two wives, local extremist Taochow Muslims began senseless looting and killing. The more progressive "New Sect" Muslims of Taochow resisted and evacuated their people, getting word of the destruction to Bob and Betty.

"The Shining One," 1999.

The Fesmires had left the city for the safer climes of the Charkhi monastery and the "friendly monks." The Alliance mission station, despite caretakers on site, was sacked again. Eventually, Chinese troops arrived and drove out the rebels; then, just as senselessly, they torched the town. Only six buildings remained standing, including the Alliance mission station. Robert Ekvall found the town in shambles; and once again, he returned in time to intervene and save what was left of the old station, though Chinese soldiers had ransacked it, taking all they wanted and destroying the rest. Except for a few things in a hidden closet, the Ekvalls lost household goods, clothing, footwear, and Bob's papers, poems, graduation thesis from Wheaton. The paper served to start fires.

Since Bob knew the Chinese general in charge of the troops, *Tung Kuan, Chi Si-chang* (Division commander Chi), he ordered his soldiers to guard the mission station from further damage. Two years earlier, this same general, a Christian, had opened the gates of Lunghsi long after midnight when the KTBM missionaries returned from the emergency evacuation furlough. His mission in Taochow did not please him, but he kept his troops occupied cleaning up the city. He had no affinity for the Tibetan "wild barbarians"[102] and wondered why Bob would waste his time trying to evangelize such savages. Despite the difference of opinion, he and Bob had a good relationship. The last time they met before he departed with his troops, they gave each other the traditional Chinese farewell, "All the road in peace," with the addendum, "The Lord protect." They never met again.

After General Chi's troops left, angry soldiers from the Chone militia (half Chinese, half Tibetan) arrived and swung into action. They went to the Islamic cemetery where between two and three thousand Muslim men were held prisoner, half-starved and weak from hunger. The militia beheaded the Muslims, swinging their short swords all day, shouting vengeance against these members of the local New Sect population, largely innocent of the senseless killing and looting done by the Little General's rebel Muslim soldiers. Since he and his troops were gone, these local followers of the prophet would do.

On the day after the Muslim massacre, Bob heard women and children screaming from the nearby New Sect compound. These were the wives and children of husbands who had days before been beheaded by the Chone soldiers. Bob ran to the compound and found the soldiers from Chone trying to break down the heavy gate of the Muslim compound to kill the rest of the families. He pushed his way to the front of the compound gate. There, he sat:

> On the doorstep with my rifle across my knees. The gun was of small importance—there were quite a number of guns in the hands of the Chone militia. Instead, I reached, as I had often done, for language and its power to drive men into reality and break up make-believe. I blistered them in Chinese, telling them the troubles they would make for themselves, and the still greater trouble I would bring upon them. In confusion, they drifted down the trail to their distant camp; the sobs of the women and children ceased.[103]

These women and children were all who remained alive from the sizeable Muslim population of Taochow Old City, saved by Bob, a Christian "man of the book."

The next day, Chinese replacement troops arrived with a new chief official, secretary and guard; the officer asked to talk with Bob. Seeing the size of the Alliance mission compound, he tried to commandeer it for his use. However, Bob responded that with "law and order" coming back to Taochow through the government troops, he, their head officer, represented protection of the mission station property and its building for church services and conferences. In addition, the Tibetan guest rooms needed repair for use by nomads who came to town to trade. The official finally gave up and ordered the postmaster to give them an armful of mail, the first received in months. One letter asked if it was safe for the rest of the missionaries to return to town, and Bob assured them it was time.

Gradually, by 1930, things returned to some semblance of law and order in the region. No missionaries lived in Taochow Old City for the next ten years. Yet, over time, more progress than setbacks occurred in the outreach effort among the Tibetans. The Ekvalls made their temporary residence in Samtsa through the sponsorship of the "smiling Buddha," Duggursjip. While sometimes discouraged, with broken promises and open hostility shown in some villages, their rotund sponsor found them a few mud-walled rooms where they could escape the bitter cold of winter. Then, traveling the familiar trail to Lhamo once more in early spring 1930, with Duggur, long-time confidante of the authorities of both *Gurdu* and *Sechu* monasteries, Bob and Betty hoped that this time they could move to their long-prayed-for new home. While both monasteries were of the same *Gelugpa* Tibetan Buddhist sect, Gurdu gompa, with its one thousand two hundred monks, looked down on their coreligionists on the opposing hillside across the valley, with "only" eight hundred monks. Occasionally, over the years, they had even fought with each other. The possibility of success in receiving permission depended on the obvious ill will between the two *gompas*. Perhaps one might give permission the other might deny, simply out of spite. That seemed a pattern observed in the past.

Back in 1927, before the emergency evacuation, a tentative promise of land from Gurdu had been made. After three long years, Bob wanted to settle the matter. With scarf-covered gifts in hand, Bob and Duggur called on the steward. Duggur, the "man of strong words," spoke while

Bob silently prayed. His presentation of Bob's petition in eloquent Tibetan oration included a masterwork of proverbs, quotations, and other rhetorical devices. Bob managed to follow the high points but got lost in the florid prose. The steward began his reply, like a steam locomotive gradually gaining speed and power. After the introductory niceties, Bob soon understood the main points. "No land will be given. The foreigner may visit. He will be welcomed as a guest. But the speaker of a foreign religion may not live in Lhamo. No. No. No!"[104]

Fed-up, Duggur stormed out while the steward was still talking, sarcastically calling back over his shoulder, "Why then did you accept the gifts?" Bob stayed till the bitter end out of respect, then returned to the dank Gurdu guest room. He found that Duggur had packed his bag and left word for Bob to meet him up on the trail the next day. Hence, Bob spent a cold night alone in prayer. Next morning, dark and rainy, Bob wondered as he crossed the swollen creek dividing the valley if he would ever live in Lhamo, seemingly as inaccessible as the surrounding sharp-toothed peaks. Suddenly, Bob heard an excited voice:

"Get a present; let's go see the Sechu *ombo* [head steward]. And don't be stingy with the gift!" Bob had no stomach for disappointment, but his friend insisted, explaining that he had talked the previous night with the Sechu steward as to why having the foreigners living at Sechu gompa was a good idea. Bob had "strong medicine" that actually worked on wounds and common ailments. In addition, the thought that Sechu, the smaller monastery, could one-up Gurdu proved a winning point. Entering the Sechu steward's warm audience room, Bob listened as Duggur argued with the monk manager. His polite reply seemed noncommittal and Bob left wondering, but Duggur, his friend of "strong words," radiated certainty. "It's all settled." And to Ekvall's delight, it was settled once and for all.

Consequently, in the fall of 1930, the Ekvall family moved into what Bob termed a "nondescript shack" with cluttered yard enclosed within a flimsy fence on the edge of Sechu's squalid trading post. Soon after moving in, their "station" boasted a yard full of horses and cattle. Nomad guests slept everywhere as Bob and Betty hosted tribal friends that had received them in their travels. At one point, Bob set up a yurt-like tent as a guestroom, where yak butter-tea flowed and the salvation story of the Jesus way explained.

The next two years, passed rapidly with an ever-widening circle of friends and friendly territory at their disposal. Whenever possible, the family traveled together to visit the different tribes and clans, often hostile to each other, but all friends of the "foreign devils." In time, Bob and Betty needed a bigger home to receive their guests and a larger lot for a proper station. After months of waiting and praying, the Sechu monastery donated a small but adequate piece of land on the hillside below the monastery looking over the rushing creek. A twelve foot wall of packed earth and rocks provided security, since they were in Lhamo, not heaven. The foreigner's "obvious wealth" challenged the thieving spirit of some of their neighbors. High walls, strong gates and several big Tibetan mastiffs made for good neighbors.

Now with a property, they needed a house; and a well-built one which had belonged to the former Gurdu monastery steward had come on the market. At the price of one hundred and twenty pieces of silver, it wasn't cheap., but it was a fine wood-frame house, easy to disassemble and reassemble on the mission property. The fact that the house was "haunted" made it more possible. Someone had died in it and the monks feared the spirit of the dead, not a problem for the Yeshu-talkers. They struck a deal and gave official permission for the sale. Bob moved in with carpenters and workers to disassemble the frame house cleverly built and held together with pegs and mortices. After removing a large amount of boards and beams, the Gurdu authorities turned around and ordered the return of the material, a demand refused by Ekvall. Stalemate set in, for two weeks; neither side would budge. That is, not until one of Bob's monk friends from the Sechu monastery sat with a gun across his legs in front of the mission property, proclaiming that he would shoot whoever tried to take back the pile of boards and beams already removed. After more frantic back and forth, Bob was counseled to take a "face-saving" gift wrapped in a beautiful silk khata to the Gurdu steward, who finally honored his original decision. The logjam broke, and next day, the rest of the house came across the creek and up the little hill to the work site. Their home, located "on the edge," was part of the dirty market town of shops and houses outside the walls of the monastery. Both Gurdu and Sechu "edges," were made up of small business owners and families who lived off the relationship with the monasteries.

Bob, David and Betty Ekvall, 1932.

The early years in Lhamo proved challenging since not everyone "on the edge" or in the monasteries was happy with the foreigner's presence. Nightly, rocks flew over the wall, gunfire interrupted their sleep, and shouted threats of robbery and ruin came from angry voices outside their barricade. Dogs howled and snarled, and sleep fled many nights. Yet, daily contact over weeks, months and eventually more than a year brought change. During the summer when big religious events took place, the twin-town population swelled and the curious came to visit. The Ekvalls served tubfulls of tea to those who wanted to see the blond-haired, blue-eyed "devil," but Betty's dark hair and olive complexion won their hearts. Little David, while blond like his dad, brought murmurs of admiration because he spoke Tibetan just like them. Bob would break out his guitar and sing of the love of the great Creator God and "salvation's way through Yeshu." Attentive crowds slurped butter-tea in wooden bowls and mixed dried cheese into their tsampa with grimy fingers When leaving, they gave thumbs-up to the hospitality of the foreigners.

In the summer of 1932, Ed and Carol Carlson plugged on in unfriendly Denga, putting up with harassment from the Tebbu tribesmen who threatened to torch their home, steal their horses or even attack them. Meanwhile, the Ekvalls headed southwest toward Ngawa territory once again. This time, Dr. Vaughn Rees and his wife, China Inland Mission workers based at the CIM hospital in Lanzhou, traveled with them. Setting off with the adults and the slow-moving hybrid yak caravan, seven year-old David Ekvall, with his little .22 rifle hung over his shoulder, rode his own pony.

On this trip, Bob and Betty's second to the distant Mei Kingdom, they went no longer as "unwanted interlopers," but welcome visitors. The queen, who had returned the New Testament on the first visit, asked for another copy, read it and asked questions about its contents. During the three week stay, formerly unfriendly neighboring *Golok* (wild nomad) tribesmen welcomed them. The leader of the *Kang Sar Goloks*, twelve days away, pleaded for Bob to visit. Another Golok chief promised access to "six thousand tents" seven day's travel west. More surprisingly, the royal family asked the Ekvalls to move to Ngawa and live there. Suddenly, barriers fell and opportunities beyond their wildest dreams appeared.

We Stared at One Another With Mutual Amazement

While visiting Ngawa, Bob met an intriguing man in the royal guest hall drinking butter tea and tsampa. Bob, wearing a Tibetan robe, met an official, obviously Tibetan "dressed nattily as a Chinese officer carrying himself with certain aloof distinction and evidently of considerable importance and privilege, and we stared at one another with mutual amazement."[105] What could have brought this unusual Tibetan official to travel so far to this distant realm hundreds of miles from Lanzhou? This strange figure, *Legs Bshad Rgya Mtsho*, a former Tibetan monk from Labrang monastery far to the north, had been Will Simpson's Tibetan teacher back in 1920. Once a rising star among his peers, Legs Bshad had learned much about the gospel and the world beyond the monastery's walls. After months of dialogue with Will, exposure to Western maps, the Gospel, books on history and culture, the monk became disillusioned after recognizing the flimsy theological fabric of Tibetan Buddhism. Despairing his fate of living and working in a religious system he no longer believed in, he won a reprieve from a double life of unbelief when appointed to work with the Chinese government as secretary of the Tibetan Affairs Bureau, with the enthusiastic approval of the monastery authorities.

As they talked together, Bob and Legs discovered a mutual connection through Will Simpson, Ekvall's first cousin. Sadly, as they met in the summer of 1932, they did not know that Will's body lay by a remote mountain road riddled by thirteen bullets. During his time in Ngawa fulfilling official duties, only once did Legs talk about Will. Only then, "did he lift the curtain of the past and reveal some of the agony of conviction and indecision that had been his. And even then he held it resolutely in the past, giving it no place in the present."[106]

In early August, after the very promising visit with the Mei royal family, the Ekvalls returned to Lhamo where they received the news of Will Simpson's death.[107] Shocked and saddened, Bob deeply sensed the loss of his cousin and colleague. The tensions raised by the arrival of AG missionaries on the Kansu-Tibetan frontier in 1918 had never hindered their relationship as "family and brothers" in Christ. Bob wrote a letter of consolation to Will's father, W. W. Simpson, dated August 5, 1932, expressing all that Will meant to him and the Tibetan people: "We can still hardly sense what our personal loss will be to say nothing of the seemingly irreparable loss to the Tibetan work. The last few years Will has seemed very close to all of us and we have come more and more to look up to him in every way."[108] All of the Tibetan border missionaries, whether AG, C&MA or CIM, lamented the loss of this godly good man. Now without him, trails that he had opened to the nomads beckoned to them.

The following year, well established in Lhamo, the Ekvalls gradually extended their influence in ever widening circles. At the annual yak caravan, they visited old and new friends, distributing tracts and gospels to those who could read, praying for the sick, stitching up wounds, and giving simple medical treatment. Each evening, they sang of Yeshu and his love, followed by a Bible story that helped the listeners understand Yeshu's free gift, "salvation's way." This offer of unearned redemption and forgiveness offended many and puzzled most. Yet, the life ministry of the Ekvalls exemplified what they preached. They served others and charged nothing. They itinerated among the tribes and never asked for offerings in exchange for their prayers, as did the monks and their holy lamas. While the soul soil remained hard, it seemed to be softening, which brought encouragement to Bob and Betty and the whole Tibetan border mission.

Near the end of summer 1933, mail from America arrived. Eagerly opening the letters, one suddenly brought another rush of sorrow and loss. Bob's mother, Helen Gailbraith Ekvall, had died on June 5 from a heart attack following complications from pneumonia at the age of sixty-three. After her husband, David, died in 1912 from typhoid, she settled in Wheaton. There, she served as "dorm mother" for male students in a multi-story residence. Known and loved by all at Wheaton College, she led a popular Bible study for students for years. Sadly, by the time this "old news" reached Bob, a couple of months had passed. Bob found comfort in the fact that his parents were in the presence of the One who brings inexpressible joy and peace.

"Do You Believe? . . . A-Ta Answered, 'I Do.'"

Despite sorrow and setbacks, the first fruits of patient planting and cultivation by Bob and Betty sprouted in a heart living in the village of Anitang, where mountain meadows meet the dark spruce of the lower valleys. There, high in Samtsa farm country where barley barely grew lived a young farmer. *A-Ta*, while poor, was held in high regard because he could read and chant the mantras that drove away the harvest-killing hail and deadly livestock disease. Not long after Ekvalls moved to Lhamo, A-ta visited there during *Losar*, the New Year Festival, and stayed in their guest room. For the first time, he heard the strange message of "salvation's way," and returned home with some Yeshu gospels. Over the next three years, he pondered the curiously compelling message of this new "way" of salvation and forgiveness of sins by grace, not by karmic merit. Bob's periodic visit to A-Ta's mountain village gave them time to talk.

At last, returning to Lhamo, A-Ta listened to the good news story again. That night, while sleeping in the mission guest tent, he dreamed that he was falling into a dark pit. However, a figure in white called to him while reaching out and grabbing his hand. A-Ta somehow knew it was Yeshu, and that he was safe. At first light, A-Ta left for his home in the hills. When his neighbors asked him to chant the protective Buddhist chants, the words stuck in his throat. With two friend whom he had told about Yeshu's way of salvation, they went to Lhamo and Bob's guest tent to hear the message again. Finally, Bob, seeing his hunger and hesitation, asked him, "Do you believe? . . . A-Ta answered, 'I do.'"[109]

Returning to his village, A-Ta cut down the prayer flags and removed the "god altar" from his house, much to his mother's dismay. The villagers, seeing his new-found faith in action, watched and waited for the worst to happen. Not long after, angry monks from a nearby monastery joined forces to chant powerful curses on him. Soon, his ox perished from an attack by wild dogs; his horses got sick and died, and he could no longer farm. Yet, he firmly resisted the temptation to go back to chanting for money. He became a woodcutter living in the forest. His two friends also took the Yeshu way and the three men constituted the first Christian fellowship in that part of the Tibetan border.

Ten long years after sensing God's first urgings to work among the Tibetans rather than the Chinese, Bob and Betty felt they were living the dream of open doors, with Ngawa calling them farther to the nomad heartlands. Just at that critical moment, disaster struck.

Early in 1935, as Bob was visiting nomad tribes in the grasslands, Betty fell ill with anthrax, a deadly disease endemic to Tibet's grassy wetlands. The dramatic circumstances of Betty's close call with death were later described by C&MA missionary nurse, Marion Birrel:

> Mr. Ekvall had been away and was returning home when he was met by a messenger sent by the gatekeeper of Lhamo, that his wife was desperately ill. Putting his horse to the test, he left his fellow travelers behind him and did a marathon over the high Tibetan mountains to Lhamo, an altitude of 12,000 feet. He found his wife alive but in a critical condition after a week of suffering. She had no help but her young son, David, who did his best and the uncouth, but faithful Tibetan friends and servants. They lay on the floor in their smelly sheep-skin garments and snored part of the night and did what they could in the daytime when she was conscious enough to tell them what she needed.[110]

Miss Birrel, then serving in distant Titao, traveled with one of the Chinese workers to the Alliance station of Lupa where the Francis Derks lived. Thrilled that someone had come who could possibly help Betty, still in Lhamo, they decided to move her to Lupa, about six thousand feet lower. They made a litter to carry Betty and arrived in Lhamo after two and a half days forced march, to Bob and Betty's joy. Marion described the journey back to Lupa:

> Betty was over the crisis, but action could occur even after a victory. So, we returned to prayer and had consultation. It was decided to try to bring Betty down to a lower altitude where more comforts were available. We had no laboratory to diagnose the illness, but she was not getting any stronger at Lhamo and this decision seemed to be the only one to take. No mule liter (sic) had ever attempted the hazardous journey before. It had to be assembled with special care. Along the route it was necessary

to hack away the undergrowth in places with swords and knives
the Tibetans carry. At other times, the liter (sic) was supported
by several men to keep it on the precipitous road.

With all possible care and speed, they trekked through the mountains, amazingly, in just three days. Surrounded by friends, Betty spent
the next month recuperating at Lupa. However, it became obvious that
she needed proper medical attention; so, another litter trip took Betty
and Bob to Lanzhou via Titao and a long stay at the China Inland Mission's hospital. When Betty's entourage arrived in Titao, she took a turn
for the worse, and Dr. Rees:

> Made a hurried trip down to see her from Lanzhou. The initial
> disease had passed undiagnosed and the heart condition and oth-
> er lingering difficulties were baffling, but the Lord heard prayer
> again and in a few days, the caravan was formed anew and we
> made our way to the capital for a stay in the hospital compound.[111]

Months later, the Ekvalls left for the United States, this time by plane
from Lanzhou. The clinical case baffled the doctors and bewildered the
KTBM mission. Yet at what seemed to be a low point, God came on the
scene in an amazing way. In Bob's own words:

> Some years later, in 1935, we were staying in Lanzhou at the
> China Inland Mission Hospital. Strange and bitter circum-
> stances seemed to have hedged us in from having any part in
> giving the Gospel to the Tibetans. Then one day at a time when
> he thought I was in Taktshang Lhamo and I thought he was in
> Sining, Legs Bshad Rgya Mtsho and I met on the [CIM] hospi-
> tal terrace and the broken thread of interrupted fellowship was
> spliced anew, and throughout the summer with every increasing
> frequency he was our visitor.[112]

After their first encounter in Ngawa in 1932, Bob and Legs Bshad
had corresponded sporadically over the next two years. On one occasion,
Legs went to Lhamo on official government business, but first visited
the Ekvalls in their simple home and they spent most of the day talking about theology, evolution, the biblical creation account, the flood,
Charles Darwin, H. G. Wells and Bertrand Russell. By then, the onetime
monk doubted belief in any god, professing more faith in materialism's
answers to the question of existence. Sadly, this rising Tibetan official in
Kansu's provincial government seemed lost to the message of the gospel.

Legs Was Conflicted and Convicted in His Heart

During those weeks in Lanzhou, the two men often met to discuss the growing menace of communism, since Mao Tse Tung's armies Long Marched near his tribal family's lands. This time, Legs, much more pensive, seemed to have lost faith in materialism in light of Marxism's menace. Their conversations centered around his Tibetan copies of the Pentateuch, Psalms and the New Testament, since the full Bible would not come out until the late 1940s. However, he had more than enough Bible to follow the "blood-stained, blood-bought path that is God's way and the only way for the sinner seeking peace." Plainly, Legs was deeply conflicted; he even shared samples of his poetical compositions and bits of Christian hymns he would write "if he were a believer." Unknown to Legs, Bob had recruited the whole Lanzhou CIM community as well as missionaries working along the border and churches in faraway North America to pray for the former monk and intercede for his salvation. Weary in body and soul, Legs told Bob he couldn't sleep as he struggled between God, or gods or no god.

> So we come to the date Friday the thirteenth of September, 1935. We were to leave very soon, and he had come to say goodbye. For once little of talk and conversation seemed possible between us. Yet he started to raise some of the old discussion, the old arguments and the old doubts, but I felt the matter was out of my hands.
>
> 'We have come to the end of words between us about the truth,' I said. 'Now you must talk to the Lord. If it is *yes,* tell Him. If it is *no,* tell Him.'"
>
> The silence that came lengthened until the suspense was as the unendurable tightening—like a wire—of our very heart-strings, and I could only pray . . . .

Bob had always believed the Buddhist doctrine of reincarnation represented the highest barrier to the Tibetan's placing their faith in the gospel:

> Reincarnation, he wrote, "makes sin a little less awful, it makes salvation a little less blessed, and it takes away the finality of the terrible state of the lost. Always with the recurrent implications of a second, a third, and even an unending succession of chances, it lulls the soul to indecision and indifference. Yet . . . the Holy Spirit used just that masterpiece of Satan—the doctrine of reincarnation—as the last urge to lead him across the border-line of decision.

He spoke—carefully, precisely—as though stating an equa-
tion of mathematics. 'If Buddha is right and Christ is wrong,
even if I follow Christ I only lose my religious chance in this life.
There will be another rebirth and I will have another chance.
But if Buddha is wrong and Christ is right and I do not accept
Christ, then I am lost to the endlessness of time. I will believe.'[113]

On that Friday the 13th, the so-called "bad-luck day" so many fool-
ishly fear, the ex-monk, ex-materialist and now new believer "bet" on his
version of Pascal's Wager, as Bob termed it, "the argument of greater good
or the lesser evil." Truly, God worked in mysterious ways, His wonders to
perform. On that most propitious day, Legs wept his way to the Savior
and sensed his sins bathed away with the fearful burden of endless hell.
At last, after minutes of prayer and confession, silence reigned, that of
peace and rest. Then like a whisper out of his once-tortured soul, Legs
Bshad Rgya Mtsho spoke from behind hands spread to hide his tears,
"All the misery has gone from my heart. Oh, I have been so miserable.'"
This newborn follower of Jesus was the decades-long fruit of two peacemakers: William Simpson and Robert Ekvall. Will plowed and planted,
followed by Bob's patient cultivation of that struggling shoot of "wheat"
pushing its way through the hard Tibetan soul soil. Both men partnered
in bringing the message of peace to Legs' tormented heart.

The Ekvalls left the borderlands in September 1935, flying to the
coast on a Eurasia Airlines tri-motor airplane. Once there, they boarded
the *S. S. President Cleveland* in Shanghai for their return to America and
Betty's long recovery which took till January 1939. Legs continued his
official duties with the Chinese government. Just before his conversion,
he had been invited, to head up a committee for the translation of the
Tibetan Buddhist scriptures into Chinese because of his scholarship
and abilities. The project, to be set up in Shanghai and Nanjing, would
have Legs as chairman with commensurate honors and perks, plus travel
abroad, one of his fondest dreams.

When Bob asked about this, Legs simply said, "Of course now, I
can't have any part of that." Over the next few years, Bob discipled Legs
by mail. He wanted to know the Bible better and even contemplated Bible
school. "What school should I attend to learn more of the Jesus doctrine,
because it must be preached to the Bod [Tibetan] peoples of Amdo."[114]
Even as the Ekvalls had to stay in America for Betty's health, a witness
remained. Bob wrote this story, *God's Miracle in the Heart of a Tibetan*,
published by the C&MA soon after the Ekvalls returned to America.

Chapter 7

Return to Reap

GOING BACK TO WHEATON, the Ekvall's stayed with Betty's family, and David began to "learn America," as his dad had done back in 1912. For the next year, as Betty recuperated, Bob traveled extensively on deputation ministry. Since Betty's illness had been widely known as well as the breakthrough on the Tibetan border, he was sought after. One of Betty's cousins wrote in a letter to *Prairie Publications*, a description of Betty's health upon return to America: "Betty's Anthrax was the gastro-intestinal form. She was sure it came from a mountain sheep's liver. There, all meat came from hunting. Betty was never very strong afterward, like someone recovering from a serious nervous breakdown, trouble sleeping, tiring easily, couldn't be in crowded places, etc."[115]

Following that first year of heavy travel, Bob was given leave by the C&MA to study anthropology at the University of Chicago, fall semester of 1937 and spring of 1938, where he also took a class in Sanskrit as the professor's only student! Because he had on-the-field experience among "real, live Tibetans," his professors actively engaged him in order to learn more about the culture of those living on the West China-Tibetan border. As a part of his study program, he presented a paper, *Cultural Relations on the Kansu-Tibetan Border* in 1939, which was later republished by the University of Chicago Press in 1964. Despite pleas from the department head for Bob to remain at the University and complete a PhD, he and Betty did not give the offer even a second thought, as their heart's desire was to return to their home in Lhamo.

Their long stay in America also resulted in Bob's writing career taking off. His first work was *God's Miracle in the Heart of a Tibetan*, the thrilling story of Legs Bshad Rgya Mtsho, published in 1936 by Christian Publications, Inc. (CPI), the Alliance publishing house. Wanting to use Bob's writing ability to its greatest advantage, the Alliance asked the Ekvalls to move to Nyack to write a history of the Kansu-Tibetan Border Mission, *Gateway to Tibet*, which came out in 1938. Then, Bob headed up a writing team that produced the history of The Christian and Missionary Alliance, *After Fifty Years*, printed the next year. Bob was not pleased by the editorial changes made by CPI and asked to have his name removed as lead writer; however, the request was denied since his name helped guarantee that the book sold well. During that long furlough, from 1936 to 1939, Bob wrote numerous articles for *The Alliance Weekly* as well as a series of poems, which were later published by CPI as *Monologues from the Chinese*.

Betty gradually regained strength, and the couple's determination to return to work among their beloved Tibetan tribesmen convinced the mission to send them back on January 27, 1939. Boarding ship in San Francisco for their third term of missionary service, they sailed to Hong Kong. From there, they took another ship to Haiphong, major port in French Indo-China. The family of three with all their baggage took a train to Hanoi, capital of the northern province of Tonkin, then, traveled south on another train to Dalat in Annam, the beautiful central highland province. There, they left fourteen year-old David to study at the C&MA's Dalat School for missionary children. After taking a few weeks to help David settle into dorm life and high school, Bob and Betty left him bravely waving as their train steamed out of the station and rolled back to Hanoi for their journey to Takhtsang Lhamo "through the back door."

They traveled north from Hanoi by narrow-gauge train up through the mountains, crossing roaring rivers and wrought-iron bridges stretched across wide valley spans, until they reached the border of China and on to *Kunming (Hunan-fu)*, capital of Yunnan Province. From Kunming, they went by road to Chongqing (Chungking), a major city on the Yangtze River. There, they met C&MA missionaries who had driven from Hong Kong to West China in two mission trucks.

Dalat MK School, 1930s.

Bob and Betty experienced the first great raid of Japan's Imperial Air Force in Chungking in May 1939, when it mercilessly attacked the poorly-defended city. From the garden of the U.S. Embassy on the south bank of the river, he described the air raid:

> The city of Chungking [Chonqing] boiled in a sudden upheaval of flying wreckage and black dust, while, with the terrific (sic) of bursting bombs which seemed to explode simultaneously, there came a fierce blast of air that bent the trees around us. The black shroud billowed over the whole rock of Chungking, and for some minutes it seemed as though the whole city had gone. As the dust settled the smoke rose above it, and in that cloud which was Chungking's sunset to a cloudless day strange red flares half a mile above the city showed the location of the fires that raged below. By nightfall the entire horizon was red with fires.[116]

The bombers had circled the city and dropped their lethal load on the southern end at the meeting of the Chialing and Yangtze rivers. In five minutes, the entire lower end of the city became a smoldering heap of crumbling walls and geysers of dust rising up to meet the flames and smoke.

> Under cover of darkness my wife and I recrossed the river and found the truck I was driving and had left in the city, miraculously intact within the stricken area and, after sitting out the

night in the cab—no movement or lights were permitted—we
pulled out at daybreak with my load of mission supplies and
gasoline, through the streets, where houses burned on one side
or both, to merge with the thousands who were fleeing what
seemed like a doomed city.[117]

From there, Bob drove one of the trucks on the "highway" northwest to *Chengdu* (*Chengtu*), the capital of Sichuan Province, a distance of
about one hundred eighty miles. Leaving their colleagues in Chengdu,
Bob and Betty rode north, crossing part of the vast "red basin" of Sichuan
before arriving at *Sungpan*. They did not stay long due to Betty's weakened condition. On the last leg of the trip, litter bearers carried Betty
while Bob rode alongside. "For days they followed in the footsteps of
one of the Communist armies in the famous Long March . . . . As they
crossed the uninhabited grasslands north of Sungpan, they saw hundreds
of skulls of soldiers who had died in that deadly stretch of land."[118]

Duggur Had Died Murmuring "Jesus, Jesus, Jesus"

Continuing northward, they left the grasslands and entered mountainous
terrain where they encountered nomads as they drew nearer to Lhamo.
They passed through villages Bob had visited in previous years. The closer they got to their mission station, the more their hearts rejoiced that
they were "coming home." Upon arrival, friends and neighbors, once cold
and devious, now celebrated their return, crowding into the courtyard
of the station to greet them. Three years of absence required hours of
tea-drinking and catching up. David's absence demanded answers about
his whereabouts and need for schooling. While not fully understanding,
the population of Taktshang Lhamo, "sacred and profane," received them
with open arms.

The joyous neighbors shared the "latest local news," births, deaths,
marriages and feuds. Bob and Betty sadly received the news of the recent
death of their Samtsa tribe host-sponsor, Dzopa Duggursjip, or just plain
"Duggur," the man of "strong words," who had argued with the monks of
Gurdu and Sechu monasteries before giving final permission for Ekvalls
to establish residence in Lhamo. Over the years, they had made many
visits to Duggur's unusual two-tent and two-wives home. Bob had often
shared the message of Christ's grace gift of salvation. At first uninterested,
Duggur gradually began to question his religion. One of Bob's poems

printed in *The Alliance Weekly*, "Aged Dweller of Tents," described Duggur's spiritual journey.

> I WISH, alas, I wish I knew
> Which way is right, which way is true.
> Four years ago [when he and Bob first met] I knew, without,
> The slightest whispering of doubt,
> Which way was heaven, which dropped below.
> Of course, I knew the way I'd go.
> It was the way of fifty years,
> It was the way, with pain and fears,
> I'd built by pilgrimage and prayer,
> And pious offerings everywhere.
> So merit—surely reckoned mine
> By gifts at every tower and shrine –
> Would balance all my sins and blots:
> Salvation by the Bodhisats.
> But Shes-rab's (Ekvall's Tibetan name] faith, his Jesus Lord,
> Was just a tale too weak, to ward
> Away the fear and painful strife
> Of all that somber afterlife.
> *I wish, my life, I wish I knew*
> *Which way is right, which way is true.*

The next three verses described Duggur's next three years. Faith in his good works gradually weakened as his questions about the grace-gift of salvation by Yeshu's perfect work on the cross slowly penetrated his heart. The poem ends with one last, long verse:

> Ah, She-rab, come within the tent,
> And talk with me, then I'm content.
> You tell me now, I must believe
> In Jesus' name, and so receive
> Salvation free—I like to hear
> That name of Jesus, in my ear.
> Its sound is sweet in song or prayer.
> I hear its whisper everywhere
> When you have told me about His love,
> And all the tent sites up above,
> Where I can pitch my tent and stay
> Encamped within the realm of day.
> Yet, how can I of surety
> Know it is meant for even me?
> And of my tribe, must I alone

Be first to call your faith my own?
For I am old; it's hard to change
To ways uncertain, steps so strange.
Suppose I change and changing fail
To plant my feet upon that trail.
Then good or bad I will have lost
My way, nor gained, at any cost,
Your faith. And so between the two
I fall, and fail to find the true.
My heart's so dark—my day is night –
Ah, Shes-rab, pray that God's own light
Will come and drive the mists away
So I may walk where it is day.
I wish, strange God, I wish I knew
Which way is right, which way is true.[119]

When one of the Samtsa tribe visited the Ekvall's guest room in Lhamo and told them of Duggur's recent death, their hearts rejoiced as he told them that their "smiling-Buddha" friend, Duggur had died murmuring "Yeshu, Yeshu, Yeshu." God by His gracious timing confirmed to Bob and Betty that their years of life and labor sharing the living Word had not been in vain. Another hard-won soul had come to Christ while they were on the other side of the globe. Duggar had read those Gospels that Bob had given him; he had meditated on the "two truths" from Buddha and the Bible, that required a decision, and God be praised, he decided for Christ.

Consequently, they began putting the hillside home in order after a three-year absence. Their housekeeper had maintained the station with an occasional visit by Ed Carlson or M. G. Griebenow to ensure that all was well, passing along the latest news from America about Shes-rab and Dorje Mzdo. Bob and Betty spent the rest of the year renewing friendships with neighbors and nomads from near and far, sharing the gospel message with all who visited their guest room. Among others, A-Ta, the powerful chanter of Buddhist mantras and sutras, who had believed in Yeshu not long before their emergency health furlough in 1935. He and his two friends he had led to Christ had remained faithful despite opposition from fellow villagers and nearby monastery monks. Each of these followers of Yeshu represented hard-fought battles won by the truth of His Word, and these living testimonies reinforced the Ekvall's desire to reach lost ones not yet in His fold.

The next year, mid-1940, Bob and Betty followed the well-traveled route south to Ngawa with colleagues, Ed and Carol Carlson, and their teenage son, Bobby. Once again the king offered them property for a mission station, lumber to build a home and permission to visit the scattered tribes of the Mei Kingdom. After a two week visit and a promise to return, Bob and Betty navigated the marshy grasslands to *Sungpan*, southeast of Ngawa in Sichuan. At the site of a CIM mission station abandoned back in 1892, the Alliance opened their newest and southernmost base as part of a renewed commitment to reach Tibetans had with the gospel. Francis and Georgia Derks had moved there with their son, Donny and were just getting started. Bob described Sungpan as "A border town with a reputation for the lawlessness of a wild-west trading post."

David Ekvall, Dalat School, 1942.

While on the trail to Sungpan, traders lugging huge loads of Chinese black tea on wooden back-frames met Bob and Betty on the trail and gave them a letter from Francis Derk. Along with the "breaking news" about Hitler's victories in Europe, they received a cryptic telegram from Dalat School in Indo-China: "David conscious, improving rapidly, no impairment."[120] With that enigmatic message weighing on their thoughts and prayers, they made their way to Sungpan as quickly as possible, arriving in eight days. There, they wired Dalat for an explanation. They received a reply a few days later informing that David had been hit by the French governor's car and had suffered a concussion. However, he had already recovered, left the hospital in good health and a letter was on the way.

After visiting with their new KTBM "neighbors," Bob and Betty set out for Lhamo, once again passing through marshlands before arriving at their station. A few weeks later, they traveled to Minchow for the 1940 mission conference where the KTBM workers agreed that they had to respond to the repeated invitations from the Mei king. Despite the distance between Ngawa and the rest of the field and the lack of postal service, the conference appointed Bob and Betty Ekvall to leave Lhamo and open up a new station in Ngawa.

On October 8, not long after the close of the Minchow conference, while returning to Lhamo on horseback, Betty began to feel ill but did not believe it to be serious. However, shortly before arriving at the station, her fever spiked, her headache became unbearable and her left ear began discharging infection later thought to be streptococcus. Upon arrival in Lhamo on the 12th, Bob battled alone trying to save his wife's life, crying out to God for healing while desperately attempting to lower Betty's raging fever. At midnight, she became delirious, talking in Tibetan, then fell unconscious for the next two days before briefly coming to. Her eyes seemed to clear and she tried to smile as she reached up to touch Bob's face. Then she fell unconscious again. At one point, her heart stopped briefly, but slowly began beating again. Over the next hours, it stopped and started spontaneously several times. At last, on the morning of the 16th, "the stoppage lengthened into silence," and she "fell asleep" and left Bob and Lhamo for a better place.[121]

Her pet mastiff, gift of a tribal chief, howled all that night, sensing his beloved mistress's suffering. On Wednesday morning at 7:20, October 16, 1940, Betty passed from the world of pain into the presence of her Lord. Bob, exhausted, went outside and found the big Tibetan mastiff, who loved Betty as only dogs can love, lying dead on the frozen ground. Left alone and devastated, Bob determined to bury her at the hallowed cemetery grounds at Lupa.

Road Over the Minshan Range, 1942.

A Lone Rider Came Through the Mission Compound Gate

Back in Taochow Old City, the Ed Carlsons still marveled at God's opening doors for advance to Ngawa. Suddenly, in mid-October, a lone rider
came through the mission compound gate on a beautiful bay horse, instantly recognized as Betty Ekvall's, but, she wasn't on it. The rider gave
Ed a letter from Bob urgently asking for some of the new sulfa drugs
for Betty, who lay desperately ill. Ed gathered the medicine and set out
immediately for Lhamo, a three-day ride. Despite approaching nightfall,
he rode as quickly as the dark trail would permit. Not long after reaching Minshan pass, he came upon Bob and his companions, with Betty's
coffin slung between two mules. As Carlson later explained: "She was
gone even before we knew she was sick." Bob had asked a local carpenter
in Lhamo to make a simple wood coffin, then held a funeral service for
the mourners in Lhamo before setting out for "God's Acre," the hillside
graveyard established by the Alliance mission decades previously. There
lay the bodies of Will Simpson, Torsten Halldorf, Al Fesmire and so many
who had died taking the Yeshu way of salvation to those on the border.
Due to the distance between the stations, only the Carlsons, Mrs. Fesmire

(recently widowed), Stan Harrison of Hehtso and William Ruhl of Minchow attended. Grief stricken, the little band of border workers sang, at
Bob's request, "Oh God, Our Help in Ages Past, "Safe in the Arms of
Jesus," followed by a brief message and Scripture reading by Field Chairman and close friend, Ed Carlson.[122]

"God's Acre" at Lupa, 2019.

As an amazing witness of the gospel's power to penetrate hearts
and stay planted, the writer visited Lupa in 2019 and met the pastor of
that local congregation, the great-grandson of the first national pastor.
The Lupa church continues to meet faithfully, fruit of the labors of the
KTBM missionaries more than a century before. While the old church
and outbuildings and "God's Acre," where Betty Ekvall later was laid,
was demolished by the government's relocation program, the church still
meets nearby weekly. Just a few gravestones of deceased locals Christians
remain where many more graves once lay.

> Meanwhile in Indochina, David—before hearing of his moth-
> er's—had a vision. He saw his mother standing beside the Lord
> Jesus who turned to her and said, "Well done, thou good and
> faithful servant." A sense of peace and consolation swept over
> David and he was at rest.[123]

For several weeks, Bob remained in Taochow and grieved as one who
had lost his soul mate. With his priceless partner in heaven, he remained
on earth, alone. Like a lost limb, he sorely missed Betty, mourning long

and hard. His colleagues feared for him and could only watch and pray, not daring violate his sanctuary of sorrow as he processed his pain. Long hours spent reading Scripture led to pacing on the mission porch and pain-filled prayer. In his room, alone, for hours, he strummed his guitar and sang to his Lord:

Oh Thou, in whose presence my soul takes delight,
On whom in affliction I call,
My comfort by day and my song in the night,
My hope, my salvation my all!
Oh, why should I wander, an alien from Thee,
Or cry in the desert for bread?
Thy foes will rejoice when my sorrows they see,
And smile at the tears I have shed.[124]

To his colleagues and friends, Bob's grief seemed almost fatal; Edwin Carlson, the leader of the mission worried about Bob. In Ekvall's own words, "He [the field chairman] had the feeling that I'd commit suicide. I didn't intend to commit suicide. I wanted to die, but I didn't intend to commit suicide at all."[125] Ed asked Bob to accompany the C&MA Mission's Foreign Secretary, Rev. A. C. Snead, as he visited the various KTBM field stations. Snead arrived at Lanzhou on November 4, frail and thin, looking like "death warmed over." The altitude, cold and harsh travel conditions had taken their toll, but God kept him alive and going till the end of his tour. The assignment seemed to help Bob get back on his feet. He judged it time to return to Lhamo before Christmas, since Betty had always shared the Christmas celebration with their friends and neighbors.

"Lord, Did It Have to Be This Way?"

He left Taochow for Dragsgumna, the friendly, secure "stone box" valley. As he crossed the Minshan range, what had, years before, seemed like a huge barrier, had become familiar, albeit difficult territory. Despite the bitter cold and deep snow, he pressed on. The trail took him through the dangerous "robber valley" where the "dog-headed" Drangwa lived. Hated and feared by the other tribes, Bob had established a guest-host relationship with one of the village families, and found safe haven with them. In the simple nomad's mud and stone winter house, a grandfather, father and son, three generations, sat around the fire commiserating with Bob.

In the midst of their conversation, the old grandfather asked Bob, 'Tell us, where is Dorje Mtso now?' The ready response was, 'She's in heaven with Jesus.' The question and the answer were repeated because the old man wanted to be very sure he was hearing correctly. Convinced, he immediately replied, 'I must believe,' and then prayed, 'God, be merciful to me a sinner and save me for Jesus' sake.'[126]

The son and grandson followed suit, and those three men became the core Christ-followers that eventually saw two-thirds of their village turn to Christ. So in the most unlikely place, "robber valley," seed patiently sown and watered bore fruit. The breakthrough that Bob and Betty had so long prayed for had taken place; but as Bob considered the cost, his broken heart cried, "Lord, did it have to be this way?"[127] Years before, in 1935, Betty, near death and battling anthrax, had told Bob that she would gladly give her life for the salvation of the Tibetans with whom they worked. And now in this painfully mysterious manner, she received her prayerful wish at great price.

Arriving in Lhamo in time for Christmas, Bob shared the old story of Christ's birth as best he could. He dearly sensed Betty's absence; she always had made it a special time for themselves and their friends. Over the next few months, Bob returned several times to visit the Drangwa believers and encourage them in their Christian walk. In answer to the grandfather's question, "Well now I must believe. What do I do?"[128] Bob told him to get rid of the amulets and religious objects hung around his neck, the wind-frayed prayer flags flapping outside and to remove the house-god altar. All the trappings of Tibetan Buddhist worship had to go. Get rid of it all, and his son and grandson would follow along, and they did. They became the Christian nucleus in Drangwa Valley, the most despised tribe in the region.

On each visit, Bob saw more villagers become "Jesus-ones." As their numbers grew, Bob encouraged them to remain good neighbors, without practicing the Tibetan Buddhist rituals. When the village planned to build a bridge and offer it to the lama, Bob urged them to participate and work with their neighbors since it served all of the villagers. However he urged them to not participate in the Buddhist ritual dedication. This met with approval of the new Christians as well as the other villagers.

Rather than join the lamas as they chanted for protection from the devastating hailstorms, Bob and the villagers held an outdoor prayer meeting asking Almighty God to protect their crops, and God answered their prayers. When the number of believers became the majority of the tribe, Bob encouraged them to be gracious, to not force the non-believers out, nor force them to convert. Tolerance had been shown them in the beginning; so now, they should show it to the minority. After months of discipling the little body of Jesus-ones, their growth and maturity persuaded Bob that they could be left on their own for a while. He strongly felt the need to visit his son, David, living far to the south in distant French Indo-China.

Thus, Bob began making preparations for the long overland trip from Lhamo to Dalat in the central highlands of Annam in Indo-China. The mission approved his plan to make the weeks-long trip by horseback down to Sungpan, on to Chengdu, continuing southeastward to Chungking, through the mountains to Kunming, plunging south through more mountains until reaching Hanoi, capital of the Tonkin Province of Indo-China. Then, a short train trip southward to Dalat would reunite Robert Ekvall with his tall teenage son, David.

Chapter 8

Hurry Up and Wait

AFTER SPENDING MONTHS DISCIPLING the newborn Drangwa church in Robber Valley, Bob knew the first anniversary of Betty's death was approaching in October, and he felt torn because part of him demanded he go to Ngawa to establish the long-prayed-for station. The young prince who he had met on the first two trips now ruled the Mei Kingdom; both parents had died. His standing offer for property, building materials and help in construction had been prayed about for years. To not go seemed almost betrayal of Betty's memory.

At the same time, David, fifteen, still at the Alliance MK School in Dalat, Indo-China, had not seen his father since 1939. Bob still grieved the loss of his wife, and he was also father of a son who had lost his mother. David needed his father, and Bob needed his son so that they could mourn together the death of the godly gentle woman who had been a strength and comfort to both of them. The C&MA mission gave Bob leave to travel overland to Dalat to spend a few months with David. Then, he would return to Lhamo by the end of 1941 and continue discipling the new-born community of Christians in Drangwa before going to Ngawa to open the new field of ministry.

Consequently, in August 1941, Bob set off for French Indo-China, now under the Vichy French government which had handed over control of Indo-China to its new "ally," Japan. Such was the situation when Bob left Lhamo mission station in the charge of a trustworthy caretaker family. In a little tract published by the C&MA in 1941, "The Trail of the

Gospel in War Times," Ekvall describes starting out on the long journey from Lhamo to Saigon in French Indo-China:

> Just at daybreak on the first of August, 1941, we were ready to start. Behind the dark, barred door of the courtyard the horses were saddled the mules loaded, and I am my companions were ready too. The gate was thrown open, but before I could start and old Tibetan woman was at my stirrup speaking to me. She is over eighty—wrinkled face, bent so she can hardly rise her head . . . She said, 'I won't see you again here. Not here, but over in the skyland of the gods [angels] where Jesus is, there I'll see you again.'"[129]

On that encouraging note, he headed southeast with his travel companions through mountain passes and rocky valleys until they came upon vast flocks of sheep in the grasslands that lead to *Sungpan*. Basically, he retraced the route that he and Betty had followed in 1939 after leaving David at the Dalat School and returned to Lhamo from their extended furlough of 1936 to 1939. They traveled for four days, avoiding robbers with stealth and haste. At night, they made "dark camps," fireless camp-site in the blackness of cloudy, moonless nights.

They rode through territory familiar to Bob. Tibetan farmers laboriously cut hay with their crude hand sickles. Little villages and monasteries grew scarcer as the land became increasingly desolate; they came upon miles of sun-bleached bones left by the Red Army's Long March in 1935. The ghastly sight reminded them that the revolutionary changes of the outside world reached even this far inland. Close to Sungpan, thousands of Chinese miners dug in the grey mud in search of gold at government-run mines. Arriving in Sungpan, the newest Alliance mission station, Francis Derks, his wife, Dixie, and their young son welcomed him. There for several days, Bob replenished his food supplies from local Chinese traders before moving on.

On the morning of his departure from Sungpan, before turning north to return to Lhamo, Bob's two trusted companions, came and said: "Peace go with you, the Lord watch over you and bless you and keep you." These men, just a few years before, had lived and walked in spiritual darkness, and now they blessed the messenger who had brought them God's light.

Well-marked trails led out of the town in all directions, and Bob set out on the southern track. Leaving on foot with carriers, Bob walked behind them pushing them as hard as he could since it would take ten days to reach the provincial capital of *Sichuan, Chengdu*. Passing through deserted country, they ate from the supplies carried on their back. Reaching one Chinese town, they were able to eat "real food" and rest before hitting the trail once again. Bob traveled through the hottest days of summer on the western edge of the Sichuan Basin with his carriers, "ragged scarecrows who lived on rice gruel and opium." Every two hours, the odd trio stopped at roadside tea houses to rehydrate, making Bob a connoisseur of different types of Chinese tea.[130]

Arriving at last in Chengdu, Bob paid off his helpers and spent a few days resting there. He visited with Canadian missionaries who taught at Western Union University, a joint effort of four Protestant missions from the United States and Canada. Then, Ekvall suddenly left the centuries-old travel trails and flew by Eurasia Airlines trimotor airplane to Chungking, China's wartime Kuomintang government capital. When they touched down at the airfield some miles out of town, the whole area was under bombardment by the Japanese Imperial Air Force. Ekvall and the other passengers had to wait for five hours until the bombing stopped. "In the meantime, we hid in the bushes along the river, on the edge of an emergency landing field, not knowing when machine guns might be turned on us from the air."[131]

On the banks of the Yangtze River that cuts China in two, Bob knew Chungking as an interesting place to visit. However, the war had changed things for travelers and townsfolk. Barrage balloons hung over the city; "take cover" sirens wailed warning of incoming Japanese bombers.

> In the hostel where I stayed, every morning each one packed a bag of his valuables for deposit in the hostel's air raid shelter, just in case the hostel were hit, but each one then went about his own affairs in a city where business and the work of the day went on at a feverish pace; interrupted only when the bombers were coming.[132]

The sandstone mountains surrounding Chungking had been tunneled and every bank, hotel, government office and business had their own "cave" where they stored valuables. The Flying Tigers operated in the region and gave some defense against the bombers, a first sign of growing U.S. involvement in the region.

Bob had little time for delay since his destination lay south in French Indo-China. Continuing on his journey, again by Eurasia Airlines, he flew to Hong Kong. The plane flew up to sixteen thousand feet into gray clouds and driving rain; after marching across hundreds of miles of hard walking under the scorching Sichuan sun, Bob

> sat shivering alone, [when] a Chinese passenger slipped from his seat across the aisle to sit beside me, sharing his blanket as we talked. His father was an old Chinese pastor and he, the son, was the head of a big government hospital far out in Si-kang, the border land of Tibet. So he told me about his father and about himself. 'I work for the government but I live for the Lord.[133]

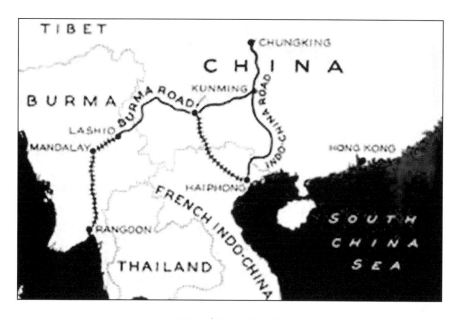

Map of Burma Road.

Having less than a day layover in Hong Kong, Bob boarded a coastal steamer, which made a brief stop in Macao, before steaming down the coast to arrive in Indo-China in just a few days. The ship anchored in Haiphong, now under the control of the Japanese military. Bob was shadowed and questioned by the police. As soon as possible, he left by train for Hanoi, and, there, he took the train south from to Dalat in the central highlands. After weeks of constant travel, the thought of finally seeing his teenage son, blond and tall like his father but gentle and quiet like his mother, loomed large.

Bob later wrote about that tense trip in *Dark Camps*, a book of unpublished prose poems:

> The train raced swiftly through the heavy hot night and toward
> the inevitable dawn. Too swiftly for him. The reckoning he had
> evaded for a month had cornered him at last. For a month, he
> had marched and moved through change, excitement, danger,
> fatigue, and the exultation of achieving the nearly impossible;
> for a month he had put off the inevitable.[134]

This same train that Bob and Betty had taken north two years before
when they left David in the care of the Dalat School director now carried
him back to his son. The beautiful town, built by the French as a summer
resort, drew ever closer. Bob remembered watching David wave goodbye
to them two years before. Now, inches taller, that same son once again
waved as Bob's train pulled into the station. The two Ekvalls, father and
son, held each other tightly as they rejoiced and wept at the same time.
Thus began their healing time together; yet, in another two months at the
most, Bob would have to return to Lhamo and the borderlands.

One year to the day after Betty's death, Bob and David found themselves on a beautiful beach looking out on the South China Sea. Bob
wrote in *Dark Camps*:

> The hour had passed and the day too was passing in molten,
> fiery splendor. The protesting sea and the dying day both said
> that hope of relief or release was dead. A whole year had done
> nothing to lessen his pain . . . . But God would not let him quit,
> she would not let him quit, and the voice too of his son calling
> carelessly from the beach was stronger than the sadness of the
> sea and the fast burning sky.[135]

Life went on and Bob pressed on though the wearisome burden of
sorrow weighed him down.

In the midst of his pain, the old adage, "the best laid plans of mice
and men often go astray" proved true once again. Bob had arrived in
Dalat in late August 1941 to stay for about two months before returning
to the Tibetan border. However, his departure had been delayed; and a
few months later, December 7, 1941, the Imperial Japanese Navy bombed
Pearl Harbor and declared war on The United States of America. Consequently, the Japanese officials in Indo-China interned all foreigners: U.S.
citizens, Canadians, British subjects, et al, classifying them as "enemy
nationals." While restricted, the missionaries continued their normal
activities. The churches in the "homeland" prayed for their safety, and
eventually the Swiss consulate sent word that all Alliance personnel in Indo-China were well. This brought Bob no comfort since he had planned

on returning to the Tibetan border, but had not gotten out before December 7. Thus, he found himself "stuck" in a kind of missionary limbo. While a C&MA missionary, but not a member of the C&MA Indo-China Mission, he felt "stranded" in a country where his command of Chinese had little use except with Chinese merchants. On occasion, he preached at the Chinese church, but his Tibetan language skills had no use at all.

Having time on his hands, Bob decided to learn French like he had learned Tibetan, by the "sound-to-meaning" immersion method. Living in a French colony full of French speakers, he walked the streets daily. He drank countless cups of coffee in the cafés, listened to the voluble French as they debated the war news, and read French-language newspapers. Within a year, he had an amazing command of French with an excellent accent despite being in his mid 40s. With David still in school, time hung heavy; so, he began writing again, resulting in two books: *Tibetan Skylines*, a travel ethnography, and *Tents Against the Sky*, a novel set among Tibetan nomads.

During this time, the Red Cross developed a plan to repatriate the "enemy foreigners" in China and Indo-China to their countries of origin, while also allowing Japanese nationals interned in the U. S. to return to Japan. Thus, some missionaries and MKs from the Dalat School, including David Ekvall, sailed on July 1942 from Saigon to Singapore, then on to Lourenço Marques (Maputo) in Mozambique. There, Japanese internees were exchanged for foreign nationals from Indo-China who boarded the neutral Swedish liner *Gripsholm* for South Africa's Cape of Good Hope and across the South Atlantic, arriving at Rio de Janeiro in early August. The marked difference in diet and comfort on the Swedish ship, as compared to the wartime rigor of life on the Japanese ships delighted the passengers.

> The entire trip was without incident, and it was wonderful for them to pass the Statue of Liberty and the ship slipped into the New York harbor. After an almost 8-week long journey, the missionaries from French-Indo China arrived in New Jersey to a grand welcome by family and friends on August 25, 1942.[136]

Temptation's Tasty Treats Were Dangled Before Him

While Bob hated to see his son leave, he was delighted to see him return to the Fischer family back in Wheaton where he would be safe, well cared for by Betty's family and able to finish high school. After David left, Bob went through a very difficult time. Having few close associates in the Indo-China mission, and immersing himself in the local French milieu, temptation's tasty treats dangled before him. At one party he had been invited to, an attractive woman with a throaty voice insinuated,

> 'Don't you remember me?' she said, and then added, 'You must be lonely at night. . . . Aren't you lonely?' In Bob's heart, 'Thou shalt not . . .' answered that question unequivocally. Yet he was not unscathed. He knew to his shame that even in laughing it off, and cutting short the visit of his guests in the room, he yet had looked longingly, for a moment that fled, for something of tenderness and affection—impossible though that might be—in the eyes that challenged his.[137]

In February, an order came from the Japanese military command that "All missionaries in Annam must reside at Dalat as of March 1, 1943."[138] Bob already stayed at the MK school, thus, no move needed. However, the Japanese authorities found the presence of the "enemy foreigners" disagreeable. Who could know what spies might be among them? Ironically, while not a spy, Bob had developed a strong relationship with French plantation owners disenchanted with the Vichy capitulation to Hitler's Japanese allies. Eventually, they took him to a local Viet Minh resistance group, which previously had sought for independence from the French. Now, their efforts aimed at subverting Japanese rule. They wanted the Allies to win the war.

On April 27, 1943, the Japanese ordered them to a detainment camp, *Mytho* in the Mekong Delta, south of Saigon. Alliance missionaries had worked in Mytho for years and knew the town and the mighty Mekong River flowing past it. The C&MA staff, forty adults and children, left Dalat by train for Saigon and then on to Mytho. They loaded all of their baggage, boxes and beds, cupboards, school library books, and even a piano, into six boxcars. Fortunately, the French colonial officers, technically allies of Japan, had long known the missionaries and treated them favorably. The Alliance personnel arrived at their not-yet-completed military-type barracks surrounded by an iron fence. In short time, the French finished the work and each family had their own room with kitchens facilities on the ground floor. The food, like the accommodations while meager, was adequate.

As a single man, Bob shared a room with other "bachelors." Accustomed to simple living in Tibet, he did not find the living conditions hard as did some others. Besides Alliance missionaries, other detainees included British and Dutch citizens, a Jewish hotel manager from Dalat, two Roman Catholic brothers and the Italian consul and his wife.

The internees had limited freedom. When he could, Bob visited the town. During this time, they received word of their repatriation in the fall of 1943. When the Viet Minh underground heard that Bob would be sent home, they asked him to take out strategic military intelligence; a potentially dangerous act. They also asked him to request that the United States not support France's post-war plans to reoccupy Indo-China. Sympathetic to their request, Bob agreed although he wondered how he could take the critically vital intelligence, due to limits on baggage as well as his two type-written manuscripts. In the end, he concluded that it was more important to pass the vital information such as ammo dumps, military installations and oil storage to U. S. military. Thus, he left the two manuscripts with a local friend, and hid the tiny rice-paper maps in the hollowed-out sole of one of his leather sandals.

The repatriation of 1942, had taken twenty-three of the forty Alliance detainees, including David. Similar to the first exchange, those leaving would board a Japanese liner, the *S. S. Teia Maru* destined for Goa, a Portuguese enclave on the West Coast of India. There, they would be transferred to the *S. S. Gripsholm*, the neutral Swedish ocean liner leased by the Red Cross. The *Teia Maru* left Yokohama on September 14, 1943 and stopped in Shanghai to pick up nine hundred seventy five passengers, including Alliance and CIM missionaries. The ship then steamed south to Hong Kong for more detainees, then on to San Fernando in the Philippines and finally Saigon, arriving on September 30, 1943. There, thirty passengers from Mytho embarked. As they boarded, French officers closely inspected each passenger.

Take Off Your Shoe, Take Off Your Sandals

In Ekvall's own words:

> I walked down the line and the gendarmes would check me out, because I was wearing a sort of safari shirt like the French and shorts, bare feet . . . , and he ran over me and then he said, 'Take off your shoe, take off your sandals.' And of course, I naturally decided to take off the innocent one and I stopped to . . . unbuckle it and he said 'No, no . . . not that one, the other one.' And then I left the thing on the ground, put my toe on the ground

to keep balance and stepped back and he watched me and then as he went down to pick it up, he kept his eyes on me. And he hesitated a moment and then he said, 'Put it back on again.' Of course, if he had taken that sandal and torn it apart, I would be six feet underground.[139]

Ray Smith, Ekvall's first cousin-once removed, described the scene with more detail:

> The Vichy were strip-searching all persons just prior to going on board. All luggage had already been searched. Bob was called into an office where a French officer . . . sitting behind a desk, ordered [Bob] to disrobe. Bob had secreted the maps in the hollowed-out heel of one of his shoes. As he stood there in just his skivvies, the office looked steely-eyed at him and told him to take off his shoes. 'Both?' 'That one,' pointing at one of his feet. It was the shoe *without* the maps.[140]

After boarding the detainees from Mytho, the *Teia Maru* sailed to Singapore, then through the Sunda Straits and west toward Goa. The Japanese ship arrived at Mormagão, port of Goa, on October 15, 1943 and the *Gripsholm* arrived a day later.

> The exchange process began on October 19 at 8 a.m. The Americans left from the bow of the *Teia Maru* and entered the Gripsholm via the stern gangway. At the same time the Japanese left from the bow of the *Gripsholm* and entered the stern of the *Teia Maru*, a much longer distance. The Japanese looked healthy and had good American clothing and luggage. They looked like tourists. The Americans were emaciated, and their clothing and luggage were in bad shape too. The exchange took 91 minutes.[141]

Among other things, 48,760 Red Cross relief boxes for other prisoners of war and internees in Singapore, Manila and Japan were transshipped from the *Gripsholm* to *Teia Maru*. A great number of casks of fish and soy sauce intended for Japanese people interned in the United States were then loaded onto the Swedish ship before sealing the holds.

The whole process proved tedious to the passengers, but the final paper signing and passenger transfer occurred without a problem. Then, began the task of finding their assigned rooms on the multi-deck ship with its labyrinth of corridors and stairs. Eventually, Bob found his cabin, #605, on "E" deck, lowest in the ship. A fellow internee on the *Gripsholm* with Bob later described the quarters:

The cabin, 3rd class, was small without much wardrobe space, but the bunks, four in number, were clean and comfortable, and the furnishings adequate—far superior to his steerage quarters on the *Teia Maru*. His three cabin-mates proved to be interesting and congenial men whom he had partially know before—one of them a Catholic "Father" and another [Ekvall] a well-known missionary, linguist and explorer from the borders of Tibet.[142]

After the poor food and accommodations on the *Teia Maru*, the *Gripsholm* was truly a luxury liner. Hot and cold running water, clean showers and toilets, bountiful food and freedom on board overwhelmed those traveling from Japanese-held Asia to North America. The same could not be said for the Japanese citizens going from west to east.

After a week in port, tug boats pushed the *Gripsholm* into the bay, which then set course for Port Elizabeth, South Africa, a twelve day voyage. Two days later, on the open sea, an American submarine surfaced near the *Gripsholm* and sailors boarded the ship to retrieve the documents from Ekvall. These documents soon reached the U.S. military, and eventually, Cordell Hull, President Franklin Roosevelt's Secretary of State. Ekvall learned some months later that U.S. carrier-based planes bombed the targets indicated on the secreted maps.[143]

Without further incident, the Swedish ship arrived at Port Elizabeth, South Africa, on November 2. Following two days in port, they left for Rio de Janeiro, arriving on November 14. Following two days visiting Brazil's beautiful capital, enjoying the delicious food and seeing the tourist sites, the passengers boarded the *Gripsholm* on the evening of the 16th for the last leg of their long voyage back to America. Bob had done little tourism since agents of the OSS (Office of Strategic Services—precursor to the CIA) had met him at the docks. They had heard about his smuggling out the secret maps from Indo-China. They also knew of his command of the Chinese language and culture; so they offered him a job with the OSS. As a result of the invitation, Bob, not wanting to compromise his role as a missionary by involvement in war work, resigned from the mission to work in Washington on strategic analysis of the war effort in China.

S. S. Gripsholm, 1943.

Following the few days in Rio, Bob reboarded the *Gripsholm* with his fellow passengers. Since the ship was scheduled to arrive in Jersey City, New Jersey, on December 1, they wondered about the winter weather. Nearing the New York harbor, the Red Cross sent out a boat loaded with used warm winter clothing for internees who had lived in the tropics for years. As they passed the Statue of Liberty and docked at Jersey City, the passengers sang "God Bless America." After their documents were checked and cleared, the passengers disembarked. The Alliance "Headquarters" in New York had a delegation present to greet the missionaries. Those from Canada were immediately taken to Penn Station and sent by train to Montreal. The U. S. missionaries were taken to the Alliance "hotel" for missionaries in transit on 690 8th Avenue. Bob, anxious to see David and Betty's family in Wheaton, soon left New York on a Chicago-bound train. More than a year had passed since father and son had last been together.

While at the Mytho internment camp in Indo-China, Bob penned his thoughts in *Dark Camps*:

> Some day . . . he would have to go back to the scenes of courtship and marriage; go to the home folks and the home town of his beloved, go to meet her dear ones and his, go to meet the friends of their earliest shared past, go to walk through the streets where he first had seen her walking, go to stand in the place where they first had known their love for each other. He would have to go, alone and without her, to the world in which she of all persons belonged, where he by comparison was truly an interloper. She would not be there. She would be—on the other side of the world—beyond the stars. She would be somewhere, but not there.[144]

Chapter 9

Onward Christian Soldier

ARRIVING IN CHICAGO AND met at the train station by his tall son, they celebrated Christmas season together with the Fischer family in Wheaton. While there, Bob revisited the scenes where he and Betty had first met, their first date and kiss, the church where they were wed and much more. The ache in his heart still throbbed as he recalled the shared joy that these places represented. Since he had made a commitment with the newly-formed O.S.S. to serve in the war effort, Bob returned to Washington and began work with the "spooks" in January 1944.

As a lifetime civilian and missionary in far-off Western China, Ekvall entered the still-new government agency opened right after the United States entered WW 2. President Roosevelt had recognized the need for better intelligence-gathering coordination from diplomatic and military sources. He chose General William "Wild Bill" Donovan, a WW I hero and top New York lawyer, to head up the "Office of the Coordinator of Information (COI)," established July 11, 1941. Unfortunately, just six months after its founding, the fledgling COI failed to alert the president in time to avert the greatest intelligence failure of the war, the surprise attack on Pearl Harbor. The COI was renamed the OSS, the "Office of Strategic Services," on June 13, 1942 and reported directly to the Joint Chiefs of Staff rather than the office of the President.

In Washington, Bob began working in "research and analysis," putting to work his expertise in Chinese and years of first-hand knowledge of conditions on the West China border. Ekvall describes how he quickly moved from a civilian "desk job" to the front lines in Burma:

> After two years of internment in Indochina, I had been repatri-
> ated two months before [December 1943] and, like many others,
> found myself in Washington trying to help the war effort. But a
> desk job, even with the Office of Strategic Services, is a poor way
> in which to help win a war, and until the meeting with [General
> Haydon] Boatner, the G-2 conference had seemed very much
> like the many other futile meetings I had attended.[145]

Ekvall's language ability and lived-experience in China caught the attention of a U. S. Army General. At that critical period of the war, the Army
desperately needed Chinese-speaking officers in Burma (Myanmar).
General Haydon L. Boatner, serving under General Joseph Stillwell, US
commander in Burma, spoke Chinese, as did Stillwell. It took just a few
minutes of conversation between Ekvall and Boatner to establish the fact
that Ekvall's superb Chinese surpassed Boatner's. Therefore, he asked
Bob directly: "How would you like to go to Burma?"

At this watershed moment, Ekvall was forty six years old. Except for
a few months of basic military training at the tail end of World War I, he
was "pure civilian," although not quite a "normal" one. Boatner wanted
to know if Bob thought he could pass an army physical; Bob, still thin
from the internment in Mytho, felt sure he would pass given his years of
strenuous life on the Tibetan border. When asked if he was willing to take
a 50 percent cut in pay, Bob agreed since he had simple needs. Boatner
promised that he would get Bob a military commission if he passed the
exam and sent in a statement of "vital statistics."

> I sent the statement and nine days later I was captain in the
> Army of the United States. Fortunately, from among the things I
> had started to learn in 1918, I remembered how to salute. They
> kept me in Washington just long enough to give me the first two
> thirds of the necessary shots and to let me finish a paper I was
> doing for the Office of Strategic Services, for that was part of the
> bargain that released me from that agency. Six weeks later, I was
> under fire in the jungles of northern Burma.[146]

Bob later discovered his field file information card which contained the interesting observation: "No formal military training; well
fitted for combat."[147]

For the next nine months, Bob used the survival craft he had acquired on the border. A lifelong hunter, his marksmanship and handling
of weapons made him an ideal instructor for army cooks and clerks who
quickly had to learn how to load and fire in battle during the siege of the

strategic town of Myitkyina held by the Imperial Army. The overall goal of the Burma military operation was to reopen the famed "Burma Road" to supply China by land rather than the dangerous flights over the Himalaya Mountains. During the months in the jungles of northern Burma," Bob led a detachment of Merrill's Marauders, lugging mortars and machine gun ammunition to the front. Working in liaison with Nationalist Chinese troops, Bob's ability to talk to the average Chinese "grunt" in common speech endeared him to them.

He Served as the "Interpreter of the Interpreters"

More importantly, Bob's ability to interpret "on the fly" helped correct misinterpretation by Chinese officers serving as English-speaking interpreters between U. S. officers and their Chinese counterparts who spoke no English. His vital coordination ensured the accuracy of the two-way exchange of information. Truth be told, he served as the "interrupter of the interpreters," which did not endear him to the young Chinese officers, proud of their command of English, who did not always get the true sense of General Boatner's attempts at keeping U. S. and Chinese troops on the same page.

Late in the fall of 1944, Bob's ability to lead Chinese troops enabled him to organize the loading of two divisions of Chinese soldiers into U.S. Army Air Force planes flying from India over "the Hump" [the Himalayas] to northern Burma. This exercise, generally a royal SNAFU, had to be done at night without lights due to Japanese bombers in the area. In the "blackness of black," Bob's moved the troops quickly while entering the cargo planes in "the fastest enplanement of troops yet know."[148] Such was the service of a former missionary, now military man. At the end of fighting in Burma in late 1944, Bob was transferred to Chungking, and promoted to major and staff officer at the U.S.-China Theater Headquarters of the U. S. Forces.

At first, Bob translated French intelligence reports before his assignment to serve as liaison officer between U. S. Army G-2 (Intelligence) and Chinese military intelligence. General "Vinegar Joe" Stillwell's undiplomatic method of working with the Chinese military resulted in his replacement by General Albert C. Wedemeyer. Bob worked with Wedemeyer to repair the breach in Sino-American cooperation. At the weekly joint staff conferences, Bob sat close to the General, not only to ensure the accuracy of the "official interpretation," but also to whisper the *soto voce* asides made by the Chinese translators, unaware that Bob understood all of their slang and slander. He later commented that that role was not glorious "but it was useful in fostering comprehension and understanding . . . ."[149]

While still serving in Chungking, Bob's son, David, 6 feet, 2 inches tall, with Betty's brown hair and eyes, enlisted in the Army on February 15, 1944, before graduating from high school. After basic training, he was sent to California for further instruction and then on to Washington. He shipped out on August 19, 1945 from Seattle for South Korea at the tail-end of the war. There, he served with the 93rd Ordinance Bomb Disposal Squad of the Thirty Second Infantry at Packch'on, South Korea, about thirty miles east of Seoul.

Bob had continued in Chungking while his son prepared to go off to war. On July 7, 1945, just before the war ended, Ekvall volunteered to accompany a Nationalist Army military operation behind enemy Japanese lines at Liuchow, Guangxi Province. "The end of the war found me in a hospital. While on a special mission at the front I had blundered into a confused fire-fight in a village street.[150] In the wild skirmish, Bob suffered a serious wound to one of his arms requiring extensive surgery. Due to the severity of the wound, the field doctors recommended amputation, but Bob rigorously objected, asking them to do all they could to save it. After stabilizing the wound, he was sent back to the United States to spend the next nine months recuperating, at the Thomas M. England General Hospital in Atlantic City, New Jersey. He was awarded the Purple Heart for the wound. The building, a seventeen-story beachfront resort, had been transformed into a military hospital with a capacity of about 2,000 soldiers. Then, once again when least expected, tragedy struck. While recovering from his wounds, Bob received word that David had been accidentally killed serving with a demolitions unit. He and four other soldiers died on December 30, 1945. No remains of David were ever found.

While preparing a demolition pit near the town of *Yonan*, thirty miles east of Seoul, a malfunction occurred detonating Japanese munitions left-over from the war. It took almost a month for the official letter notifying Bob of his son's death to arrive at the hospital. The news hit Bob like an avalanche. Years before, in 1912, his dad had suddenly passed away from typhus; then Betty had died just a few years before in 1940 to an unidentified infection, and now, this! His only remaining family, his son whose gentle smile and radiant personality warmed his heart, gone, without a vestige to bury. Perhaps, at this point, Robert Ekvall began to seriously question God's dealings with him. Why this Job-like loss of loved ones? What was God trying to tell him? Only silence answered.

PFC David and Captain Robert Ekvall.

The February 16 issue of *The Alliance Weekly* published the shocking news of David's accidental death in South Korea. The sad news spread throughout the Alliance. Bob's former colleague and field chairman of the Kansu-tibetan Border Mission, Rev. Thomas Mosely, wrote him a letter of condolence from his office at the Nyack Missionary Training Institute where he was now president. For all who had served on the field with Bob and Betty, the tragic report of David's death brought great sorrow.

Subsequently, in early 1946, Ekvall received sick leave from the military hospital while still recuperating. Depending on the results of his rehabilitation and final evaluation, he would either return to China or be discharged from the Army. During the leave, Bob traveled west to Omaha to visit the Omaha Gospel Tabernacle, his "home church" and Rev. R. R. Brown, who had "adopted" Bob and Betty years before. They had become members on their way to the field back in 1921. "The Tab" had supported the Ekvalls in prayer, love gifts and special offerings which helped finance the purchase of the hybrid-yak caravan for travel among the Tibetans. Doubtless, in conversation with R. R. Brown, Bob shared his heart pain and the testing of his faith. Ekvall spoke at the Sunday night service of his nineteen years as a C&MA missionary on the West China-Tibetan border. He told the congregation of the visible effects of the gospel witnessed first-hand by GIs scattered all over the world during the war.

> And everywhere, whenever he [the G.I.] has found honesty and decency among strange peoples and in far off places, he has found that missions and the results of missionary work are the sources from which the decency flowed. Kachin tribesmen in Burma, wooly-headed Papuans in New Guinea, or Chinese villagers performed deeds of mercy because they were Christian.[151]

He Was Bitter for a Time

Sometime after Robert Ekvall's visit to Omaha, the combined emotional weight of Betty's traumatic death in 1940 and the senseless loss of David in 1946, Bob started on a different journey. Rev. Bill Kerr, a friend from his earlier days with the Alliance, later described this new direction after visiting Ekvall in his mid 70s. "He deliberately chose to take a different road than the road he had followed as a missionary; but he emphasized that he did not give up his faith at that time nor since. He was bitter for a time and inferred that he lived the life of a worldly man.[152]

After Bob returned to Atlantic City for his final health evaluation, fully recovered, he reported for orders, a three months stint of "limited-duty" at an Army base in Georgia for re-acclimatation to Army life after nine months of hospitalization. Enroute to his new posting, Bob stopped off in Washington to look up some friends he had made in Burma and China and who now worked at the Pentagon, "Headquarters of all Head-quarters." Amazingly, in that huge labyrinth of hallways and floors, he ran into a Colonel Dusenberry whom he had known while serving in 1944 and 1945. When he learned of Bob's new orders, the Colonel encouraged him to "get on the embassy staff in Nanjing as Assistant Military Attaché.[153] Bob, a "civilian in uniform," knew nothing about the role and duties of such a position. Rather than the "gilded creature" that attended glittering social functions, cocktails or teas, the Colonel, a kind of military talent scout, suggested that Bob employ his proven skills as an intelligence officer with exceptional knowledge of both Chinese and the culture. Ideally, Bob would travel throughout the interior of China, keeping his ears clear to hear and eyes wide open to see the real situation on the ground rather than what over-optimistic "experts" opined from their chairs.

Captivated by the idea offered by Colonel Dusenberry, Bob agreed to begin filling out multiple forms and answering questions in numerous interviews. Roaming through the vast seven-floor headquarters of the United States Department of Defense, Bob lost and found himself many times while running into old friends from his two years in Burma and China. They filled him in on the intricacies of military bureaucracy and urged him to pursue the attaché position.

Since the post required proficiency in Chinese, Bob had to be tested, but there was no time for a formal language examination before reporting for duty in Georgia. When asked who might be able to vouch for his language ability, Ekvall drew up a short list of former officers and colleagues. From the list, a Colonel Dickey, Bob's commanding officer in Chungking, gave a glowing reply that left the examining officer, dazed. He put down his phone and said, "What a recommendation! We'll waive the language examination."[154] Colonel Dickey wanted to talk with Bob right away. After another walk down a long corridor and one more elevator ride, Bob found himself talking to his former G-2 boss from Chungking US Army Headquarters.

The Colonel was amazed that Bob had gotten out of the hospital so soon, since he had been told that Ekvall's wound was so bad that likely he would require up to fifteen months of treatment. Bob demonstrated that his arm and hand were fine, and proceeded to fill the Colonel in on the possible posting as a Military Attaché. Colonel Dickey replied: "The duty I have in mind has priority over any Attaché assignment, and you are a natural. I'll talk to General Carraway about it. Haven't you heard of the Marshal Mission to China?"[155] Obviously, Bob had heard; by the end of W II, everybody had heard of General George Catlett Marshall, President Roosevelt closest military adviser, a five-star general with military experience since the First World War.

From December 15, 1945, to January 1947, Marshall served as the US special envoy to China in a last ditch attempt to negotiate a coalition government between Chiang Kai-shek's Nationalists Kuomintang government with the insurgent Communists forces of Mao Tse Tung. While Bob, a lowly Major, had heard of the Marshall Mission, he never imagined that he would be considered for such a lofty role. However, that same evening, Bob received a call from an officer staffing the mission. With a full "bird colonel" guiding him through the maze of red tape, Bob, supposedly on "limited duty," eventually found himself facing the Surgeon General of the Army, General Kirk.

> I was told to peal off my shirt, and with professional pride, he [the General] fingered my scars. 'We did a good job on that arm. So you want to go to China, do you? Spread your fingers. Make a fist. You'll do, but this will probably cut out any disability payments in the future. If General Marshall wants you in China, he can have you.[156]

They then sent Ekvall to Walter Reed Hospital to meet with their board of doctors in order to change his status from "limited duty" to "full duty," in order to fulfill Army regulations.

At Walter Reed, the full board went over his record from the England Military Hospital in Atlantic City dictated over long-distance telephone. All of his hospital papers were in order. Before the board, Bob saluted the colonel in charge who told Bob to sit down and then asked how he felt. Bob responded that he felt "Fine, sir." "How is your arm?" "Fine, sir." "Make a fist." "Yes, sir." "Spread your fingers." "Yes, sir." "Fit for full duty."[157] With that official pronouncement and another salute, Bob's examination ended and he was on his way back to China. After three shots in each arm and more than a "touch of fever," Bob left the hospital and returned for a quick visit at the Pentagon to tell Colonel Dickey about the posting to the Marshall Mission. "Yes, we had heard about it. We can't hold you for an attaché job if the Marshall Mission wants, but when you're through, we'll be waiting for you to take the matter up again."[158] The date for this change in orders was March 25, 1946; and accordingly, Bob was sent with high travel status to Peking, China's capital.

For the next nine months, Ekvall served on Marshall's mission staff, which he judged as well intentioned but which failed because of the irreconcilable conflicts and animosities of the Chinese civil war between the Nationalists and Communists. Beside interpreting at conferences and cocktail parties, Bob prepared and delivered a daily briefing to the U.S. Commissioner and staff, detailing the day-to-day developments of the continued combat in northern China between the Red Army and the Nationalists. He also prepared a daily "confidential" summary sent directly to General Marshall. Weekly, he prepared an "analysis of trends" for the top brass. When Marshall visited the Headquarters, Bob had the awesome assignment of briefing the "Old Man" himself.

In the course of negotiations involving tripartite conference meetings with Nationalist and Communist Chinese officers, Bob interpreted for the U.S. negotiators. His ability with the language and insistence on accurate translations from English to Chinese and Chinese to English earned him the gratitude of the Nationalists and the enmity of the Red Army officers, who had to yield to Bob's dogged insistence on the accuracy of interpretation concerning issues being discussed. He would later meet some of these same officers in other venues.

During the months in Peking, Bob met freely with both Nationalist and Communist officers. While not working formally in "intelligence," he wandered the streets and markets picking up "murmurings of change." His facility in understanding everything spoken while dressed in formal Army uniform left the people believing that he understood nothing. This ruse proved invaluable over his time in China. By January 1947, the Marshall Mission had thrown in the towel; the "Big Boss" had returned to America. The Mission staff officers began their career-advancement moves, leaving Bob to wonder if the military attaché job was still viable. And just at that time, the Senior Assistant Military Attaché from the U. S. Embassy looked Bob up. Because of his unique skillset, Bob fit the bill for a Chinese-speaking officer who could spend months away from Nanjing as the Office of Military Attaché's representative, an ideal posting for a single man, however . . .

Somehow, during all of the conferences and briefings while serving the Marshall Mission in Peking, Bob met someone at the Shanghai U.S. Consulate who changed his life, Eva Maria Kunfi, a young Jewish refugee born in Breslau, Germany and raised in Hungary. Her father, Tibor, a dentist, saw Hitler's growing hostility toward Jews in the 1930s. Consequently, with his wife, Anna and young Eva, they left Budapest. Unable to find a country where they could stay, the Kunfis emigrated to Shanghai and became part of the sizeable Jewish community at the "International Settlement." The Settlement became the "Shanghai Ghetto" in 1941 when the Japanese army forced all Jews to live in approximately one square mile in the southern part of the city. The community centered around the *Ohel Moshe Synagogue*. Surrounded by barbed wire, overcrowded and lacking basic necessities, it became the poorest area of Greater Shanghai with 23,000 Jewish refugees in the ghetto. American Jewish charities and rich local Jewish families assisted their fellow residents with food and clothing.

This Was No April-to-September Romance

At the war's conclusion, Eva's excellent English, as well as German, Hungarian and "Shanghai" Mandarin made her a valuable asset and earned her a job at the U.S. Consulate. There, the very attractive brunette, twenty-three years old and "stateless," met Major Robert Ekvall, a forty-nine-year-old widower. This was no April-to-September romance, more likely early-March-to-late-November. Family sources indicate that Eva's parents were not thrilled about her marrying an older man a year younger than her mother! Over time, the Kunfis came to accept Robert and the families became close through visits and constant communication

Years later, Ekvall described Eva as young, beautiful, educated in Austria, England and Shanghai, and . . .

> endowed with a zest for living and rare courage. She was also an athlete and horsewoman. Our first date had been a ride through the streets of Peking and into the countryside to the Temple of Heaven where the paved courtyard had echoed to the sound of our horses hooves.[159]

Somehow, during Bob's futile nine months with the Marshall Mission, he found a new love of his life, and she proved up to the challenge of being his wife. Possessing no passport or official papers, her family's flight for safety had left her "stateless," an unenviable status for a refugee from Europe.

Personal biographical information on Eva is sketchy, and none suggest she ever became a believer in Jesus Christ. At this point, the reader might ask: "Why? Why would this called-of-God Christian man marry a young Jewess who did not share his faith?" A hint of an answer to this hard question may be found in his unfinished manuscript, *Attaché Trek*, which describes his life as a military attaché in China in 1947 to 1949. He writes: "For some years I had been a loner, with all the advantages and disadvantages of that state, for my wife had died in 1940 and my only son had been killed in December of 1945 during the occupation of Korea."[160] In that matter-of-fact statement might lie the answer to the "Why?" question.

After Betty's death, Bob had been a "loner," but not a lone wolf, for more than six years. Gregarious and sociable, he liked people and enjoyed making friends. Losing Betty to a dread infection alone in Taktshang Lhamo, and then suffering the added loss of his son to an absurdly unlikely military "incident" in South Korea clearly unsettled him and shook the foundations of his faith. He had traveled his "Job journey" for years and had wearied of traveling alone. Then, Eva came into his life as a partner, a friend, a lover and companion on his journey.

"I Love Thee, Darling"

In *Dark Camps*, Ekvall's little book of unpublished prose poems, his last poem, XXII, answers the question.

> 'I love thee, darling.' The words newly spoken, and their coun-terpart in his own heart marked an end and a beginning. All the tenderness, sweetness and beauty of the past remained, but the pain began to go—was gone. Once, when in the valley of the shadow, she [Betty] had prayed in all her unselfishness for that. 'When the pain is passed that God will give you someone to love and care for you.'
>
> But she had not known that only with love would the pain pass. The answer too was different from her prayer; maybe from her choice if she could have made a choice—and yet? 'I love thee, darling.'[161]

Eva Kunfi Ekvall, 1947.

Betty, on her deathbed in Lhamo, had prayed for Bob that God would give him "someone" who would love and care for him. Bob recognized that Eva was likely not Betty's choice, yet she loved him and he loved her, and they made their life together.

They married in a civil ceremony on February 26, 1947 at the U.S. Consulate in Shanghai, where her parents lived. The Vice Consul, Lee B. Williams, signed their marriage certificate at the Glenline Building located on the Shanghai Bund. The fact that Eva had no "proper documents" made obtaining the marriage license process a bit more difficult, but, eventually, with paperwork completed, they received permission. It didn't hurt that during the war, she had risked her life to help British internees held by the Japanese and the *Kempei* (Imperial military police). She often had carried Red Cross parcels to U.S. prisoners of war held in Shanghai prisons.

As he and Eva navigated Army bureaucracy in order to marry, Bob received orders to report for duty in the Office of the Military Attaché, at the U.S. Consulate in Nanjing. Suddenly, Bob's status as a "single officer," which had made him the ideal candidate for his new job, changed. His new "situation," just engaged and soon to be married, caught the Office of the Military Attaché in Nanjing by surprise. After waiting a few days as the Army absorbed the "new news," official permission came through with the commanding officer's restrained blessing and his fellow officer's congratulations as he left Peking for ten days of leave in Shanghai and the "holy state of matrimony."

When Bob returned to Nanjing on March 8, after his ten-days of marital bliss with Eva, she remained back in Shanghai. Now married, the question as to whether Eva could be regarded a "security risk" required consideration.

> Eva had] lived in the welter of intrigue that was Shanghai: where Nazis, Communists, Russians—both white and red—renegade Frenchmen, turn-coat Chinese, refugee Central Europeans, occupation Japanese, allied internees, prisoners of war and spies of every hue and allegiance had had contact with, and schemed against each other in a thousand plots and counterplots that crisscrossed the International Settlement as it seethed under the Japanese occupation.[162]

Bob found himself in the "doghouse" with the officials at the Nanjing Office of the Military Attaché. He decided to wait patiently and study the thick volume labeled "Office of the Military Attaché Standard

Operating Procedures" to find the Military Attaché's job description. Since the Marshall Mission had just shut down its Peking operation, Bob had "liberated" several bottles from the mission's lavish liquor locker and brought them in his Army A-4 bag. As a result, he quickly made friends and influenced people at Nanjing with his contribution to their meager libation locker. Clearly, Bob's years in the Army had given him a different perspective on liquor, given his parent's raising him in a "tee-totaling " household during the years of Prohibition. The fact that he would transport the "raging strong drink" to his new post represented another step in his journey.

Captain Robert and Eva Kunfi Wedding Photo, 1947.

His commanding officer, General Robert H. Soule, gave Bob a guarded but friendly reception, not making any promises about Bob's future. He asked if his wife had a "place in Shanghai," since adequate officer's quarters were in short supply in Nanjing. Bob informed General Soule that Eva, an "old China hand," had "traveled much and roughed it well and might be able to travel with [him] and be of assistance." This comment prompted an unenthusiastic reaction. At this point, Bob ran into one of the Army's golden rules that "we take care of our women," and no "white woman" should be exposed to the hardship of travel in China's interior.[163] Bob decided to bide his time and study the Operating Procedures Manual. By the end of the week, he was told to return to Shanghai and spend time exploring the book stalls looking for military manuals or anything of intelligence value and to return on Thursday of the next week.

Unbeknownst to Military Attaché command, Eva was on her way by train to spend the weekend with Bob. He looked forward to her arrival, after which he would return to Shanghai with her to do a deep dive in the book stalls. His plan for their weekend included a horseback ride with Eva, followed by lunch at a restaurant of Bob's choosing. Surprisingly, after the General's initial dissent to the idea of Eva living in Nanjing, Bob was told to see if there was any "suitable housing" available. The normal rental offices were notorious for their extortionate dealings with Army officers needing housing, and international hotel rates far exceeded Bob's salary. Yet a ray of light remained since one Chinese-owned hotel, *The Nanking*, was listed as "suitable" by the Army. Yet, not even the General had ever managed to get a room for a guest. Nevertheless, with Eva's arrival, the possibility of establishing their own "home" in Nanjing seemed feasible. So, they visited The Nanking Hotel, once one of the top places in town, but it had fallen on hard times during the war.

A Room With Bath Required Negotiation

Bob, born and raised in China, knew how to negotiate. In his impeccable Peking Chinese, he convinced the reluctant manager that lodging an American Army officer at his establishment would increase the "face" of the hotel, even though it was somewhat rundown and seedy. When the manager realized that he was dealing with a "half-Chinese" American born in Kansu, just married and seeking Chinese hospitality, he promised Bob a room, contingent on the "young wife's" acceptance of the bridal chamber. The Nanking was large and put on "airs," but Bob saw that it was not too clean and very noisy. A room with bath required negotiation and the occasional bill-in-the-palm handshake. In the end, he secured "suitable quarters" with the assurance that his young wife would not pine away in Shanghai while he labored in Nanjing.

Their horseback ride to Nanjing's Purple Mountain took them over dusty roads heavy with traffic; they crossed dikes and rice paddies that circled the city. Despite the less than ideal conditions, the horses were eager and the outing was a success. Back at the Club, they trotted into the enclosed ring to test the skills of horse and rider. Their mounts, full-sized horses left by the Japanese cavalry had seen better days, but still had some life in them. They did some jumping and then put their mounts through their paces, finding them good trotters. Wanting to show Eva the "Tibetan trot," learned from the horsemen of the upper Yellow River basin, he loosened the reins and his horse began trotting faster as Bob adjusted to the horse's motion. Then he heard someone calling, "*Shes Rab btSon aGris.*" Twice, he heard the call and looked among the bystanders until he spied a familiar Tibetan face, the political manager of the Panchen Lama, second only to the Dalai Lama.[164] They had met two years before in Chungking, when Bob was stationed at G-2 Headquarters. Instantly, the friendship made two years previous and the bond of speaking in Tibetan drew them together. Bob introduced his Tibetan friend to Eva and they set a date to meet at The Nanking to share "Chungking perfumed duck."

Major Robert Ekvall, 1947.

At dinner that same evening in one of the restaurant's private rooms, the two friends caught up on their comings and goings over the past two years. Eva, left out due to their use of Tibetan, concentrated on the delicious fare. The Tibetan official expressed his fears regarding the future, whether the Nationalists won the civil war or the communists. He invited Bob to meet his "lama" at Kumbum Monastery not far from *Xining*, Chinghai Province's capital, if the hoped-for Military Attaché assignment actually occurred. The meal also introduced Eva to what was in store for the next eighteen months, both thrills and chills and dull, dead days. That night, as the newlyweds talked aboard their train rolling back east to Shanghai, she commented: "It [the conversation with the Tibetan] sounded as though it must be frightfully important and interesting. I wish I could have understood what was going on."[165]

Returning to Shanghai by the "Express" with Eva, Bob spent the next few days checking in at the local Military Attaché Office. Inevitably, he had to attend an official cocktail party, "a well-lubricated polyglot babel" where Bob swapped Chinese epigrams with important officials, followed by a luncheon. He kept his ears attuned to the gab and gossip since this was now part of his purview as a "military spook." His browsing the second-hand book stalls resulted in a tattered "Eighth Route Army Manual on Tactics" produced by the Chinese Communists' wartime presses in faraway *Yenan* for their peasant soldiers. Another evening he spent a few hours in "Blood Alley" nursing his drinks—surreptitiously pouring them into the handy spittoons—and listening. While the material he gathered might serve as an interesting subplot in a Chinese thriller, he found no military intelligence of any value.

By the time Bob returned to Nanjing, "Bob's General," had resolved any doubts he had regarding Bob's role as a "roving" Military Attaché with Eva as traveling partner. Although it took some days to bring into focus what Bob would do and where, his unique combination of Chinese language and culture, lived-experience in China and intelligence-gathering expertise was too valuable a resource to waste on the traditional military-diplomatic "cocktail circuit." Standing before a map of China, Soule pointed out cities and regions where the Office of Military Attaché had no presence west of Nanjing: Sian, Chungking, Kweiyang, Kunming, Chengdu and Lanzhou. Bob recalled later: "Each one was for me more than a dot on the map, for I had visited all of them repeatedly and they were places in well remembered settings."[166]

General Soule took Bob and two other Military Attachés to the Nationalist Ministry of Defense in Nanjing for their "formal presentation," replete with gold braid and all their service medals. And who should the Minister of Defense be? General *Chen K'ai-ming*, the Chief of Intelligence in the Chinese General Staff in Chungking when Bob served there in 1945. Even more amazing, this same Minister had been the Nationalist Government's Commissioner in the Marshal Mission Executive Headquarters in Peking, where Bob had recently served. In both places, Bob and Chen K'ai-ming had worked together closely on a regular basis. Bob's General was amazed how the normally taciturn Chinese official broke formal protocol, going over to Bob, shaking his hand and quizzing him on his comings and goings after his injury while serving in Chungking. After the official presentation ceremony had ended, Bob was asked to go to the General's office where Colonel Dau, the Executive Officer commented: "We hadn't know you were on such good terms with the Minister of Defense. You seem to be quite a pal of his." During the official visit, the Minister had said to General Soule through the official interpreter—"This one [Ekvall] . . . I have know him for a long time. He is half Chinese and should work for me."[167] That remark nearly wrecked Bob's hoped-for assignment to travel through China's interior for the U.S. Military Attaché Office.

After some half-hearted debate about the value of keeping Bob in Nanjing to "gather intelligence" from the Minister of Defense, the OMO decided to send him to Kunming, capital of Yunnan Province, a place of strategic value which had no Military Attaché. The plan included Eva going with Bob. Since she enjoyed living at The Nanking Hotel, gaining "heroine" status in the eyes of some, General Soule's office declared that she was "just the kind of 'white woman' who could get along in the interior, without being wrapped in cotton wool and labeled 'fragile.'"

With the decision made, myriad matters had to be cared for in a very short time. The head of the Army motor pool produced a brand-new Jeep, a four cylinder, four-wheel drive all-purpose light military vehicle. To help carry their baggage plus all they needed for the proposed "trek," a purpose-built light trailer loaded with spare parts, tires, jerry-cans of gasoline and a big can of grease came with the Jeep. Sufficient fuel for about nine hundred miles was on board. With a proposed itinerary in the thousands of miles, an official document produced by the Chinese Ministry of Transportation gave Ekvall permission to obtain more fuel from the authorities as they traveled.

The First Secretary of the U.S. Embassy remedied Eva's lack of passport and official ID by producing a beautiful official document, in English and Chinese, presenting Bob's titles at length, and Eva, as his wife. Complete with pictures and the the embassy seal, plastered with red wax stamps and ribbons, the lavish document was stapled within an official U.S. folder and made "authentic beyond challenge." During their eighteen months of travel throughout China, it was never questioned, and rarely examined. Consequently, the date for their departure was set and first-class tickets were purchased on the Chinese river liner, the *S. S. Minchuan*. They attended a frantic round of cocktails and receptions before boarding their river steamship.

Chapter 10

Trek for Two

As the jam-packed *S. S. Minchuan* cast off and powered into the powerful current of the Yangtze, clearly the legal capacity of one hundred souls had been multiplied by twenty since more than two thousand passengers somehow had gotten on the ship. With decks covered with people and bundles and the holds filled to capacity, the crew begged them to move slowly since the top-heavy ship could capsize. There was no room for Bob's Jeep and trailer; so it remained behind to be sent on the next ship going upriver. Ekvall had reserved two "staterooms," one with baggage from floor to ceiling, and the other also piled high for him and Eva. They could just squeeze in and climb to the two top bunks. Between their two "first class" cabins, they had thirty-three pieces of gear, including a field safe and bucket of axle grease. Such was their home for the next five days.

The Yangtze River is one of China's two continental waterways, the other being the Yellow River. It serpentines across northern China while the Yangtze runs from the Tibetan Plateau parallel to the Mekong and Salween Rivers before turning east for the coast. In reality, the Yangtze divides China between the hardy Han-dominated north and the smaller happy folk of the south. Chinese history had been made on and around this mighty "Son of the Outer Ocean River."

Deep, wide and powerful, the strong current forced boats, large and small, to travel close to the banks or tack back and forth across it rather than charging full speed ahead. Since their packed room was stuffy by day, they sat on the upper boat deck where the few useless life boats afforded them a place to rest in the shade. Despite the circumstances, decent meals were served on time. Each day, they met a new character, businessmen, government officials and the rich returning to their homes after visiting in Nanjing. One little boy, perhaps eight, begged Eva to take him as "her little boy" since she didn't have one. Daily at lunch, they would ask the waiter for an extra big bowl of rice with vegetables and pieces of meat and fish. This they took outside the little dining room and gave to the famished child. For three days, Eva cared for "her" little boy, who soon disappeared when Bob suggested they could get the boy into school in Hankow, where they were to dock for the night. Whenever possible after tying up, Bob and Eva would walk hand in hand through the town to "see the sights." Often, local policemen followed behind discreetly. Apparently Bob's Army uniform told them that he was someone who shouldn't get mugged on their streets.

Arriving at the huge city of *Hankow*, last port of call for the *S. S. Minchuan*, they disembarked late at night. Bob had been told that someone from the American Consulate would be there; so, he forced his way to the rail in the midst of a mob of people as the ship swayed precariously. He shouted his name into the darkness, and immediately, his name echoed back; someone was there! The man fought his way up the ramp with some husky "coolies" who shouldered their way past the crowds to Ekvall's rooms and carried off all but their personal baggage. After late dinner with the American consul and wife, they overnighted at the consulate's cramped flat.

Much refreshed by a good night's sleep on a real bed, Bob informed the consul that they had to wait for their jeep coming on the next ship from Nanjing in ten days. Not wanting to stay in the tiny flat, Bob "knew of a missionary hotel and business agency run by an old friend," where they could stay with their baggage safely stored in the agency "go down," (storage room).[168] All along the way on their eighteen month trek, Bob would fall back on longtime relationships from missionary days. While the presence of his attractive "new" young wife young raised the eyes of a few former friends, they were well received. At times, they even stayed at unoccupied mission stations whose caretakers, shocked seeing an Army officer at their doors, immediately recognized the Chinese-speaking officer as a friend of "their missionary."

Since they had a wait in Hankow, Bob told the surprised consul that he wished to "pay his respects" to General Ch'eng Ch'ien, Personal Representative of President, Shang Kai Shek. The consul had never gotten close to an audience with such a lofty figure but humored the request;

to his amazement, the request was granted. Recalling the "Manual," he remembered there were things to observe and things to report. The trick was to know which was which. The SOP for the Military Attaché was to develop relationships and personal rapport, whenever possible with government officials. Secondly, he had to keep his ears tuned and eyes pealed for intelligence at all times wherever they were. Since no one dreamed that the blond U.S. Army officer understood their dialect, much valuable information found its way in Bob's reports.

Bob's courtesy call with General Ch'eng Ch'ien, a sizable, sleepy-looking man, would not take more than fifteen minutes. The General appeared just awake enough to let the Chinese-speaking American know that his visit wasn't worth much time. Try as he might, Bob got only a few mono-syllabic remarks from the man who had played a large role in the history of the Nationalist movement. However, Bob chanced to quote from a poem written by Mao Tse tung that caused the heavy-lidded eyes to open wider, and they began talking about Chinese poetry. With appropriate modesty, Bob mentioned, *en passant*, that he had just published his first volume of poetry, *Chinese Dialogues* the year before. The result of this chat came at the end of the visit. "You must come and have lunch with me tomorrow. Real Hunan food. You will taste how good it is. I will send a car for you."[169] Back at the U.S. Consulate, the consul was astounded, never having heard of such a thing.

Many Toasts of Fiery *Mao-T'ai* Served in Tiny Jade Cups

The next day's two-hour luncheon proved to be the high point of their stay in Hankow. Regaled with spicy Hunanese dishes and many toasts of fiery *mao-t'ai* served in tiny jade cups, the General talked and talked. Like everyone else in China, the General wondered who was going to win the civil war, "Old Mao" or "Old Chiang." He told Bob that the Americans had done right by trying to mediate between the two Chinese leaders. What China needed was peace, not more war, and it was a shame that the honest U.S. effort had failed. Like all thinking Chinese, he wondered and waited.

One other high point during their stay in Hankow was running into George Findlay Andrew, OBE (Order of the British Empire). China born, ex-China Inland Mission educator, ex-famine relief administrator, ex-director of public relations for Butterfield and Swire, a British steamship company, and First Secretary of Her Majesty's Embassy in Chungking, Bob first had met him in 1945 while at the U.S. Military Headquarters. The old "China hand" also wondered who would win the war? He was not sanguine about the Nationalist's chances nor overly hopeful regarding the Communist's intentions. Long overdue for retirement, he was leaving China and strongly objected to Bob "taking a girl like this into what you may get into. If things break up too fast there is going to be complete chaos." He doubted that Bob would get back to his birthplace in Kansu because the governor in Lanzhou, Chang Chih-chung "doesn't like Americans." As the old man gabbed on, Bob filed away in his mind names and places which might be useful in the future before parting company.

When the jeep finally arrived, Bob had it loaded onto another smaller river boat that same evening. Amazingly, their vehicle and trailer had arrived intact; nothing had been taken, gas still in the tank, and battery untouched. The *S.S. Ming-yuan* was much less crowded and the deck free of people. From the throb of the engine, Bob could tell it was geared for the roaring gorges upstream. On this leg of their trip, they met Mr. Shang, a Sichuanese businessman and high official. Discovering that Bob spoke French, the loquacious little man entertained them with stories, local history and sly comments about Eva's good looks. Discovering that she loved to dance, he asked Bob to play the *Merry Widow Waltz* on his guitar while the Franco-Sino gentleman squired Eva around the deck. He told Bob who he should see in Chungking and also in Chengdu, capital of the province. With him, conversation never lagged, mostly from him, and almost always, in faultless French.

After passing *Ichang*, the river narrowed and gained strength; the high cliffs on each bank rose up. They watched the great rice junks transporting the harvest of the vast fertile red basin. "With sweeps manned by as many as twenty men—coming through the gateway as though they were fleeing from the foaming rapids and swift eddies of the fearsome upper gorges. And the only sound was the faint echo of the harsh tunes to which the long sweeps rose and fell rhythmically.[170] Bob recalled his parents telling him about their fleeing Kansu due to the violent Boxer Rebellion in 1900 when Bob was just two years old. They came downriver on one of the same kind of barges, and Bob felt an odd sense of ownership as he pointed them out. Immediately, Eva wanted to ride on one, but they had gained speed and stopping was out of the question.

The next day, their ship barely crept forward against the current. Angry brown water resisted the ship as it swung from bank to bank to avoid the mid-stream flow. Junks loaded with cargo crept upriver hauled forward by towline-coolies who sang their mournful dirges as they hauled on the bamboo cable fixed to the junk's mast. Bob had heard that an international engineering firm had even surveyed the narrow gorges of the Yangtze, predicting that one day a great dam would be built there, taming the river's annual floods and producing three fourths of all the electrical power needed to propel Central China forward as a modern nation. That prediction materialized when the Three Gorges Dam became operational in 2012.

After passing the relentless rapids of the Three Gorges region, they entered smooth waters. Not long after, the great river city of *Chungking* abruptly appeared straight ahead. China's wartime capital after the fall of Nanjing in 1937, it had swollen with the rapid influx of government offices, foreign personnel, U.S. Army installations, and refugees fleeing the coast after Japan's takeover of China's coastal territory. Now with the war over, the Nationalist government capital went back to Nanjing. Chungking was less hectic and electric.

The *S. S. Ming-yuan* dropped anchor about a half mile from shore, and the passengers swarmed onto the waiting *sampans* with their belongings. Cargo was hauled up from the hold and loaded into lighters for transport to the docks. Bob hailed a free sampan which took them, bag and baggage, ashore. However, he found no sampan large enough to transport the Jeep and trailer. Bob and Eva took a rickshaw up the winding streets to the Victory House, a war-time hotel still in business. After settling Eva in the room, Bob set out to find a junk owner who could get the Jeep and trailer onto land. At a nearby tea-room, the proprietor, a stocky, barefoot woman, assured Bob that her husband was up to the task. After a quick bowl of noodles and tea, Bob went to the docks and found the junk owner.

In just a few minutes, he had his crew and boat alongside the *Ming-yuan*. Using long, sturdy bamboo poles, the Jeep and trailer slid down the poles. Part of the crew stayed on the deck of the *Ming-yuan* securing ropes that lowered the Jeep and trailer down the angled poles. Although the bamboo bent and bowed, and Bob feared his transportation would end up in the river, the vehicles slipped jerkily down the poles and landed safely on the deck of the junk. Raising sail, they glided up to a nearby landing where the highway came to the river side. Bob held his breath as he turned the key. The battery woke the little four-cylinder engine, which coughing and sputtering, quickly roared into life. Then he drove the jeep and trailer from the deck of the junk down two wide planks to the shore. And, voilà, they had transportation for their trek—12,000 miles over the next 18 months. Driving into the city, Bob smiled as he pulled up to Victory House, marking the first of more than one hundred overnights at inns, hotels, houses and other accommodations.

A Small Squad of Rats Froze in the Light

The hotel furnished a night watchman to care for the jeep and supplies piled in the trailer. Glad to be on land, they had a delicious meal, sampling the delicious *shab-hsing* sherry-colored rice wine, like *saké* but much better. In their room, they doused the floor around their bed with insect-powder and then enjoyed a well-deserved night's sleep. Then, in the early hours of the morning, they awoke to a sniffing, snuffling sound. Bob, service revolver in one hand and flashlight in the other, shined a beam onto the floor where a small squad of rats froze in the light then disappeared.

The next morning, they planned for eating on the road: chopsticks and a spoon or two. At restaurants and roadside food stalls, they would ask the proprietor to pour scalding water on the serving dishes; and use 150-proof *kaffir-corn* liquor to wipe off the chopsticks and spoons. The drink was lethal to the unsuspecting stomach and even more deadly on germs.

Checking in at the U.S. Consulate for any mail or new orders for Bob, the consul was delighted that they had arrived safely but decidedly not in favor of their staying at the Victory House. He moved them to his commodious house on the outskirts of town. Since no mail or orders awaited them, Bob went to the consulate and found two large filing cabinets, unlocked, containing documents left over from the war. The consul thought there "might be some confidential information" in the them. As Bob went through the files, he found most of the documents marked "Top-Secret" or "Confidential." A telegram from the Embassy in Nanjing ordered Bob to "Inspect and certify destruction of all classified material not considered worth keeping."[171] For the next four days, Bob burned the damp documents that persistently defied incineration. Then, for the next four days, Bob and Eva were wined and dined at a series of cocktails and luncheons, the local whirl of diplomatic social doings. The mayor of Chungking invited Bob to his office; there, the worried government official shared his concerns about China's future and the "who will win" question.

At the end of the stay, they headed northwest toward *Chengdu*, about 180 miles northwest on a badly worn two-lane gravel highway, notable for its potholes. Built during WW II, it featured truck drivers who seemed to play "chicken" with oncoming vehicles. Decrepit alcohol-powered buses and single-axle freight carts pulled by four men went down the middle of the highway. In addition, pedestrians, rickshaws, shoulder-yoked carriers hauling bags of rice and farmers struggling under the dead-weight of wooden "honey buckets" for their fields, jammed the road. To make things even more interesting, an occasional water-buffalo might exit a roadside rice paddy and simply walk into the traffic flow. It took a whole day before they reached a tributary of the Yangtze, the *Nui-kiang*. The ferry boat lacked a full-size gangplank to access the flat-bottom scow, just two sturdy planks the width of the Jeep and trailer's tires. Fortunately, Bob's nerves of steel managed to get the Jeep and cargo hauler on and off the ferry.

They found their stay in Chengdu pleasant but busy since Bob knew the city well, having traveled there several time as a missionary. Now in the U.S. Army, he and Eva moved into a "modern apartment" built for Army Air Force pilots during the war. The move to "little America" put Bob and Eva in the midst of a swirl of social gatherings. In addition, duty required Bob to enter another "world" of diplomatic protocol, leaving his card at the offices of Chinese military and civilian officials with follow-up visits and receptions. Bob also wanted to revisit a third "world," the campus of the West China Union University, a product of the cooperative efforts of four Protestant missionary boards. Bob knew many of the missionaries who taught at the university; and although his uniform clashed with their memories of him from "another life," he spent pleasant hours with them.

Who Will Win the War, and Then . . . What?

At China's "West Point," the National Military Academy in Chengdu, Bob met with the head of the school. As in so many other discussions on the long trek, the conversation inevitably led to the the big question: Who will win the war, and then . . . what? The climatic diplomatic event, a farewell dinner served at the Academy, gave Eva opportunity to dance with a file of Chinese officers. Bob, sweating like a stevedore in the hot dining hall, had to dance with a bevy of charming young wives of the officers lined up to dance with Eva. That was a night to remember for the former missionary who, doubtless, had learned to waltz from his young bride who had lived in Vienna, home of the waltz. Like liquor, dancing, verboten in his missionary days, had become part of his new reality.

The gala event ended with the military band gallantly producing a fair rendition of the U.S. national anthem, which required all to stand stiffly at attention till the last note died. The academy's commander gave Bob a beautiful, scroll painted by a noted local artist. It portrayed two swallows wheeling and diving in the sky above trees bowed and bent by a storm. Swallows, the symbol of marital happiness represented Bob and Eva, flying high above the storm about to roar across China.

While navigating the whirl of three competing worlds in Chengdu, Bob found time to visit tea houses and talk with and listen to the "common people," like the burly men of "bitter strength" who pulled the heavy single-axle cargo carts. From them, he learned much about road conditions in the region, the amount of commerce requiring transportation and local food prices. Bob shared tea and salted watermelon seeds with a rail-thin peasant farmer in town to sell his just-harvested grain. A sharecropper, he paid sixty percent of his yield to the landowner, having to provide seed for next year's crop from his share. In this very fertile land of the "red basin" of Sichuan, most farmers owned little or none of the "good earth," and their families, were always hungry. This cold reality provided fertile soil for local Communist agents. All of this went into Bob's reports sent to Nanjing. Always, the perennial question about who would win, Old Mao or Old Chiang, occupied everyone's mind.

The other thing that Bob took away from Chengdu related to the heavy-handed American "advisers," who made it clear that continued logistic support for the Nationalist Army depended on their acquiescence to training methods and military doctrine from the U.S. Army's "American Book." The issue strained the relationship between the sometime allies, concerning Bob. The Chinese military greatly admired U.S. military hardware and always wanted more, but they preferred their Chinese "grass sandals" to heavy American combat boots.

At the end of their stay in Chengdu, Bob and Eva retraced their route back to Chungking. Their return had the feel of déjà vu, like a film run backward. The fields promised a good harvest and hopeful prospects for next year's crop. Yet, the back-breaking plight of the peasant sharecropper poisoned the relationship between farmer and land owner. Bob sensed that sooner or later, this toxin would eventually destroy the "social soul" and result in catastrophic upheaval.

Back in Chungking, Bob wrote a detailed account of what he had seen and learned while in Chengdu. A few social event, like the dinner worthy of a "chef manque" prepared by the French Consul, broke up the time otherwise spent reading his notes and typing up his report for the Office of the Military Attaché (OMA) in Nanjing. He reported on the Military Academy and the commander's concerns about the "American book" for soldiers and the "Chinese way." These reports later got Bob in some hot water with the U.S. brass since he shared the Chinese official's frustration at the inflexibility of the U.S. military's philosophy of soldiering and war. He gave his assessment of the Nationalist troops' readiness, the state of the highways and how that affected military transport. He shared the viewpoint of the burly cart-puller on commerce in and around Chengdu, as well as the sharecropper's frustration at an ever-diminishing return on their labor in the fertile fields of Sichuan. Not having a "proper" military background, Bob's reports told of "matters more of behavioral science interest than such things as data on 'battle order' to gratify Pentagon experts."[172]

While the round trip to Chengdu and back had proved the viability of travel in a four-wheeled Jeep, the next leg of their odyssey proved much more challenging. Taking the ferry across the Yangtze to the south bank, they left relatively flat land for a region of narrow valleys, hog-back ridges and high passes. They traveled a badly-worn road poorly maintained. Hairpin turns required considerable maneuvering around and up the steep inclines to the next pass. The lightweight Jeep struggled to pull the overloaded trailer which threw its weight around making the steering light and erratic. At best, they made about fifteen miles per hour on the wartime "highway," which still had some inns and restaurants, even repair shops, making travel easier.

The farther south they drove towards *Kwei-yang*, capital of backward Guizhou Province, the more they saw evidence of the many "minority tribes," the Miao, Yao, Yi, etc.—pushed back into the mountains to farm steep slopes. In their colorful, distinctive clothes, they thronged the market towns they passed. Most of the road-repair workers were obviously non-Chinese. The "anthropologist" in Ekvall observed and noted their costume and listened to their mostly unwritten languages. They struggled to maintain their identity despite the government's attempt at the Sinicization of the minority groups.

The Desperate Need to Find Medical Care for Eva

After days of travel over red dust or red mud when it rained, Bob and Eva were about a day's drive from *Kwei-Yang* when the first cloud of sorrow blotted out their sun of fun. "Too much jeeping on too rough roads on the wrong day of the month brought on the threat of a miscarriage—a very early one but frightening nevertheless. We reached Kwei-Yang with the desperate need to find medical care for Eva, and knowing little where we could find it."[173]

The provincial hospital was a "sprawl of low buildings" with an all-Chinese staff of dedicated, highly skilled doctors and nurses who took excellent care of Eva, charging very little. The staff considered working in an off-the-road place like Kwei-yang their duty and privilege. Due to Eva's condition, the doctors decided that she needed treatment followed by bed rest. They stayed in the back-water capital city, which afforded Bob opportunity to observe how China assimilated her minorities.

The governor of Guizhou, Tang Shen, a short, trim Han Chinse with a firm handshake had a penchant for seeing "his people" strong, healthy and regimented. He ordered the city population to do morning exercises, something of a surprise to Bob since he had visited the sleepy town back in 1939 as he and Betty returned to Lhamo after leaving David at Dalat School. The thought of the local populous awaking to bugle calls "by the dawn's early light" to do calisthenics amused Bob. Yet, "being strong" obsessed the governor. He wanted his people strong to resist the foreigner and intermarry with the Chinese and drive Guizhou forward. As in Chengdu, the local military officer complained of having to confirm to the "American soldier book" during the recent war. The south of China had seen thousands of U.S. troops, part of the Burma Road construction and U.S. Army Air force bases, with their wealth of equipment and manuals telling how to use them. A major gripe of the Chinese soldier concerned the Army combat boot, a heavy leather affair that their light feet didn't appreciate. "In sandals a Chinese soldier can walk faster and longer and carry a greater weight than any American soldier, but in heavy boots that are always too big—what feet the Americans have—he can't walk like a Chinese."[174] The simple dry-grass sandal made by the Chinese soldier every other day proved superior to the footwear of the big-footed foreign devils. Bob included these candid observations in his next report to Nanjing after reaching their goal, Kunming capital of Yunnan Province in June 1947.

Kunming, last "stop" on the road, became Bob's "permanent station," until new orders dispatched them elsewhere. Pulling into the city, strategically valuable during WW II at the end of the Burma Road, it had supplied much of the Nationalist Army by land and air. Kunming had:

> received the 14th Air Force pilots, who had flown the hump with nylons and lipstick in their flight bags . . . .
>
> Flying from India over the Himalayas with freight, fuel and materiel for the fight on Chinese soil against Imperial Japan, these pilots stayed at the Hotel du Commerce, "a semi-European relic from the days when French influence and the French presence, which had come in with the railroad from Hanoi into this southwestern corner of China, [which] had created a miniature and authentic French colony."[175]

In addition, OSS agents had crowded the hotel bar to drink and hatch schemes against China's enemy.

The Ekvalls chose the Hotel du Commerce, a leftover bastion of French cuisine and culture, as their home until the U.S. Vice-Consul located permanent quarters. While rather run down, it still offered chateaubriand steaks and crepe suzettes on the menu, something the competing Chinese hostels could not match. In addition, the "suites" had bathrooms with real "running water" which flowed both hot and cold in and out of the tubs, something most hostelries could not boast.

On April 1947, Bob, quickly set up his U.S. Military Attaché "branch office" in the consulate complete with typewriter, files and a field safe. He settled into the busyness of official paper-work. All this had happened little more than a year after a chance meeting with a colonel at the Pentagon. Since that time, he and Eva had visited and seen many faces, civilian, military, of high status and lowly station. They had gained new insights, lived new experiences, and acquired new perspectives, and "always the sheer lusty joys of wandering, old within our natures yet refreshingly new in each day's wayfaring."[176]

No longer vagabonds, Bob and Eva soon fit into local "high society," foreign and Chinese. The sizeable community of foreign legations in town, U.S., British and French maintained full-blown consulates, as well as a smattering of businessmen, missionaries and "wandering scholars" of various nationalities. Opportunities abounded to meet new people. From friendly French expats, Bob learned of France's attempts to hold onto their former colonies in Indo-China while negotiating with Ho Chi Minh, head of the communist Viet Minh, the same guerrilla fighters which asked Bob to smuggle out strategic maps in 1943. Thus, from the French Consul, the manager of the Banque de l'Indochine and a longtime French professor at the provincial university, Bob learned of France's desperate efforts to negotiate in Hanoi with Bao Dai, the devious ex-emperor of Annam and Tonkin who had worked with the Japanese when Vichy France fell in 1945. From these three contacts, he established what he called a "three-point fix on fact."[177] All this found its place in the Nanjing reports.

While his first contacts with Chinese officialdom, civil and military yielded little more than a few business cards and cursory introductions, Bob bided his time. Scanning the local press, he discovered articles authored by an extremely insightful writer who, in elegant Chinese, reported on the many "minority tribes" in the region. When Bob looked up the thin-faced writer in a cluttered room at the local newspaper, he startled the writer. Just the fact that an American Army officer could read Chinese, much less that he had sought out the writer, caused the man to share his story. From the *Wa* people, whose traditional lands lay hard on the border between China and Indo-China, he had decided as a small boy in a little town in the hills to "learn the learning" of the "master race" in order to meet the arrogant Chinese and their four thousand year civilization. He studied Chinese since his mother-tongue was not yet in writing. In a real sense, he gave voice and visibility to scores of other tribes—Cheo, Meo, Mu, Nhu, Kha to name a few. He became a scholar, a historian and ethnographer of those who, while native to China, were not considered Chinese. As a result, Ekvall began studying the tribes of China's southern border region. He learned that Yunnan had many other tribes, remnants of the Thai kingdom whose capital once lay near Kunming. "The Lolo in the north on the border of Tibet; and the Pai-Li-su and other peoples along the Burma border who [were] ethnically matched by people beyond the frontier."[178]

Since the Japanese Did Not Win the War, Who Did?

At one social occasion, Bob met a Chinese professor of history at the local university. While Ekvall had studied Chinese history since his boyhood, he had never had it explained to him by a Chinese scholar. He elaborated on China's four thousand year history while applying lessons learned from the past to China's present problems. The question came up: "Since the Japanese did not win the war, who did? Can it be that 'Old Mao' did?

Where does he belong in Chinese history?" The professor answered the question with another question relating to the critical problem of land reform in China, something already in Bob's sights.

"Land reform in China should follow Chinese ideas. We do not need foreign ideas and thinking to solve our Chinese problems. Is 'old Mao' Chinese or has he swallowed a foreign idea-system? That is the important question."[179] While he did not answer the question with another question, the Chinese history professor's "answer" became the theme of another long report to Nanjing. His insightful query as to whether Mao was Chinese or had swallowed a foreign idea would help determine China's future wellbeing.

During those halcyon days in Kunming, each day seemed to bring Bob and Eva something new. Such exotic experiences as an "arsenic-drinking" party, or hours-long feasts featuring two dozen courses with birds'-nest soup, shark fins, pigeon eggs, deer sinews, bear-paws and rare fungi which tickled or tortured their taste buds. Multiple toasts with the best of French cognac and Chinese "liquid fire water" left them dazed and drowsy. Invariably at such encounters, Bob would meet a new contact, perhaps the richest businessman in Yunnan, which would open a whole new gamut of questions: Is there still a market for tungsten in the United States? Will Burma gain its independence or will Great Britain seek to control the tin markets in the newly independent Federation of Malay States. Questions regarding international banking, transportation, and the "manipulation" of government officials often came up at cocktails and banquets which demanded Ekvall's presence. The host of the arsenic-drinking party (a Chinese health ritual) candidly stated that he wished to open Yunnan to international business. He pointed out that WW 2 had cut off the French from South China and destroyed the railway to Hanoi and Haiphong. Yet, the same war opened the Burma road, built new airfields and changed the political situations in Burma and Yunnan. He also foresaw a way to develop the mineral wealth of his province.

In the long conversation, Bob noted that the man seemed to be blind to two "blank spaces: the workers and their human condition." From all accounts, the tin miner's life was miserable and the mines, terrible places to work. It seemed that no one realized that they all lived under the "looming shadow of Mao." Bob later mused: "If power corrupts, wealth, on the other hand, may create a strange blindness."[180] Bob's report back to OMA in Nanjing about Mr. Miao and his empire building was long and detailed. While not a cloak and dagger spy, Robert Ekvall had developed into a perceptive and persistent intelligence agent for the U.S. Army.

Eventually Eva's parents, Tibor and Maria, fled the heat and humidity of Shanghai for an extended visit with Bob and their daughter. Tibor spent his days busily taking pictures of the city and surrounding area. A first-class photographer, he made an extensive record of his visit before returning to Shanghai. Sadly, his photographic register of their visit did not survive. During their long stay, the presence of Tibor and Maria Kunfi with Bob and their daughter, made the Ekvalls a "two-adult-generation family," lending dignity to their social gatherings. For Eva, having her parents brought her joy since she and her parents had lived and traveled as a family to many lands before finding refuge in far-off China. The parents dearly missed their daughter as she did them, even though she had found the love of her life in a man old enough to be her father.

Eva spent long hours with a Chinese teacher to free herself from a "deaf-mute's" life on the road. While she loved the rootless life in China's backwater provinces, she had no desire to be a silent partner. As a Central European born and raised where intrigue was a way of life, she had a "nose for sniffing out hints of plots and double meanings in situations and conversations, and intuitively could tip [Bob] off on leads."[181] While they enjoyed their life in Kunming, and Nanjing had no complaints about Bob's reports, he sensed it was time to get back on the road and among the people of the land to find out what was really happening, something not learned while "on station." After Eva's parents returned to Shanghai, they had no good reason to stay in Kunming any longer. They had squeezed that orange dry and garnered much "juice" which had been concentrated and sent on to OMA in Nanjing and then on to Washington, D.C.

Bob let it be known that he planned to follow the newly opened auto road northward over the mountains in Sichuan to where the Yangtze no longer permitted river boat traffic. While Bob had experienced little surveillance in Kunming, he quickly heard from the security apparatus that such a trip was not a good idea. "Too dangerous" was the explanation. "Road was unsafe—too many bandits."[182] After haggling for permission to leave town for the countryside, it was suggested that they drive up to *Weining*, "A very interesting place and the nearby mountains are pleasant to visit in the summer time." It was about 250 miles northeast in neighboring Guizhou Province.

With their trusty Jeep and trailer loaded, they set out on the new "gas-cart road." Looking like a fresh red scar on the landscape, the just-finished road did not follow the old lay-of-the-land footpaths but struck out on a new and shorter course. This resulted in no eating places or inns on the roadside. Lunch required them to stop at a crossroad and hike across some fields to buy hard-boiled eggs and tea at a little village food stand. Seeing no fresh tire marks on the gravel, they wondered if they might find a bridge out or a landslide. Yet, this was not the case and they finally sighted Weining after going down a steep descent into a wide valley.

"Are You a Pastor and of What Mission?"

Arriving at dusk, the motor road funneled into a muddy street with no gutters or pavement. It appeared to Bob, a life-long veteran of travel in China's interior, as one of the dirtiest towns he had ever visited. They found the local "inns" filthy and falling down; the owners showed no concern. About this time, with their Jeep surrounded by curious crowds in the muddy street, someone came up to Bob and asked, "Are you a pastor and of what mission?" Bob quickly replied, "No, I am not a pastor but is there a 'Good News Hall' here in Weining?" There was, and since the resident missionaries were absent, the caretaker of the mission offered them a refuge in their time of need. Whether Bob whispered a prayer or not that night, clearly, some One had looked out for him and his young wife. All the caretaker asked for was a letter for the missionary to relieve him of responsibility. Once again, Bob's missionary background saved them from a cold night in the Jeep. After getting the jeep and trailer over the high threshold of the mission compound and through the narrow gate, with two inches to spare, they cleaned up while the caretaker and wife brought food from a local restaurant.

The experience that night in Weining reminded Bob of his childhood back in Minchow, Kansu Province. The Alliance mission station in that largely Chinese town was the place where any foreigner was directed. If they spoke English, whether missionaries, explorers, scientists, business men, refugees, or consular officials, they all headed to the Ekvall home where his father and mother entertained the visitors. Little wide-eyed Bobby longed to hear news from the world beyond his narrow world of experience. As he and Eva enjoyed the hospitality of the missionary, even though absent, Bob could sense a covering presence accompanying his travels.

The next day, sunlight streaming in the window revealed the streets of Weining, no better, no worse, than so many other interior towns that Ekvall had visited, just another small town in China's vast interior. After breakfast, they visited the local markets to observe the produce and prices. The worried secretary of the mayor found them and invited Bob and Eva for dinner that evening. Like so many eating affairs, the meal began in the mid-afternoon and went through dusk to the late evening. Not knowing why they had been invited, the guests enjoyed the mayor's hospitality. Some of the school teachers present reported of the state of the school system and education in their region. When Bob asked about the "security situation" on the gas-cart road, they immediately told him that it had no bandits. In times past, yes, but not now "since the establishment of local self-government in the villages, banditry had all but disappeared."[183]

With his curiosity piqued by the thought of self-government, something rare in post-war China, they told Bob that some months earlier, a directive had come down from Nanjing to the mayor's office decreeing "democracy" at the local village level. Rather than the mayor arbitrarily appointing a village leader, the villagers themselves would elect their headman to collect taxes for the region, execute policies and represent the interests of the villagers when dealing with the mayors office. Considered newsworthy by the guests at the mayor's residence, this experiment in democracy seemed well-received. The villagers liked the idea since it made the headman responsible to them, and not just a henchman of a far-away mayor.

Recently, one village, disenchanted with their elected headman who showed no concern for their rights, summarily "fired" him and elected another headman without telling the mayor. Amazingly, the decision stood and the mayor recognized their prerogative to expect responsive leadership. The ousted headman had appealed his case to the mayor but the local peasants argued for their rights and presented such a unified testimony that the headman who had "eaten too much profit" lost his appeal. This novel development became one of the main features of Bob's next report to OMA in Nanjing. While some of the more well-to-do townsmen did not appreciate the "half-cooked" democratic ideas of the peasants, it appeared that the winds of change were stirring up centuries of undemocratic dust. The mayor, trying to keep all sides happy, explained that he had done what he had been told to do by Nanjing, and he did agree that the countryside was safer and calmer than before.

The next day, Bob decided to see the new social experiment closer. Asking the mayor if he could drive into the hill country to "vacation" near the copper mines, the mayor "regretfully" informed him that the roads in that part of the district were impassable for a Jeep. Bob countered by saying that they could walk in if baggage carriers could be found. Caught off guard by Bob's second request, the mayor agreed that Bob could go in with mules and horses for hire, with local guides. The next day, they would set out for the copper mines.

While Bob hoped to visit the "democratic village," he felt it too obvious to ask the guides to detour to the town. However, that night, Bob's luck held; he met a farmer from that very town at their over-night inn. On his way to market with a shoulder-pole load of produce, he gladly talked about the local politics. He explained that when the decree had come from Nanjing to the mayor's office and filtered down to their village, the locals understood it to mean they were to simply confirm the long-standing headman appointed years before. Taking his "election" as a sign that he had more power than ever, the headman, wealthy by the villager's standards and able to read and write, began to exact more from the villagers. Two village youths in school at Weining returned with clearer understanding of the policy which they had read about in the newspaper and discussed at school. They learned that such things as "people's power" meant they could do something about the unjust arrangement under which they lived. Other peasants in town could read and write and file reports for the mayor. Consequently, they took another village vote, "threw out the bum," and elected another headman of their liking. As the farmer explained the story to Bob, his weather-beaten face reflected both satisfaction and amazement. The new headman is more honest than the previous and knew that he was being watched. "Strange and wonderful" indeed is this "people's power."[184]

There Are None So Blind as Those Who Will Not See

Bob's updated report to Nanjing on "people's power" and "self government" contained the on-the-ground testimony of a villager who had seen it happen. Some months later at a cocktail party in Nanjing, Bob was charged with gullibility. "The first secretary of the embassy and the two New York times correspondents in Nanjing—China hands all—faulted me for being naïve; despite my language capability and many years in

China."[185] As goes the old adage: There are none so blind as those who will not see. Unfortunately, the "old hands," jaded by years of observing corruption, high-handed officials and political chicanery, did not believe that Chinese peasants on the local level could take seriously a government mandate and make it work. While some laughed at the "half-cooked barbarians" in the hill country of Yunnan, others believed that change could happen, even in China!

The day after Bob heard from the villager of his experience with a ground-level "democracy," he and Eva arrived at the copper mine hours after the sun had gone down. In the pitch black darkness, they stumbled onto the headquarters compound and into the glare of electric lights and a very warm welcome by the director, Dr. Li, who spoke English fluently. He enthusiastically showed the Ekvalls around the operation. This particular copper mine had produced sufficient copper for the province's needs for centuries. At the same time, the need to increase production through economy of scale and modern technology was apparent. In order to keep up with present demand, the mine continued using the old ore pits and tunnels and charcoal-fueled furnaces. The miners worked the mines in the traditional way and were paid by the old salary scale. At the same time, the mine administration had begun to introduce new technology and methods, increasing production to meet the growing demand caused by heavy industry which moved west during the war. They needed a more efficient, less destructive energy source than charcoal, and electric power could provide it since they had no local source of coal.

The staff, experimenting with these new ideas, had jerry-rigged a small hydroelectric dam and generator which ran a very efficient small electric furnace. However, another stream nearby had much more energy potential. The director gladly showed Bob the site of a hoped-for dam. Ironically, this source was very familiar to Bob. "That river was the same Son of the Ocean we had followed from Nanjing upward to Chungking, but here called 'the River of Golden Sand, as it squeezed its way from Tibet through the forested mountains of Lolo land."[186] Bob had crossed the Golden Sands River many times on his visits to Ngawa years before. The mine director wondered out loud if Bob could somehow help him get the needed equipment to realize the plans for expansion. While sympathetic to the man's needs and in agreement with the plans in view, Bob's purview as a Military Attaché did not include "venture capitalist."

The short three-day stay in Weining had some personal benefits. Since they did so much walking, both Bob and Eva lost "some of the flab of easy living" in Kunming. Their friends at the U.S. Consulate and others they met at the next dinner party hosted by the governor all commented on how they had slimmed down. Bob felt that the short jaunt to the hill country had given him a much better understanding of life in the average village, as well as the potential for mineral production in Yunnan and Sichuan. At the same dinner affair, Bob learned of Chu Shao-liang's coming to Kunming in the near future. This Nationalist government figure was one of Chiang Kai Shek's closest and most trusted associates. Bob had been told that he should seek to meet and interview him since he had overall responsibility for China's four southwestern provinces of Sichuan, Kweichow, Yunnan and Sikang (Tibet).

Twice Bob had tried to meet him in Chungking, but had not succeeded. This time in Kunming, his chances, though slim, were better. For a mere Major in the U.S. Army to try and seek an audience with one of the highest ranked Nationalist generals was more than a bit presumptuous. However, Bob Ekvall, never one to shirk a challenge, went to the crowded railway station platform where the illustrious figure was to arrive. Since there was no prescribed place for him to observe the arrival of General Chu Shao-liang, Bob devised a plan. He told the anxious protocol officer, not knowing what to do with the smartly uniformed American officer bedecked with medals and ribbons, that he only wished to greet the General and present his card. With no protocol to follow, the official let Bob roam free, giving him a chance to smartly salute the General and present his card. Bob explained that the Minister of Defense in Nanjing, Chen Kai Min, had told him to meet the just-arrived General. Noting Bob's name dropping, the General ordered his aide to jot down Ekvall's name for a visit the next day.

The long interview began, over cups of tea, with the General probing to learned more about Bob as Bob tried to do the same with him. Chu Shao-liang had long and loyally served Chiang Kai Shek, from the pacification of the Muslim Rebellion led by Big Horse in 1928–1931 to the present day. Gradually, the interview grew warmer. This American, who spoke Chinese better than most of his aides, impressed the General. After conferring on whom Bob knew in China's military and civilian hierarchy, their talk turned to the present conundrum, "Who's going to win? What will happen next?" The "shadows" of Old Mao and Old Chiang loomed over their conversation, and Bob ventured to ask the General who "he thought" would win. The reply:

It has nothing to do with winning: it is the question of how the people of my country—people of the common womb—will live and be governed. The solution is only three tenths a military one: it is seven tenths a political one."[187]

Chinese traditional wisdom historically seemed to reject imposed military solutions rather than political solutions taught, implanted, nurtured and given a chance to bring people into agreement to form a polity.

As had occurred in other conversations on this long trek, the General spoke of land reform. "Root and base, the polity has to do with the problem of fields-earth: who tills them and what about ownership, because those who farm are very important." The General felt that the problem of land use and ownership had worsened in the past century (from 1840 onward), producing a landless populous that moved to the cities creating an urban proletariat. This displacement of the peasantry made for misery and anger, resulting in riot and rebellion. Bob gently probed to get a clarification on the "three tenths-seven tenths" equation. He received a "revolutionary" one because it was not a foreign idea imposed by force, but a return to an early principle of land ownership and use from the past.

All farm land—the fields-earth—is to be taken back and become the possession of the state, and solely of the state. No one can privately own any piece of fields-earth. The right to till the fields will be bestowed on the peasants . . . , but not to individuals: only to families, and in extent, according to the number of mouths in each family. Just as the fields-earth cannot be sold so the right to plow and reap cannot be sold. It cannot be mortgaged; it cannot be loaned to anyone. It must stay solely with the family as long as the family exists. If for any reason the family dies out and ends, that right must go back to the state and the state can then assign it to some other family whose needs have over-passed its original portion.[188]

General Chu Shao-liang shared with Bob, a Major in the U.S. Army, a political solution that a "clique" of Nationalist officers and officials had developed and were about to present formally to President Chiang Kai Shek and the National Assembly in order to pass a law to settle the fields-earth problem "once and for all." The odds of such a radical solution were not good, but the General felt they had to try despite the President not yet persuaded as to the wisdom of the solution proposed. Clearly, China's future hung in the balance, between Old Mao and Old Chiang's armies and ideologies. Within the next two months, the solution-law had to be made.

This interview took place in the summer of 1947. With time short, Bob, finished his nth cup of tea and said: "Does the general say only two months until he will know? At all cost I will beg instruction from the wisdom of the One-under-the-canopy when the time is right." By that courteous phrase, Bob indicated that he hoped that he could talk again with this highly-placed General, "under-the-canopy," of Chiang Kai-Shek's authority, to learn if the clique's "fields-earth" political solution had been made into law.

His "Performance So Far Was Being Rated 'Superior"

In early October 1947, Bob was ordered back to Nanjing for "consultations." Eva remained in Kunming with her many friends and Chinese-language study. His tiresome flight to Nanjing required three stops. Once he arrived, the OMA staff received him with surprising deference. Bob learned from General Soule that his "performance so far was being rated 'superior,' that top-notch ultimate official approval.'" His reports were being given to the American Ambassador, John Leighton Stuart, a "China hand" older than Bob. Born and raised in China by his parents, who were among the first Presbyterian missionaries in the 1860s. General Soule took Bob to Ambassador Stuart who proceeded to ask "numerous and some very searching questions; many of which centered on my report concerning Chu Shao-ling,"[189]

When not consulting with the heads of the Office of Military Attaché, Bob received dozens of invitations to cocktails and dinners, most of which produced a "no show." Those he could attend had him "going from party to party with the naïve enthusiasm of a country boy in the big city." The next OMA decision focused on "what to do with Ekvall?" There were three options: The first would send Bob by Jeep to Hong Kong via Canton. Obviously, the question of Eva traveling with him no longer came up. Where Bob went, she went. However, the Hong Kong option dissolved like ice cream in July when Bob informed his bosses that Cantonese was very different from Mandarin, thus negating his most valuable resource, his language skills. With the option discarded, two more options remained, one "over-the-top" crazy, and the other, the adventure of a lifetime.

Right after Bob had arrived in Nanjing, he ran into the Tibetan Delegation sent from Lhasa seeking some kind of formal legal recognition as a distinct national state. Tibetologist John Bray explains:

> Tibet became a protectorate within the Qing (Manchu) empire in the 18th century. It always exercised a high degree of internal autonomy, and increasingly so as the power of the Qing state declined in the course of the 19th century. The Tibetans always maintained that the relationship was conditional on the Emperor's support for the Dalai Lama.
>
> The Dalai Lama's administration in Central Tibet had achieved *de facto* independence in 1912, following the collapse of the Qing Empire the previous year, after which it expelled all Chinese officials from Lhasa. However, it had never achieved formal *de jure* recognition of its full independence from any foreign government. As long as it faced no immediate threat from China, the ambiguity about its status was of no immediate concern to the Lhasa government. However, the prospect of a Communist victory in the Chinese civil war raised new concerns about possible future Chinese intervention. At this point, the Tibetan government belatedly took steps to seek formal international recognition of its legal status as a fully independent state.[190]

Now in Nanjing, fearful of what might happen when either Old Mao or Old Chiang took over, the delegation ran into Bob Ekvall, known to some of them.

In brief, the Tibetans wanted Bob to return to Kunming, something already decided by the OMA. Then, he and Eva would travel on side trips until they got near to the mountainous Sino-Tibetan border. There, "Tibetan bandits would "kidnap them," take them across the border, then "rescued" by government troops which would take them safely to Lhasa. There, due to "bad weather" or "tribal wars" in the border region, the Ekvalls would remain indefinitely, cared for by the Dalai Lama's retinue and the *Kashag* counselors. The Ekvalls would remain there for an indefinite period, establish a "temporary office" of the OMA, in effect, giving Tibet legal diplomatic cover from none other than the United States of America! Bob duly reported this exotic plan to General Soule and his top aide. Their reaction was a blend of astonishment, skepticism and sympathy for the desperate Tibetans. The "proposal," duly encoded, was sent to the Pentagon for its disposition.

The alternative opportunity required another trek, a long one, from Kunming, where they would close the office, to Lanzhou in Kansu Province, and then back over the Old Silk Road to Turkistan, or *Xinjiang*. This option seemed the most viable, despite the fact that the governor, Chang Chih-chung was notably anti-American.

On Bob's three-leg flight from Kunming to Nanjing just a few weeks previously, he had flown with a very talkative official who spoke with great admiration of the enlightened rule of Governor Chang. He had shown great administrative skill by nipping a rebellion of dissidents in the bud; he had supported Turki-language schools and newspapers, making the Turki language equal to the Chinese tongue in all official proceedings. He also gave open support to Turki drama, music and dance groups. Different than the treatment of other minorities that Bob had seen first hand, this governor did not diminish the regional culture and language. Instead, he defended their right to maintain their identities within a multi-cultural Chinese state. Bob decided that he wanted to meet this man, and if possible, obtain permission to travel through his region.

Bob's uncle, Rev. Martin Ekvall, C&MA missionary, had known Chang Chih-chung years before. With that pretext for an introduction, Bob telephoned the Governor's residence in Nanjing and mentioned an extensive article that the Governor had written in China's most important monthly journal. Somehow, the confused aide, hearing Bob's perfect colloquial Chinese, gave the phone to the Governor. In a few minutes, the general himself granted Bob opportunity to "pay his respects" to talk about the magazine article.

The "Folly of Great Han Chauvinism"

The interview had been granted, but the impressive official displayed a frigid reserve. He admitted having known Bob's uncle but beyond that, he spared the small talk. Seeming to find no common ground for conversation, Bob brought up the magazine article which he had read carefully before their meeting. He complimented the Governor on his recognition of the "folly of great Han chauvinism," the penchant of the Han Chinese to devalue the other "minorities" of the great Central Nation. As the great revolutionary of 1911, Sun Yat-sen had proclaimed, China, the home of all peoples in the "all-under-heaven" nation. The magazine ploy worked and gradually the glacial governor began to open up.

When Bob expressed how he would love to see the enlightened administration first hand, Chang Chih-chung countered with an invitation: "You should come to the Northwest and see what I am planning and doing: not only for the Turki but for the Tibetans, Mongols and other minority races. I invite you to come."[191] With the die cast, they spent the rest of their conversation establishing the itinerary and timeframe of the visit. The Governor called the Minister of Defense to inform him that he had officially invited Ekvall to the Northeast. He asked that all military posts on the route northward be informed and render all assistance necessary to the United States Major driving his Jeep and trailer. Bob had no time to consult with "his general" and staff. Within a few minutes, the details were resolved and Bob returned to the OMA headquarters with the "what to do with Ekvall" question resolved. The Pentagon had already nixed the bizarre "Tibetan snatch" scheme. All agreed that the most strategically beneficial "use" of Major Ekvall entailed travel to the Northwest of China and *Xinjiang*.

A few days later while flying back to Kunming, a twenty-four hour forced layover in Chungking gave Bob opportunity to interview General Chu Shao-liang, to follow up on their meeting in Kunming two months before. This time, the grim-faced General expressed out-spoken hopelessness. He and his group had not managed to persuade Chiang Kai Shek regarding the rightness of their proposed legislation. He admitted that the "landlord-merchant clique bought up too many votes." Thus, the seven-tenths political solution would have to give way to the three-tenths military resolution. The General went on to say "Military strength is not enough to save our nation. Old Mao certainly will win for he does have a field-earth plan—not drastic enough but a plan."[192] Despite his pessimism, the disheartened general said he would fight for the Nationalist side as a loyalist rather than a realist. With this dark cloud slowly forming on the horizon, Bob flew back to Kunming and his wife with her much-improved command of Chinese.

Chapter 11

Burma Road and Back

UPON BOB'S RETURN TO Kunming, he immediately began planning a survey trip down the Burma Road from Kunming to Burma's border. Eva and her close friend, Ce Roser, had also been "planning together." Ce, barely five-feet tall was wife of U.S. Consul, Hal Roser, a six-foot-four graduate of Princeton. She, Philadelphia born and third-generation Chinese-American, represented a unique amalgam of U.S. and Chinese culture. Bob described her, "as American as chewing gum and as Chinese as a stick of incense."[193] The couple's multi-year experience on the border warranted their providing "the long and the short of " of almost any questions posed to them. For whatever reason, the U.S. State Department had decided that this strategic post at the end of the Burma Road and the beginning of China's southern transport system had no need for a full-fledged "Consul." Over time, the couples had become close friends.

At the start of their travel preparation, a warning came from a doctor just back from *Pao-shan (Paoshan, Baoshan)* , between the Mekong and Salween rivers, half-way to the Burma border. An epidemic, "bubonic, pneumonic and systemic, 100% fatal," had broken out, and the region had been quarantined. The doctor, flown in by the World Health Organization, had come to investigate since the Pao-shan region had a long history as a vector point for the "Black Death." After an intensive inoculation campaign had reached a sufficient number of the population, those properly inoculated could travel through the area.[194]

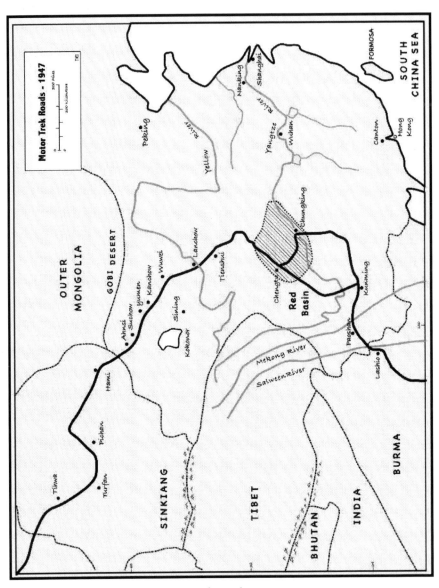

Motor Trek Roads—1947.

As he prepared to travel, Bob discovered that Eva and Ce had conjured up a "plan" not on his radar. Ce would accompany Bob and Eva on the trip. He could see some positive points in their scheme, especially, Ce's impeccable Chinese, which would provide Eva with a handy interpreter when Bob was otherwise occupied. Ce commented on the irony of "never having seen anything of Yun-nan while, Eva goes everywhere." Ce and Hal Roser had been in Kunming since the "glory days" of the Burma Road in WW 2. The creation of herculean efforts by thousands of Chinese coolie labor in the late 1930s, it was closed by Japanese forces in April 1942. Renamed the "Stillwell Road," it reopened in October 1944 through the combined forces of the Chinese, British and U.S. armies. Having lived in Kunming at the terminus of this amazing road, Ce swore that she would "died of frustration" if the historic route fell into disuse before she saw it. Hal, enjoyed seeing Bob squirm under the combined arguments of the two women and readily gave his consent, but only if Bob was OK with the arrangement.

And exactly that "arrangement" troubled him. One U.S. Army officer traveling in a U.S. Army vehicle flying the American flag with "two women" next to him on the front seat! How to explain that "arrangement?" Ce suggested, "Just introduce me as *Lo-Si-erh* (transliteration of Roser). . . . That will give them something to think of—a Chinese with a foreign surname. Maybe they will think I am the old Number One accompanying you, . . . the young Number Two . . . ."[195] In the end, the "arrangement" caused no problems. Eva had a close companion and Ce got to see the Burma Road. Bob knew that Ce's bicultural background would help explain things to his wife, and give Bob a competent counter-perspective to what he was seeing.

Trailer loaded with tires, parts, fuel and baggage for three rather than two, they began "speeding" over the Burma Road at 25 miles per hour! Now a lightly used highway, worn and potholed, it needed maintenance. In two days driving west, they drove to *Ta-li (Dali)*, a town famous for its translucent cloudy-grey marble. While the two women scoured the shops, Bob made his customary "courtesy call" to the mayor, who gladly talked about "his city." He had no complaints since the town's trade of stone cutting and polishing marble products brought a steady income for the population.

The next day, the mayor arranged a luncheon with town leaders who explained their trade. A school teacher spoke of the problems of teaching Chinese to children of tribal minorities. A scholar-historian spoke of the city's two-thousand year history while two enigmatic guests eating food especially brought, told the history of the rise and fall of their Muslim forefathers and a revolt put down by Chinese soldiers, with more than fifty thousand of their forefathers cut down in the streets of Ta-li. The hours-long luncheon and conversations left Bob with much to mull over later as he pecked out his report on his portable typewriter. His "ladies" came back with three hampers weighing more than 250 pounds! Bob left the heavy baskets to pick up on the return trip with a local police officer.

They started out at the crack of dawn. By driving hard and stopping little, they reached the plateau with the Mekong River behind and Pao-shan, center of the epidemic, not far away. After having their inoculation certificates checked and speaking with a doctor, they entered the city. The doctor warned them about fleas, talking with the locals up-close, and not picking up hitch hikers. Pulling into town, they drove to a big inn with a huge courtyard big enough for many vehicles, a vestige of the war years' traffic.

After arranging for their night's stay, they walked down the empty street and met a French priest who greeted them in Chinese and French, and then led them to a good restaurant. For twenty years, he had lived in Pao-shan; and in his fluent Chinese with rolling French r's that sounded like a drum, he entertained his new friends. He spoke of his wartime experiences and the struggle to build the Burma Road, its closing by the Japanese, and its reopening by the U.S. and Chinese forces. He talked about "his flock," their problems of faith and faithfulness and much more. He remembered when Pao-shan was "little more than a gigantic garage and repair shop."

"Democracy on the Village Level"

The French priest and Bob talked about the decree from Nanjing regarding "democracy on the village level." Father F. laughed as he told about a village which had heard about the new directive for electing headmen. The richest man in the town had never been one. Consequently, he invited the community leaders to his home for a twenty-course meal with plenty of rice wine. After hours of eating, one of the guests, feeling no pain, stood and proposed that they elect their generous host as the new town headman. The nomination, made and quickly seconded, passed with unanimous "ayes." The Catholic cleric's response seemed somewhat cynical, so Bob asked if the new arrangement was superior or inferior to the previous method. The priest admitted that while this election had not birthed "liberté, égalité, fraternité," it showed promise "but in order to know whether it has taken place in reality one must wait nine months."[196]

The next day, the Ekvall "trio" reached the Salween River, another huge waterway that began on the Tibetan Plateau not far from the sources of the Mekong and Yangtze Rivers. While the Mekong's tawny torrent had roared in its channel, the Salween River, a "jade ribbon" in a deep gorge, ran beneath the steel bridge which crossed it. Guards at both ends of the bridge checked their documents and let them continue on their way. Climbing slopes for hours until late afternoon, they arrived in *Lung-ling*, on Burma's border. The road condition had worsened, and clearly the once-vital link to China's survival no longer had much strategic value. While a few inns and truck repair shops still looked for business, the swollen lines of trucks had died out.

Lung-ling turned out to be interesting since the county magistrate, notified of Bob's arrival, made a courtesy call while he worked on his Jeep. He invited Bob and the ladies to a community festival. After clean-up and rest, they went to a large Buddhist temple-monastery packed with the local *Pai-yi* people, related to the *Shan* in Burma. Once again, Bob's infallible nose had led him to a fascinating night with a new ethnic group. While they spoke Chinese, they definitely were not Chinese. The temple abbot sat with Bob and gave him a "master class" on how the Pai-yi strived to maintain their identity. When asked how they had fared during the Japanese occupation, he stated: "The Japanese were generally very mild with the Pai-Yi because they are not Chinese. They treated the members of the sangha [Buddhist community] well. The Japanese are also 'within ones' of the Eightfold way."[197]

This memorable night included a savory vegetarian feast. While noteworthy for the absence of liquor, they drank tea of the finest vintage. The abbot asked how the Japanese were being treated after the war, since they were "within ones;" such was their affinity with China's fiercest former enemy. A local school teacher spoke with Bob about his research in local archaeological finds, and the recurring issue of using the official curriculum to teach Chinese to those not Chinese.

When the festivities ended, the school teacher led Bob and the ladies back to their inn. The ladies retired, and Bob and the professor discussed his years of research, a book he was writing and, possibly, its publication in English. The professor, a Han Chinese, but remarkably open to other cultures, commented on the Pai-Yi. "They are good people—gentle but also very strong. We should have kept them within the 'all under heaven' of the Central nation, but with the Han, the matter of independence is difficult."[198] In answer to Bob's question about the Pai-Yi and "old Mao's" policy and politics, he said they knew about communism, since Burma had "several sets of communism" and they understood its implications.

The next day, they visited another town, *Mangkha*, scene of a multi-tribal market where the Pai-yi sold general merchandise to buyers clothed in a range of colors representing the *Lissu*, *Mossu*, and *Kachin* tribesmen. The Chinese restaurant owner pointed to, "those with crossbows—some very raw southern barbarians whose names are of no importance."[199] Bob was about to start the jeep when a group of armed young men stopped him. Their leader, the *T'u-si* (hereditary chief) presented his card to Bob who responded in like manner. He asked Bob to visit his home. Begging lack of time, he promised to stop by on the return trip.

A Six-Foot King Cobra Sunning on the Warm Asphalt

The road from Mangkha to the border town of *Wan-ting* begged Bob to "step on it" since the smooth blacktop let the trusty jeep run as fast as it could go. Driving in the heart of high-grass and cane country, heat waves shimmered on the road. As they rounded a curve, a six-foot King Cobra sunning on the warm asphalt highway reared up and struck at the Jeep's grill before the wheels thumped over its fat body. Bob saw the wounded snake slither into the elephant grass. Since they were in tiger country, Bob did not let up on the accelerator.

Not long after pulling into the busy border town of Wan-ting, they saw drivers and border officials vying to see who could deceive whom. Trucks sat parked everywhere, veterans of the Burma Road. After settling into their "roadside inn," they went to the border and persuaded the Chinese guard to let them cross into Burma. Bob's U.S. Army uniform helped convince the hesitant officer. Crossing the bridge over the Irrawaddy River into Burma, they met a smartly dressed Burmese major. They had a "spot of tea" and chatted while Bob tried to keep count of the number of trucks crossing back and forth over the border, and which side had the longer line of vehicles. The data helped him calculate balance of payments and the variety of trade merchandise between the countries.

It appeared that more trucks entered China than those entering Burma, which did not bode well for China's financial situation.

Back at the inn, the manager worried out loud about the nightly "inn inspection" by Chinese soldiers. Bob assured him that his flag-be-decked jeep out front and his card with his name in English and Chinese, title and rank, would guarantee them a good night's sleep. Unfortunately, Bob's prediction failed. In the wee hours of the morning, a fierce pound-ing on their door rudely awakened them. "Inn inspection! Open the door for inn inspection!" Roused from deep sleep, Bob was enraged that any-one would make such a ruckus when his card informed the soldiers of who was in the room. How dare they wake up an "American officer from the American Embassy in Nanking?"

One of the inconvenient consequences of Ekvall's perfect Chinese is that it passed the "no-see" test. Innumerable times, when people could not see Bob's face but only heard him, they naturally believed the speaker was Chinese because he had no accent. Consequently, the guard de-manded Bob to open the door.

> Never mind about the name card. Anyone can fake a name card
> and you are no American. Americans don't talk like you do.
> How do I know who you are? Open the door, you fake Ameri-
> can, or we will break it down.[200]

Fit to be tied, Ekvall opened the door and peered into two rifle bar-rels. Bob flicked the light switch, illuminating his face; the officer accom-panying the guards blanched; he choked off another shout. Mortified by the obvious fact that Bob was indeed an American, the rifles dropped, the officer apologized, and the innkeeper walked them to the door loudly complaining. Bob slammed the door shut, still steaming. He would have a formal apology, get that officer "busted" and make a full report when he got to Nanjing. This incident became known as the "Wan-ting affair" or "the Wan-ting mistake" when Ce Roser described the event to her husband later.

The next day at breakfast, Bob sensed that Eva was sympathetic to his anger, but Ce seemed strangely non-committal about the whole thing. He went to the nearby Chinese Army post to see the Commanding Offi-cer. Receiving Bob with impeccable politeness, the officer informed Bob, after the exchange of greetings, that the most unfortunate incident had been cared for. "He had already reprimanded the officer involved. Fur-thermore as the superior office responsible for his subordinates, he now tendered his formal apologies." His silence following that explanation made it apparent that this was all Bob would get from the meeting, but Bob wanted more. He wanted that officer "busted down" at least a rank, and a formal, public apology. Ekvall's adrenalin high led him to raise the ante, stating he, Major Robert B. Ekvall, would report the matter to the U.S. Embassy in Nanjing, and inform Lu Han, governor of Yun-nan and Bob's personal friend, of the incident.

The Chinese official looked Bob in the eye and stated that he too would be making his report to his superiors. He questioned who had given Bob permission to cross the border to talk with a Burmese official when relations between the countries were unsettled and tense. At that point, Bob realized that the better part of valor was to quit the field and beat a hasty retreat. He later commented: "The mistake in Wan-ting had been roundly completed and I had been taught a lesson of when not to press too far—even when fuming."[201]

Thus completing his "official visit" to the Chinese-Burmese border, Bob and company jeeped back over the silky blacktop road to Mangkha to visit the T'u-si chief. Living in a residence resembling a mini castle in a bamboo grove, the pistol-packing guards let Bob and the ladies in. The home was half-Western and half-something-else, not Chinese but also not primitive tribal. Their cultured and well-informed young host, was chief of his Pai-yi tribe and spoke excellent Chinese. After a delicious noon meal, he opened brandy, and they spent much of the afternoon talking about the Pai-yi and the Shan of Burma, the same people divided by a border. In Burma, the government recognized the Shan and treated them well, while not so for the Pai-yi in China. The Burmese called their leaders "princes" while the Chinese authorities merely called the young chief a "local leader." During the war, the Japanese had treated them well, with a Japanese general staying in his home. However, when the Chinese military came through after driving the Japanese out, they showed little respect. Putting all that aside, his major concern was the "after," whether Old Mao or Old Chiang would win the war, then what? As had happened in so many other conversations, the T'u-si's question of "then what" produced an unexpressed hopeful feeling that the United States would provide a good answer. Bob could do no more than toast his ideas; "Cheers!" After the third night-cap, Ekvall and entourage parted.

Turning homeward, they began climbing from the low borderland toward the ever-higher mountains. Bob feared that the jeep might break down since the oil pressure gauge indicated an oil leak, but Bob could not find it. While able to do the minor grease-monkey maintenance, an auto mechanic he was not. Also, the engine ran roughly, indicating an ignition problem. Another worry, totally out of his hands, concerned the road conditions. The Burma Road, much of it built with conscript labor, was in bad shape. Hasty work done during the war resulted in frequent "slippage," when long stretches of hillside road would break loose due to heavy rainfall, sometimes sliding down dozens of feet. And torrential rain drenched them that day as they rode in their open jeep. Suddenly, the oil seep became a surge as they limped into a roadside town with no repair shop in sight. Fortunately, a bystander sidled up and offered his services.

He quickly located the leak and repaired it with a bamboo plug, hammered home and held in place with tape. He fiddled with the engine for a few minutes and the engine coughed, cleared its throat, and ran smoothly as the oil gauge held steady. When Bob asked him where he had learned such skills, he replied:

> With the Americans in Burma. . . . [This] is only a makeshift repair, for you need some repair parts. The plug may blow and then you will have to plug it again, like I showed you, before you get to Pao-shan. In Pao-shan there are parts.[202]

The two men looked at each other and contemplated a mutually beneficial arrangement. Bob needed a mechanic till he got to a repair shop, and the man needed a ride. They quickly made a deal, and the ladies moved to the rear seat while the providential mechanic rode alongside Bob.

"You May Try a Try."

Bob's other concern regarding road conditions materialized as they began to ascend a curving slope before getting to the Salween River. Three loaded trucks had pulled off the road and they could see that a stretch of about one hundred yards of the road's edge had slid down the hill. While passable for smaller vehicles, farther ahead lay a section hundreds of yards long that had "slipped" down the slope. The two ends of the stretch were four or five feet below the original road surface. The road gang could do nothing without dozers and graders, but they had leveled out the breaks at each end. People could walk back and forth on it but not trucks. However, the foreman thought the light jeep and trailer could get through if the passengers walked and only Bob drove. He expected that when the rains started again, the slide would let loose and the road would need days to repair. He told Bob: "You may try a try." So, the "mechanic" and the two ladies walked the length of the break and signaled Bob to "try a try." "With muscles twitching for a possible jump, I drove jeep and trailer across; making, or leaving, no sign of disturbance."[203]

They reached Pao-shan just before another downpour. Knowing that they had at least of day of repairs before them, they returned to the same inn where they stayed before. The next day, worried about the repair and the monsoon rains, Bob found a street with dozens of repair shops. He saw hundreds of carcasses of GMC "Deuce-and-a-halves," Dodge four-wheel stake-bodies, Ford and Willys-built jeeps and other military vehicles. Two local mechanics had built a "new jeep" from the stockpile of the avenue of broken "gas carts." From the vast assortment, "Bob's mechanic" found the needed parts and made the repair. Job done and mechanic well paid, they parted ways.

Since Kunming was "only" 255 miles distant, Bob hoped his rejuvenated jeep could make the trip in one day if they left at sunup. For a short while, the jeep and almost empty trailer bounced down the deserted gravel road before stopping at the police post to get the three baskets of marble stoneware. After a quick breakfast with the helpful officer, they pushed on, eyes pealed for bandits and road washouts. Passing up lunch, they kept on going, arriving in Kunming well after dark after eighteen hours in an open jeep under heavy rain. At the U.S. Consulate, Ce's husband, Hal, gave a shout of relief since he had heard the road had washed out and would take weeks to repair. During the last hours of the marathon drive, they thought of nothing except a warm bath, dry clothes and hot food and a good night's sleep. The took care of the first three items quickly, but the long night's sleep was postponed by a lengthy, story-packed "debriefing" for Hal's benefit. Each of the travelers gave their favorite funny moments, the "Wan-ting affair," delicious meals eaten, and much more.

Bob, It Is Not Fair . . . What You Do to the Chinese

Ce's final observation summed up Bob's uncanny ability with interviewees:

> Bob, it is not fair. It is not fair what you do to the Chinese. You question and talk with them until they forget that you are foreign, and you get them to turn themselves inside out to tell you everything—even what they shouldn't tell. For the first time in

my life I begin to feel defensive on behalf of Chinese when they
begin to talk with an American. It's not fair.[204]

As she spoke of this rare talent, the unwitting humor of it dawned
on her as she, a Chinese-American, sat in that uncomfortable position of
observer of a skilled American-Chinese intelligence operator.

Chapter 12

Northward Bound

AFTER THE SUCCESSFUL BURMA Road trip, which provided valuable intelligence for the Office of Military Attaché in Nanjing, the next leg toward the northeast faced them. After living in Kunming for many months, Bob and Eva had to divest themselves of possessions no longer needed for the trip. In addition, Bob's "office" equipment, i.e., safe, files, office typewriter, etc. had to be packed for shipment to Nanjing with unneeded personal effects. Extra fuel, tires, engine oil, grease and spare parts had precedence. Thus, Bob worked on his "to do" list with three priorities: First, the jeep front "bench seat" was very uncomfortable and needed replacing. Second, they needed warm winter clothing, either from Army stock or what they could acquire locally. Thirdly, Bob wanted a "ride-along" mechanic. Although Ekvall could fuel the car, change the oil, grease the ball-joints, and change a blown tire, the ability to diagnose and repair the engine and other vital parts were beyond him.

Consequently, Bob made finding a mechanic top priority, and soon found a small, frail-looking mechanic from Southern China, near Canton, far to the east. He applied for the job offered at the U.S. Consulate, despite the fact that it would take him precisely in the opposite direction of his home. Ch'ui, affectionately known as "Lao Ch'ui or Old Chui," had served in the Chinese Army during WW 2 and had been trained by the Americans in Burma in jeep maintenance and repair. He proudly owned his own set of tools and proved to be the ideal candidate. He accepted the long-term engagement since it paid well and would give him a chance to see North China. Hired, he immediately removed the uncomfortable front seat and replaced it with a custom-made seat for three, leaving the back open for baggage. He overhauled the jeep, stocked up with vital spare parts and made the vehicle like new.

They packed heavy cold-weather clothing, including olive-drab overcoats and long-johns, sweaters, wool socks and oversized boots. Local furriers produced "fox-fur coat-liners, collars, fur-lined gloves and socks. Bob, as an Army officer, took along full-dress uniforms with medals and aguillettes to go with Eva's silk-lined gown and fur-lined satin jacket for formal events. Since they were going to horse country in the Northwest, they packed boots and breeches and Bob's well-worn saddle. Following a series of farewell parties, they set out on a cool day in the fall of 1947. They followed the highway built during the war going northeast toward Chungking, then turned off on a little-used gravel road heading north toward Chengdu, capital of Sichuan Province.

Lao Ch'ui Literally Rode "Shot-Gun"

The seldom-used road climbed over the *Sha Kiang-Wu Kiang* watershed on the upper stretches of the Yangtze River. This route took them dangerously close to the Tibetan border. "Lololand," was a region of tribal minorities related to those met while on the Burma Road trek. It happened to be the same area where the Tibetans in Nanjing had plotted the crazy Ekvall "kidnap caper". Being full of bandits and fierce tribes, the travelers carried arms. Bob's M-1 hung right behind him. Eva sat in the middle with a carbine between her knees, and Lao Ch'ui literally rode "shot-gun" with a double-barreled 12 gauge at hand. They rehearsed what to do in case of an attack, quickly exiting the jeep to take up positions to direct fire against any raiders.

Throughout the day, they drove through the wildly beautiful country under bright sun and high winds. In time, they crossed the watershed and gradually the sun gave way to grey cloud-cover. With bandits and wild tribes behind them, they stashed their armory in the back of the jeep. As always, Eva carefully noted Bob's observations relating to "highway conditions—down to minutest details about streambeds, bridges and abutments, road surfaces, grades and curves—of the full length of our route."[205] These copious notes became part of his final report to OMA. Eva proved to be an excellent scribe and observer in her own right.

On their third day of travel out of Kunming, they traversed the fertile "red basin" of Chengdu and arrived at the provincial capital. They had planned on staying only a day or two, but General John P. Lucas, Commanding General of the Military Advisory Group working with the Nationalist Army changed their plans. Visiting Chengdu, he met Bob at a banquet held in the General's honor. When Lucas discovered Bob's competency in Chinese and his knowledge of the land and culture, he tried to "hijack" Bob to his staff. When Bob's "General" got wind of the move by Lucas, he appealed up the command "ladder."[206] While temporarily acting as Lucas' private interpreter, Bob served as a language bridge between the U.S. Army brass and their Nationalist Army equivalents. The U.S. military advisers tried to persuade their Chinese Army counterparts to make their armies copies of the U.S. forces. The Chinese, wanting U.S. military hardware, finances and air support, promised much but had no interest in copying the "American book" of military doctrine. Ekvall interpreted from English to Chinese and the replies back to English. Hearing and interpreting the formally spoken and also the *soto voce* asides, Bob noted that "the strangely unreal official dialogue went its course, until I began to feel like the criss-crossed exchange in the proverbial 'dialogue of the deaf.'"[207]

Once it became clear that General Soule in Nanjing refused to let General Lucas pirate Ekvall, Bob made plans to leave Chengdu before anyone could change their mind. Someone suggested that Bob's "armory," an M-1, an Carbine and a 12-gauge shotgun lacked sufficient firepower. So, a .50 caliber machine-gun on a swivel-post behind the front seat enhanced their arsenal. Bob's mechanic said that his new weapon suited him better than the shotgun. After five days in Chengdu, they set off on their journey.

They made a side-trip to visit the beautiful *Kuan-hsien*, where the Chengdu plain meets the Tibetan plateau, with foaming gorges and beautiful scenery. Late in the afternoon as the Ekvalls walked around the town window shopping, Bob's past met him on the street. Unexpectedly, he saw a "sunburned begrimed figure whose dirty sheep-skin coat hung from one shoulder, leaving most of his torso bare. He was no beggar. The silver and the precious stones on the handle and scabbard on the sword he wore made that clear, but otherwise, there was little hint—except in his calm assurance—as to what he might be."[208] The Tibetan saw Bob in uniform and Eva in her warm satin jacket. Bob greeted him in what he guessed was the man's dialect, and the man's response showed no surprise.

More than fifty years later, interviewed at the Billy Graham Center Archives at Wheaton College, Bob related the story of *Legs Bshad Rgya Mtsho*, the Tibetan monk-turned Chinese government official, who came to Christ after fifteen years of gospel witness.[209] In the interview, Bob told how "a number [52] years ago in Szechwan . . . he [Legs Bshad] was coming out of one of the big satin stores. This is . . . very close to the Chinese border. He'd come down, he was the son of a chief, had a small tribe and he'd come down getting material and stuff for his tribe. And he showed me that he was still a Christian and that he was trying to get his tribe to become Christian."[210]

It had been thirteen years since they last talked following Legs's dramatic conversion in Lanzhou in late 1934. Since then, they had not seen each other, and much had changed. It took a bit of time for the two to acknowledge each other. Bob, now dressed in the uniform of a U.S. Army Major with a beautiful young woman at his side, confronted the former high Tibetan-Chinese official, now a tribal chief wearing the sheep-skin robe of a nomad in Kuan-hsien leading a grain-purchasing caravan. His packed yaks were just outside the walls of the town. When Bob asked him if he knew the new king of Ngawa, the Tibetan chief replied affirmatively and said that he would go there soon. Bob asked him to take greetings from *Shes Rab*, which he readily agreed to do.

He Asked if Eva Was Bob's "Girlfriend or New Wife?

Bob replied to the question about where they were going, "far to the Northeast." As the chief looked admiringly at Eva, he said "there is much danger on the roads in these times. You carry weapons of course?" He then asked if Eva was Bob's "girlfriend or new wife?" When Bob indicated that she was his wife of several months, Legs Bshad said: "On your way go slowly in peace. You have a woman with you, so take care." Then, he spread his palms politely and went on his way with the rolling gait of a horseman, with hand on his sword.

Bob relished the moment as he shared with Eva a bit of the world he had lived in for twenty years with Betty. "Did you ever see such poise and assurance. The Tibetan nomads are like that—completely unflappable. They refuse to be astonished."[211]

Two days later, they drove under the grey clouds of Sichuan, skirting various chains of mountains separating Sichuan and Gansu. Gradually

Chengdu's lush Red Basin full of rice paddies gave way to the wheat fields of the north. Frost crept down the slopes and snow salted the fields. Traffic grew as they drove northward meeting columns of loaded troops. Driven at suicide pace, they forced the little jeep and trailer off the road. On the fourth day, traffic lightened as they took a less-used road to *Tienshui (Tianshui)* where Bob planned a stop before arriving in Lanzhou.

Climbing up to a last high pass, the travelers looked down on the wide Wei River valley, wrapped in a haze of talcum-fine yellow dust. *Tienshui*, home of the Chinese Nationalist Cavalry School, was high on the list of places Bob needed to visit. His other focus of interest took him back to his missionary days, the China Inland Mission station. For the next three days, these places held his attention. The strategically-vital city marked . . .

> the beginning of a no-man's-land zone in which units of the PLA [People's Liberation Army] moved quite freely at times. They could intermittently threaten, or block, traffic between Si-an, where Hu Tsun-nan was maneuvering his divisions to stop any southward movement of the PLA troops, and Lanchow . . . ."[212]

The CIM missionaries, British and American, looked on Bob not only as a friend and former C&MA missionary, but also as knowledgeable representative of the U.S. government. From him, they hoped to receive up-to-date information from someone "in the know." Equally, Ekvall expected to collect some "intelligence" about the PLA's movement from the missionaries since they had many reliable contacts among the Christians living across the province who observed the Red Army's movements up close. Despite the tenuous times, the missionaries "stayed put" since they lived off the beaten path, and their commitment to "the work" rested on faith in the One who called them there.

The staff at the Cavalry School also saw Bob as someone from the U.S. Army who might know if the "Generalissimo," Chiang Kai Shek, had plans for the horse brigade: Would he fight to protect the city and their school, or retreat to another line of defense? These "horse soldiers" were the only cavalry unit of the Nationalist Government in the region. Ekvall concluded at the end of the visit to the Cavalry School that he "had learned much about the Cavalry School and all its concerns, its forebodings and its needs . . . but [he] had learned virtually nothing"[213] of strategic intelligence value. In reality, the CIM missionaries had solid information from pastors and church members around the region.

As they prepared to leave for Lanzhou, a young CIM couple bargained with Bob for a place in the back of his jeep in exchange for loading several hundred pounds of Ekvall's baggage onto the truck hauling the couple's personal effect to Lanzhou. They covered the last two-hundred mile stretch of gravel road in two long days, staying overnight in *Anting* where they overnighted at an inn with rooms dug into the *loess* (silt-sediment from wind-blown dust) hill which provided sleeping quarters much warmer than common inns offered.

The next morning, the jeep needed help getting started with the temperature well below freezing. After an hour, they got it running by pouring boiling water into the radiator and placing a pan of burning charcoal under the engine to warm its "innards." With a cough and sputter, the faithful "four-banger" roared into life and off they went in a cloud of dust. At noon, they entered the city gates and rolled down the streets of Lanzhou. The grateful missionaries invited them to the CIM headquarters. The Ekvalls already had reservations at the *Hsi Pei Ta Hsia* (Northwest Great Mansion), but they availed themselves of a quick cleanup at the mission and tea before driving to their "mansion" on a hilltop that commanded a view of the city. Their trek from Kunming to Lanzhou ended on December 4, 1947. They remained in Lanzhou for the next five months.

As Kansu's Provincial capital, Lanzhou had a population in 1945 of about 330,000. It still looked like an "old Chinese" grey-brick walled city, double-gated and guarded by tall drum towers. Tall poplar trees looking over the grey-tiles houses lined the wide streets. The West Gate opened onto the Yellow River traversed by a long steel-truss bridge. Giant waterwheels drew up river water and poured it into a complex irrigation system. "At the far end of that bridge the highway forked: the right fork following the left bank of the river toward the plains of Mongolia; the left fork turning northwestward toward the 'Kansu corridor" and distant Sin-kiang."[214] Here, Bob and Eva would meet new friends and encounter others from years past.

Soon after arrival at their hilltop home, Eva began making their two rooms "homey" for the next months. Bob, in full dress uniform, had Ch'iu drive him to the U.S. Embassy to report in, and send a telegram to the U.S. Embassy in Nanjing announcing their arrival. He then began the round of "paying-respect" visits. The first, at Governor Chang Chih-chung's headquarters, revealed that the governor was not in the city, but the aide suggested that Bob visit the Commanding General of the Northwest Pacification Bureau, who would assist Bob in his mission. Consequently, Colonel T'ien was assigned to "care of all Bob's needs," meaning that he would be the tip of the sword for constant surveillance of Ekvall's comings and goings.

Bob and Eva Ekvall at Lanzhou, 1947.

Ekvall next visited Kansu's Governor Guo Jiqiao, which proved cordial and straight forward. During his years of rule, the governor's administration had pacified a province notable for outbreaks of violence. While bordering two provinces led by Muslim warlords, Kansu lived in relative peace, despite tense conditions in neighboring Shaanxi Province, home of Mao Tse Tung's communist government. Since Bob was "Kansu born-and-bred," the relationship between the U.S. Major and the governor, also from Kansu, grew quickly. He promised that "Major Ai," (Bob's Chinese family name) and his wife would be received at a forthcoming dinner and that his wife would "call on" Eva at their "residence." When Bob returned to the hilltop hotel and told Eva of the visit, she had already created a "reception-parlor" in their two-room apartment.

Next day, while Eva entertained the governor's wife, Bob received two telegrams at the Consulate. One congratulated him on their safe arrival in Lanzhou. The second, encoded, gave him a "specific intelligence directive"...

> the first since leaving Nanking nine months before. "There was an urgent need to know just what was taking place in their border area between Kan-su and Shen-si where—persistent rumours in Nanking had it—the Peoples Liberation Army was maneuvering into what threated to be a full-scale offensive toward the Northwest."[215]

The directive ordered him to "use all means" to obtain and send all information regarding such actions. If such an offensive were to occur, "don't get caught." The "road talk" picked up earlier in Tienshui confirmed Nanjing's concerns about communist troop movement.

Obviously, Bob did not share that message with his "constant companion," Colonel T'ien. However, he did overwhelm the colonel with requests for interviews with various Chinese intelligence officers for briefings on security issues. Ekvall specifically asked T'ien to accompany him to each interview, making it easier to keep his eye on Bob, who sought to convey the idea that he was rather inept.

That evening, he picked up Eva and they drove to a cold and dusty street that he knew well, where the food shop's signboards pictured a kettle, signally that the place served "halal" food ritually clean for Muslims. They dined on hand-stretched noodles boiled in a cauldron for five minutes, then doused in hot, spiced ground-meat sauce, which warmed them up on the cold December evening. It was the first time Eva had felt warm that day. She asked Bob to bring them back again for another meal with their movie camera to film the noodle-stretching ritual. While in the Muslim section of town, Bob took Eva to the Lanzhou office of the Taochow Islamic movement, the New Sect, founded more than five decades before.

This rather strange Islamic reform group had doses of mysticism, communism and the belief that Issa (Jesus) was coming back to reform Islam. It had originated in Taochow with an illiterate cart-driver who fancied himself as Jesus who had returned to earth to finish the task of converting and unifying the world. While fiercely opposed by the orthodox Muslims, the sect survived and became a strong social-economic movement. Conversion to the sect meant turning over all worldly wealth, working according to one's skills and capabilities, and receiving wages commensurate with the work accomplished. This "pre-Marx communism" untainted by violence, succeeded and flourished in Tao-chow Old City, where the C&MA mission had begun work in the late 1890s. David Ekvall, Bob's father, and his uncle, Martin, had known the New Sect Muslims well. Bob did also and was very well known by the New Sect community in Taochow.

The Aging Manager Did a Double-Take

Bob commented to Eva that the New Sect was a "well-run society. He explained that the leaders were somewhat in his debt:

> "When Tao-chow Old City was occupied and partly looted by government troops in the spring of 1929, I successfully inter-vened on their behalf and arranged with the Chinese General for the payment of a negotiated fine, instead of outright and complete confiscation. Later that year when Tibetan troops burned the city, I again was able to save the buildings of the Sect as I saved the mission compound from destruction. We'll be well-received whether I know the manager personally or not."[216]

Bob's candid account of those two occasions, when he literally saved the day for the New Sect as a missionary, now worked to his advantage as an Army intelligence-gathering officer. And well-received he was.

The manager of the Lanzhou branch of the New Sect Muslims, *Min Lao Yeh*, one of the sect's leading lights, was the very man who Bob had escorted to the Chinese General's quarters in 1929 to successfully negoti-ate with the general and save the New Sect Muslims from confiscation of all their wealth by the Chinese army. The aging manager did a double-take as he recognized Bob's face, but stared at the military uniform and the lovely young woman at his side. When the shock subsided, they greeted warmly and talked over "old times." On occasions like this, Eva realized that the middle-aged man at her side had lived another amazing lifetime when she was a little girl. Min Lao Yeh had been present in Lhamo, in late 1940, when Betty had lost the fight against the mysterious infection that took her life. He went to Bob's house as one of Bob's friends, "to say or do what [he] could—with sharing of sorrow—to keep me from despair; urging me ever to live and be strong through my wife . . . ."[217]

The smiling Muslim manager addressed Bob with his Tibetan name, *Sherab Tsondru*. "No that is your Tibetan name that went with Tibetan-stye clothes. Now it should be *Ai*—what is your rank? Ah yes, Major Ai, how is it that you are in Lan-chow and an officer in the American Army?"[218] Thus began a very cordial conversation with Bob introducing Eva to the Muslim gentleman. Since the two men were literally "old friends," Bob got right to the point. He told Min Lao Yeh what he needed, i.e., any information available on the border region between Kansu and *Shensi (Shaanxi)*. In addition, Bob asked about General Ma P'u-fang, leader of the Muslim troops fighting for the Chinese Nationalist Army. Were his forces involved in any maneuvers or fighting? The manager, recognizing the implications that Bob's uniform represented, did not hesitate long. He stated that General Ma P'u-fang preferred to fight on the neighboring province's borders than on his own, and had sent a sizeable force of soldiers to the Kansu-Shensi border frontlines under the command of his son.

Min Lao Yeh took Bob to the Chinghai provincial government and he received a full briefing of the military situation. Glad to have a direct link with the U.S. Army in Nanjing, the commander gave Bob all the intelligence he could desire: reports, field dispatches, maps, battle-order and estimated troops. They made arrangements for day-to-day updates on the developing situation. In that one afternoon, while Bob's "watchdog," Colonel T'ien lined up interviews and meetings, Bob had developed his own sources, superior and more honest. He had the dream of every intelligence officer, i.e., information coming from two distinct sources on the same subject, each source unaware of the other which allowed for confirmation of details.

Since the long, detailed telegrams required laborious encoding, Bob longed for access to a "diplomatic pouch" to save time and to send maps and full texts of intel directly. Not long after, Bob met two former U.S. Army Air Force pilots at the hilltop "mansion" who solved the problem. They flew for China National Aviation Corporation, an affiliate of Pan Am. Bored, tired and glad to meet someone who spoke English and even had a pot of coffee in their rooms. They became fast friends, and Bob and Eva's sitting room became their haven when in Lanzhou. They provided Bob with copies of the Shanghai English-language newspapers in return for Ekvall's hospitality. They also brought the occasional package sent by Eva's parents in Shanghai, and maybe a bottle or two of their favorite scotch or goodies from the Army PX. In time, they carried Bob's reports and on-the-ground intel to the authorities in Nanjing. Bob shared the military situation with the pilots and let them pore over maps furnished by the Chinese and Muslim intelligence sources so that they knew where the hot spots of the war lay, vital information for those flying long distances in China with worn-out WW 2 airplanes.

Over the following months in Lanzhou, Bob led a rather clandestine "double life" in order to keep Colonel T'ien occupied with "needs" in character with the persona that Bob had created, i.e., a bored military officer who would rather play than work. Bob pestered him for weeks about getting some horses, good trotters, not pacers, for him and Eva. They also needed a saddle, not the strange and uncomfortable Chinese saddle, but a true English-style saddle for Eva. As the weather grew colder, he sent the long-suffering officer on a search for ice skates so that he and his young wife could glide on the frozen ponds and canals. When spring arrived, tennis rackets and balls and a complete court filled his "to-do-list."

Perhaps his biggest "ask" was for permission to hunt blue sheep, famous for their skins and horns, found twenty kilometers northwest of the city, among the ravines and cliffs. Eventually, permission came and Bob and Eva, complete with a police officer to "protect them," drove to the rocky streambed where Bob left Ch'iu and the police officer, and the couple scrambled over the rocks for three hours, sighting a few blue sheep in the distance. They bagged none! However, after many visits to the site, the police escort ceased, and they roamed wherever they wished.

All these activities gave Colonel T'ien the impression that Bob was a bored playboy, sports nut, disinterested in "real work," and on a "joyride" through China. At times, Bob's strange requests and the colonel's earnest desire to "help" coincided. Bob had heard about the beautiful polychrome pottery "Shang pots" to be found in the many shops that sold authentic "ancient things." The colonel was a true afficionado of such earthenware. Thus, he gladly spent hours with Bob and Eva searching the ancient-things shops in the backstreets of the city. They also scoured the flea markets looking for antique rugs made with local wool and natural dyes from saffron and indigo rather than chemical-based aniline dyes.

Dilettante Rather Than Diligent Intelligence Officer

As they approached the last month or two before heading to the northwest, Bob asked for someone to teach him Turki, in his "sound-to-meaning" method. Refused at first but later granted, the language work proved somewhat helpful on their future travels. All in all, Bob gave an Oscar performance of a dilettante rather than diligent intelligence officer. In his words, "Gaily abetted by my wife, I was an incorrigibly feckless and irresponsible combination of sports maniac and indefatigable party-goer . . . Eva and I were swingers in Lan-chow society and had a hilarious time swinging."[219]

In the spring of 1947, Bob revisited an old experience on a new stage, as he and Eva drove out to Lanzhou's airport, built by the U.S. Army Engineers during the war. Apparently, Bob and Eva had gone out to the airport to meet their pilot friends. And while there, they ran into a group of young C&MA missionaries flying in, the first new KTBM recruits in many years. Some of Bob's old Alliance colleagues, like M.G. Griebenow and Ed Carlson also were there awaiting the flight coming on CAT's (Civil Air Transport) old Army C-46s. One of the pilots who flew the route from Shanghai to Lanzhou described flying into the city:

> Our shadow, circled by a rainbow, ran along with us until the clouds broke up over mountains, and we saw a valley of the Yellow River and Sian. Another two hours put us within sight of giant waterwheels near a city of wide streets and rows of poplar trees and an encircling wall that was twenty feet thick and bristled with parapets and watch towers.[220]

Malcolm "Mac" Sawyer and his wife, Helen, flew in on the old Army transport equipped with canvas bucket seats, with two other couples, Gene and Cleo Evans and Wayne and Minnie Persons, as well as William Carlsen. They, along with Jack and Jean Shepherd, already on the field, had been recruited by Nyack Missionary Training Institute's president, Rev. Thomas "Tibet Tom" Mosely. His efforts resulted in new blood for the field. Sawyer described arriving at Lanzhou in an interview for the Billy Graham Center at Wheaton in 1983:

> Well, we flew across China, and there were no trees whatsoever . . . Just brown, brown dirt everywhere in central China. And as we went farther inland, all the mountains are terraced right to the top. Came down in Wuchang part way for refueling. There wasn't a house in sight anywhere on this . . . on this grass runway. And . . . then the mountains got higher and higher as we looked out . . .
>
> So they got to Lanzhou, the capital of Gansu Province. We came down, and when they touched down . . . what a swirl of dust. Dust was that deep. There was no rain up there for months. And so you couldn't see. I had no idea how the pilots saw to land. And incidentally, again, at that time, Robert Ekvall was there

with the plane because of his friends. He wasn't a missionary in
those days, but he was working for the American Army in intelligence. And he's remarried (His first wife had died in West China.
We'd been to her grave) He married another lady. And she was
with him in an open jeep with a . . . with a big machine gun . . .[221]

Sawyer commented that Ekvall "was impressive" not just because of
the Army uniform, jeep and new wife, but for the many articles and publications in the *Alliance Weekly* magazine over the years. In fact, Sawyer
said that he had first heard Ekvall at Old Orchard Camp and there had
first felt called as a missionary to Tibet. From his interview, Sawyer stated
that Ekvall's new role in "military service . . . in the intelligence . . . that
was his work" had removed Bob from missionary service. While there
with his C&MA friends, they asked his advice regarding the fluid military
situation in their region and any news on the PLA's drive into the northwest. The friendly visit with old and new friends, was likely strained by
Bob's new role in military intelligence and the strangeness of his having a
new wife, brunette like Betty, but very different.

For the rest of their time in Lanzhou, Bob and Eva concluded their
time there with a round of social gatherings. They received permission
to visit the supposed location of Genghis Khan's burial site in a Tibetan
Buddhist temple east of the city The abbot of the small monastery took
Bob and Eva into a chanting hall where twelve monks sat on the floor
intoning a . . .

steady rumble of mantras" for a pagan warrior who was not
Buddhist. Yet, because his grandson, Kublai Khan had become
a Tibetan Buddhist, the temple was built to hold the enormous,
unadorned black sarcophagus lit by flickering butter lamps illuminating a black and white, life-sized picture of "the man who by
a strange combination of slaughter and rule held—in terror and
power—half the known world for his own horse-pasture . . . ."[222]

In addition to frenetically mixing pleasure with official business
under the smiling tutelage of Colonel T'ien, Bob gathered a great deal
of intelligence from the missionary community. With few permanent
foreigners living in Lanzhou besides the missionaries, they provided the
best sources for collecting incidental information from their contacts,
which when integrated, gave an accurate picture of the situation. Bob sift-
ed through the comments and observations from members of the China
Inland Mission and the newly-arrived Seventh Day Adventist medical

missionaries. The Roman Catholic Mission's German Bishop Budden-brock asked: "Isn't America going to do something to stop this menace to Christianity and indeed to civilization itself?"[223] He, in fact, had voiced the question that all three missions had hoped Bob could answer.

At the end of their stay in Lanzhou, General Chang Chih-chung, while critical of U.S. military intervention in Chinese affairs, expressed his appreciation for Bob's understanding of the Chinese people, his knowledge of Tibetan and his desire to learn "Turki" (Uighur). At their meeting's close, he gave Bob some vague but disconcerting advice. "Be careful where and how you go around. There are many factions and many agents. Some do not like Americans and this is a region where violence is common: banditry, kidnapping and sometimes even assassination. Be small-hearted always."[224]

There Was a "Communist Plot to Assassinate" Him

About that same time, Bob's driver and mechanic, Ch'iu, came to him with rumors picked up while visiting the jeep "parts depot" on the back streets of Lanzhou. He told Bob that some of the contacts had asked about Ekvall's mission and whereabouts, even offering cash for information. Colonel Ti'en, Bob's official "helper" and unofficial spy on his activities had, in a round-about-way warned Bob of some "strange Turki of unknown allegiances [who] had arrived in the Turki community, and were asking questions about [you]."[225] He said that the Security Section of the local Army Headquarters had been told that there was a "communist plot to assassinate him." All of these hunches caused Bob to begin wearing his .45 caliber pistol in a shoulder holster under his ever-present Eisenhower jacket.

In early April, the winter snow squalls and bitter winds from Mongolia eased, and Bob and his mechanic prepared for the next leg of their trip from Lanzhou to *Urumqi (Tihwa)*in *Xinjiang (Sinkiang)*. Ekvall had begun his immersion-method of learning the Turki language. A quick trip to nearby Xining, capital of Chinghai Province, gave Bob opportunity to get General Ma P'u-fang's perspective on the military situation and his guess as to what the future held for Muslim military men like himself if Old Mao's PLA prevailed over Old Chiang. The tough old soldier's analysis did not drift into overt pessimism nor unreal optimism. His soldiers had fought many battles with the PLA and he knew they could fight. The Chinese Nationalist soldiers did not have the same fervor nor military prowess of the communist forces. Consequently, this did not bode well for the future.

While in Xining, Bob and Eva visited the famous Kumbum monastery nearby, where Bob met with the Panchen Lama and his political adviser, *Jigs Med Dorje*, the same Tibetan who had dreamed up the scheme for Bob and Eva's "kidnapping" by Tibetan bandits and taken to Lhasa to be the "official representatives" of the U.S. Office of Military Attaché. In all of these conversations, the Holy Lama evinced a vague feeling of euphoric hope tempered by unspoken fear.

Before leaving for *Xinjiang* , Bob and Eva, returned to Nanjing and were received as "social heroes by reason of absence." While still a Major on active duty, his future "reserve rank" was raised, meaning that he would eventually retire as a Lieutenant Colonel. They received overdue leave and took some time to "relax and play" before returning to Lanzhou. When they got back, Bob found that the situation in Western China had deteriorated, with communist forces closing in on *Sian* in Central China. Despite the possible danger, the Embassy had decided that they should return to Lanzhou ASAP and to "take all chances to remain in the northwest and get through to *Xinjiang* if possible."[226]

At the end of April 1948, Bob, Eva and their faithful mechanic-driver Ch'iu, returned to the road heading northwest along the historic "Kansu Corridor," a chain of narrow basins lying along the foothills of the Nan Shan mountains for about one thousand miles. This relatively narrow stretch, also known as the "Imperial Highway," followed the route of the famous Silk Road. Bounded by deserts on each side with occasional oasis, the corridor begins in Lanzhou and goes on to Urumqi, capital of *Xinjiang* Province, home of the Uighur people. Before reaching Urumqi, they would pass through towns that dotted the highway: *Wuwei, Kanchow (Ganzhou), Suchow (Suzhou), Ahnsi, Tun-huang (Dunhuang), Hami (Kumul)* and *Turfan (Turpan)*.

With their jeep and trailer loaded to the hilt, they left Lanzhou. While spring was "just around the corner," the weather remained cold and overcast. The promise of warmer weather would wait another day. The one hundred seventy miles from Lanzhou to Wuwei could be made in one day over the unimproved gravel roads if travel conditions allowed. As they drove between snow-capped mountains and desert, they experienced how precarious travel in an open jeep could be when it broke down in a snowstorm. Fortunately, Ch'iu, always resourceful, had a spare part in the trailer and made the repair under pelting snow. Pulling into *Kankow*, once an important city on the Silk Road, they found welcome refuge in a roadside inn and defrosted in the warm, aroma-filled restaurant.

They Had Been Reported for Dead

When the Ekvalls arrived in the next town, *Suchow*, a transportation center in the middle of "nowhere," they heard that a plane would arrive soon and looked forward to getting mail and newspapers from their CAT pilot friends. When opening their mail sent by the OMA in Nanjing, much to their surprise, Bob and Eva discovered that they had been reported for dead in the newspapers. Unfortunately, this "fake news" traveled far and wide and required a lot of letter writing to anguished friends and family.[227] Despite the unexpected report of their premature decease, the next stopover at nearby Yumen, was not a complete bust.

Discovered in the late 1930s, the Yumen oil fields produced China's first wells, and the subsequent drilling, storage and refining facilities brought a large influx of Chinese workers. Bob learned much when he visited the "forbidden oilfields." For whatever reason, General Liu, the local military authority, disregarded instructions to restrict Bob's movements. Enjoying their new sense of freedom, Bob and Eva drove on to the next big town Suchow, home of Chinese military installations.

Suchow, located in the middle of the Kansu Corredor, marked the westernmost point of the Great Wall. The nearby Jiayuguan Pass, a strategic point, had been a major hub on the old Silk Road. Close by Suchow, they visited the famous caves of *Tun-huang* located in a small oasis town surrounded by high mountains. It had more than five hundred caves with ancient manuscripts and religious objects precious to Buddhists, Muslims and Christians. The Ekvalls spent many happy hours tramping around the area.

More days of travel through desert sand and wind, with nightly stops at roadside inns, took them to *Hami*, a second military outpost on the highway and official entrance into *Xinjiang* Province. There, Bob met General *Yulsbar Khan*, also known as "*Yolbas*," a Uighur chief and head of the Nationalist forces in the region. He saw the influence of the nearby U.S.S.R., since almost every town had "White" Russians who had fled Russia after the 1917 Revolution. They also saw evidence of "Red" Russian communist influence since, during WW 2, the Soviet Union had built a highway from Moscow across Russia all the way to Xian in Central China.

Before the war, *Xinjiang* had been the scene of raging battles in the 1930s between the Chinese military and the legendary Muslim figure, General *Ma Chung-Yin*, also known as "Big Horse." This same man, years younger had terrorized the border areas around Tao-chow Old City. Bob knew the then-teenage leader as the "Little General," and their relationship went back to Labrang Monastery in 1924 when he first met the teenage military prodigy who grew to be an Islamic scourge in Kansu and later *Xinjiang*.

As they traveled the ancient caravan road, Bob found that there was an unreported rebellion in the region. It had begun in 1944, among the Turkic peoples of the *Ili* region in the north of the province bordering the Soviet Union. The Soviets took advantage of the Muslim *Ili* people's discontent and supported their rebellion against Kuomintang rule. When Ekvall arrived in the region, the rebellion was being put down by Chinese Hui Muslim fighters allied with the Nationalist government.

Arriving in Turfan, "the heart of Asia," they gave the jeep a once-over before starting the last leg of their thousands-of-miles trek. They climbed rough roads toward Urumqi, the capital, through the Tien-Shan Mountains, which stretch fifteen hundred miles from southwest to northeast with peaks over twenty-four thousand feet. However, Urumqi, at an altitude of twenty-four hundred feet had a pleasant climate. Suffering mechanical issues on the way, their jeep limped into the capital of *Xinjiang* on a wish and a prayer in early June, 1948.

Over the next four months, Bob and Eva Ekvall, and faithful Ch'iu, began "operating in Urumqi." They stayed in a hotel due to the the US Consulate's modest installations. The consul, J. Hall Paxton, son of Presbyterian missionaries in China, served as the Consul from 1946–1949. From his post he had observed the jousting between Chinese and Russian Communist factions seeking military and political ascendancy over the area. Paxton filled Bob in on the recent events which he had witnessed.

Xinjiang, "backward and undeveloped," despite efforts at modernization, seemed both oriental and middle eastern at the same time. From two mountain climbers, Eric Shipton, British consul in Kashgar, and Bill Tillman, a famous South African mountaineer, Bob learned about the attempted secession of Iling. Muslim rebels had established the "Provisional Government of the Second East Turkestan Republic" in 1944 which lasted till 1949. The Soviet government provided arms and aid to the rebels who desired to break away from Chinese control and unite with Turkey, which they still considered their "homeland." The roots of the Turki language which Bob had begun to learn reached back to the days of Turkish caravans traveling the Silk Road. He considered the mountaineers as "mad of course but with ears to the ground," from which he gathered valuable intelligence. The Ekvalls attended the usual cocktails, their presence in demand because of Eva, a rare Western woman in this forsaken outpost. The Chinese governor of the northwest of China, *Chang Chih-chung*, invited them to national art and dance exhibitions sponsored by his administration. If more Chinese leaders had shared his liberal view of recognizing the "minorities'" culture, language and their past history, the present tragic state of Xinjiang today would likely be different.

The Soviets Set Out to Eliminate His Fierce Muslim Fighters

With tennis the rage among the expat community, Bob and Eva enjoyed pleasant afternoon matches while keeping eyes and ears opened for information to go into Bob's intel reports to Nanjing. Amazingly, he attended the debriefing of *Osman Bator*, the Kazakh tribal chieftain, who, in 1944, had revolted against Russian influence in the region. Eventually, he fled south with about ten thousand Kazakh horsemen after the Soviets set out to eliminate his Muslim fighters. Bringing tanks and artillery to bear on the Muslim horse soldiers, Osman lost about three thousand of his men in four separate battles.

Later, Bob visited one of the battle sites Osman Bator had mentioned, *Beitashan* or *Pei Ta Shan*, northeast of Urumqi, where the Muslim Hui calvary attacked Mongolian and Soviet positions. There, Russians and Mongolians troops drove out Bator's Kazakh forces. After more than a year of hard driving, their faithful jeep began to show its age. They broke down again, this time in the desert, and had to ride the pony-sized horses on Mongolian saddles to safety. While waiting for new wheel bearings to arrive, they visited the front lines of the battle. When the parts arrived, Ch'iu repaired their jeep and they drove all night back to Urumqi.[228]

Arriving there, they found that some wandering Americans had appeared, including U. S. journalist, A. Doak Barnett, of the *Chicago Daily News* and the Institute of Current World Affairs. Another missionary

kid, Barnett, raised in Shanghai where his father headed up the Shanghai YMCA, spoke fluent Chinese. Together with CIA "spook," Douglas
Mackiernan, they shared information regarding the gradual erosion of
the Nationalist Government's control of *Xinjiang*. Inevitably, the questions of "who wins?" and "what next?" shaped their conversations. Since
the State Department planned on closing the Urumqi Consulate soon,
Bob sensed that their time in Urumqi had come to an end. So, he and Eva
readied for departure. Things were tense in the city, and they had a long
trip back to Lanzhou ahead of them since the Nationalist government
refused to permit the U.S. Embassy plane to fly into Urumqi.

They took a side trip to visit a cavalry outpost in T'ien Shan where
Kazakh refugees languished following the defeat of their troops. Just as
they left there, one of the axles in their jeep, with brand new bearings,
broke! Out of options, they put the jeep on a Chinese army truck, and
rode into Hami for repair. In short order, with a new axle and new bearings, the old jeep made the long journey to Lanzhou. On the way, they
stayed at a Chinese Army Camel Corps camp and went on a gazelle hunt
before arriving in Lanzhou.

The city that Bob knew so well seemed strange, with whiffs of Nationalist defeat and Old Mao's victory hanging in the air. The Chinese
authorities had wearied of the Americans who had similar feelings. Despite continual harassment by the governor, who did not like his "allied
friends," the Embassy plane finally came and picked up those leaving the
region. With the communists closing on Lanzhou, Ekvalls and their consulate compatriots flew out on of the last flights to Nanjing.

However, not all Americans had departed, including the Consul J.
Hall Paxton. He stayed at his post in Urumqi until ordered by the State
Department to close the consulate with the takeover by the communist
government imminent. On August 15, the order came from the Embassy
in Nanjing:

> Consul Paxton led an exodus, famous in State Department his-
> tory, that included all Americans except Mackiernan. Paxton's
> wife, Vincoe, Vice Consul Robert Dreesen, and more than a
> dozen local employees went out with Paxton . . . . theirs was an
> amazing journey south around the western edge of the Taklam-
> akan Desert, in western Tibet, and then through the Himalayas
> into India.[229]

Eventually, Paxton gained national attention after he fled over the Himalayas to escape advancing Communist troops. One of the last things that Bob did before boarding the Embassy plane was " leaving remains of jeep for Mckiernan (sic)."[230] With the remaining spare parts, fuel and best wishes, Mackiernan returned to Urumqi.

For almost another year, Mackiernan, an MIT dropout and brilliant agent, spied on the Soviet atomic bomb test site across the border at Semi-palatinsk in Kazakhstan. He eventually had to flee China after Chiang Kai Shek's government fell. He, with five Russian comrades, followed the same route as Paxton across Tibet. However, when they reached a region not far from Lhasa, Tibetan soldiers shot four of them, including Mackiernan, thinking they were Muslim marauders from north of the border. Only one Russian survived. Douglas Mackiernan became the first CIA agent killed in action, although the CIA kept this kept secret until recently.

In the meantime, Bob and Eva arrived in Nanjing in October 1948, and he immediately reported for orders. While Washington tried to fig-ure out what to do with Ekvall, Bob visited General Chen K'ai-min, who he had last seen months before. The General now faced a vastly different situation. With no more illusions, the seasoned soldier "tells me truth and gives time table of Communist take-over of Nanking."[231] The Pen-tagon's role for Bob envisaged him, to "meet them [the PLA] when they come in [to Nanjing]and make first contacts" [for the United States] with Mao's victorious forces.[232] Since Ekvall's knowledge of the language and people had no peer in Nanjing, this seemed to be the best course of ac-tion. Many times before, he had been able to defuse dangerous situations with the spoken word.

Because the fall of Nanjing did not seem imminent, Ekvall received orders to return to America for rapid debriefing and then "right back" to China. However, once in the United States in November, the debriefing, apparently delayed by the Thanksgiving, Christmas and New Years holi-days, changed Ekvall's orders. By late January 1949, the persistent victory of Red forces all over China made Bob's return there less and less a prior-ity or even a possibility. Then, on April 23, 1949, Mao's People's Libera-tion Army (PLA) captured Nanjing, capital of China and headquarters of the Nationalist Party. In just a few more months, it became clear that the country would fall. The preparations for evacuation to Taiwan previously made by the Kuomintang's government took precedence. And Bob's ca-reer in China came to an end, at least for a while.

Chapter 13

Off Again, On Again

WITH THE DEFEAT OF Generalissimo Chiang Kai Shek's Nationalist Chinese forces and subsequent evacuation to Formosa (Taiwan) in the South China Sea, Lieutenant Colonel Robert B. Ekvall's hard-earned experience and expertise suddenly became a moot point. "Old China hands" were no longer needed. The intensive debriefings at the Pentagon, abruptly interrupted by the eruption of another Asian hot spot, brought radical change to the Ekvall's future. A somewhat promising, although unlikely, military career threatened to go off the tracks.

With return to China ruled out, Bob received orders to report for duty at Fort Lewis, not far from Spokane Washington, where he was assigned to the Second Infantry Division as Assistant G-2 (Intelligence). Eva was expecting a baby; and as they traveled to their new assignment, both remembered the loss of their first child three years before.

At least this time, spring 1950, their travel by plane and train proved much more comfortable while going to their new base in Washington. While housing was not luxurious, their new home had electric lights, a full kitchen, indoor plumbing, and no danger of dysentery from drinking tap water. After a few days settling in, Major Ekvall took up his duties while Eva began preparing a room for the newcomer scheduled to arrive in just a few months. Sure enough, on June 16, 1950, Eric Ekvall was born at the Fort Lewis Base Hospital. At age fifty two, Bob Ekvall was a daddy once again, and Eva, at half her husband's age, was a twenty six year-old first-time mother.

In 1945 at the end of WW 2, the U.S. had argued with Kim Il-Sung and the U.S.S.R. over the reunification of Korea, since it had been occupied by Japan for more than fifty years. Not able to come to a satisfactory decision, the two major powers split the difference at the 38th parallel and war broke out five years later.

On June 25 Just eight days after baby Eric Ekvall was born, seven crack divisions of elite North Korean Army (NKA) invaded South Korea, intending to conquer the southern half of the peninsula in three weeks. The United States and UN allies were caught off guard; South Korea's capital, Seoul, was overrun, and the small garrison of U.S. soldiers was driven far south to the "Pusan Perimeter." Despite terrible losses from initial lack of preparation and resources, the U.S. and the United Nations mobilized. Commanding General Douglas MacArthur's brilliant amphibious attack at Inchon in September cut off the NKA supply lines and freed the capital Seoul, leading to the capture of hundreds of thousands of NKA troops. Gradually the UN troops under the leadership of the US Army drove the North Korean soldiers back north, all the way to the border between North Korea and Communist China at the Yalu river. Despite warnings of possible Chinese Communist intervention, the U.S. Army pressed on.

Suddenly, they came under attack from hundreds of thousands of China's PLA soldiers, suffering one of the most devastating debacles in U. S. military history. The American and UN forces found themselves trapped at the Chosin Reservoir before managing to escape south to safety. Eventually, the US and allies fought the North Korean and Chinese PLA armies to a standstill. Instead of a three-week war as envisioned by the North Korean dictator, Kim Il sung, the "Korean Police Action," as President Harry Truman euphemistically called it, slogged on for three long years until the adversaries battled on to a stalemate. A ceasefire brought on peace negotiations which led to an armistice on July 27, 1953. This "police action" was later termed "The century's nastiest little war," by one, and "a sour war" by another."[233]

The Korean War, as Such, Had Passed Me By

The first U.S. Army unit sent to fight alongside Allied forces already stationed in Korea rushed in from Japan, then followed by troops from Fort Lewis, Washington. The 2nd Infantry Division, known as "Second to

None," arrived on 23 July, almost a month after the start of hostilities. Lt. Col. Ekvall did not go with them. The new wartime reality made it clear that Bob Ekvall's days in the Army were numbered. In his words:

> The Korean war, as such, had passed me by. The army had recalled on 'extended active duty' young company grade officers to lead patrols and command combat units. It had no further use for lieutenant colonels who were more than mature and also somewhat irregular. According to army standards, I was very much a 'citizen soldier' even when in uniform, although my physical characteristics and certain mannerisms, acquired from experiences in strange places, helped me masquerade at times almost as a West Pointer. The army, I was sure, had no further use for me.[234]

Since Ekvall's age prohibited sending him to Korea, he received orders to serve at the Seattle Joint Armed Forces PIO (Public Information Office). For someone who had fought with distinction with Merrill's Marauders in WW 2, served as General George Marshall's personal "briefer" during the Marshall Mission after WW 2, and had also worked as a high-level intelligence officer all over China after the war, transfer to an Army PR office to serve out his time before retiring as a Lieutenant Colonel had to be a letdown. With relief, and perhaps regret, Bob stored his military uniforms and returned to civilian life in 1951.

About this same time, Bob's "past life" in Tibet resurrected with an invitation from the Committee for Free Asia (CFA). The organization, founded in San Francisco with CIA funding, purposed to contain communism in Eastern Asia. Since Bob had seen its result in China at first hand, he accepted their call for his unique services. The committee had been in contact with the oldest brother of the Dalai Lama, a lama like his younger brother and known as the "Takster Rinpoche." Thubten Jigme Norbu, his given name, had been recognized at age three as the reincarnated abbot of Kumbum Monastery, one of Tibet's most important, in Qinghai Province.

Major Robert Ekvall, Seattle, 1958.

Aided by British Plymouth Brethren missionary, George Patterson, Takster escaped from India and arrived in the United States on July 6, 1950. He had fled after the Dalai Lama asked him to go to America and request help to keep Tibet free from Communist China. The Committee for Free Asia sponsored him. Takster traveled ostensibly for medical treatment only available in the United States. After the Chinese PRC ambassador to India tried to interfere with his trip, he left Calcutta for London on July 5, arriving in Idlewild Airport (JFK Airport) in New York City the following day. "Next day, the newspapers carried the front-page story of the dramatic arrival in the United States of the Dalai Lama's brother, and speculated if this meant the Dalai Lama himself would follow."[235] After deplaning and clearing immigration, Norbu and his long-time servant, Jentzen Thondup, were "shocked to be greeted by a white man speaking in their native Amdo dialect. Their chaperone, Robert Ekvall, had a fascinating personal history."[236] Bob took Norbu and Jentzen to the posh Waldorf-Astoria hotel for a night's rest, telling the reporters of Norbu's infirmity (rheumatism) and intention of going to California to study at

Berkley. Before flying west, Bob took his Tibetan charges to Washington for meetings with the State Department and the CIA. Bob acted as Norbu's "mentor," helping him adjust to life in America and aiding in communicating with U.S. officials.

For the next six months, Bob and Eva, with little Eric, hosted Norbu and his servant at their rented farmhouse in Fairfax, Virginia. During that time, he received treatment for "a minor lung condition" and other issues.[237] Norbu's meetings with CIA and foreign service officials were inconclusive. While sympathetic to Tibet's plight and the Dalai Lama's original plea for help, they did nothing. The Dalai Lama, who had fled to India, later returned to Lhasa after finally accepting the *fait-acomplit* of China's rule over Tibet. After six months in Virginia, Norbu headed west to California and began language study at the University of California, Berkeley. Still on retainer with CFA, Bob moved his family to a sleepy valley just over the hills from Berkeley. While his Tibetan charge studied English, Bob began work on "The Universals of Tibetan Religious Observance and Their Function," which proposed to show how "religion," i.e. Tibetan Buddhism, shaped and dominated the doctrine-centric society of Tibet in all aspects of life and culture.

Call Washington and Ask for Operator Sixteen

In July 1952, Norbu and his servant went to Japan to attend the World Buddhist Conference in Tokyo. Ekvall continued working on research and writing. He had published *Tibetan Skylines* that same year, a book focused on life on the Kansu-Tibetan border, which received good reviews in newspapers and literary journals. Bob and Eva and their growing boy lived a simple but idyllic life.

With Norbu's leaving for Japan, Bob's relationship with the Committee for Free Asia ceased as did its support. Since he had returned to work on the universals of Tibetan Buddhism begun years before, Ekvall renewed ties with the Department of Anthropology at the University of Chicago, where he had studied in 1937–1938. Consequently, he was made a non-resident research associate and later charged with setting up a study program of Tibetan culture and language for the Department. Perhaps Bob had visions of pursuing the PhD opportunity that he had rejected in order to return to the Tibetan border area in 1939. Unfortunately, it was not to be, something he regretted in later years. The

University of Chicago Press eventually published the work, "The Universals of Tibetan Religious Observance and Their Function," in 1964.

Before Norbu's departure, Bob had happily divided his time between the University of California Library and "lengthy sessions of fact finding and argument with the brother of the Dalai Lama . . ."[238] After a session of hard writing, he would take a break and play a game or two of tennis at the local sunbaked courts. Like their little son, Eric, his next manuscript grew a bit more every day. Best of all, their little hideaway had no phone! Yet, one beautiful spring day in 1953, that all changed as Bob returned home from a visit to the post office. As he strolled through the town, everyone he saw told him that "the sheriff is looking for you." Startled, he quickly returned home to find a note telling him to call Washington and ask for "operator sixteen."

Using a friend's phone, Bob dialed the number and asked for "operator sixteen;" a voice responded:

> "Colonel Ekvall? This is General Powell, G-1 [Personnel]. We've had quite a job locating you. Finally called your publisher in New York and they gave us your address." Bob, almost standing and saluting, replied, "Yes *sir*." General Powell was brief and blunt: "We need you at the truce negotiations at Panmunjom. We would like to call you back on extended active duty. That is, with your consent."[239]

Few times had Bob ever been "asked an order," but he knew that his request for consent meant that this was urgent. Immediately the questions ran through his mind. "What about Eva and Eric? What about my teaching engagements for the fall of 1953? Do I want to go back to the country where my only son, David, lost his life in the most ignoble, stupid manner possible?" Those and many others came to mind. At the same time, he knew what he had to do. He could not stay in his Sunshine Valley hideaway working on a book that only a few might read while he could do something important that might help many in Korea. Six days later, with three painful shots in each arm, Bob took off for the Far East and the war-torn peninsula of Korea.

The 1952 U.S. presidential elections saw Democrat Governor Adlai Stevenson running against WW 2 hero, General Dwight "Ike" Eisenhower, the Republican candidate, who won in a landslide. He campaigned on the promise to stop the fighting and get out of Korea as fast as possible. The on-again, off-again negotiations got serious, and Lt. Col. Ekvall landed in South Korea and joined his colleagues as the "interpreter and Chief, Language Division, Armistice Commission."[240] Ekvall described the "Back-in-the-army" experience:

> I was really back in the army, I was on my way to the Far East and Panmunjom (English translation—the Inn with the Planken Door), that little island of truce talks in the midst of a battlefield, that place where men talked across a green-topped table of truce, an armistice, and peace. But as they talked on in the three equal languages—English, Chinese and Korean—time went fast and agreement came slowly and artillery and mortar fire raised clouds of dust on the nearby hills while other men died.[241]

The "hot war" had cooled down and the negotiators had made little progress other than the exchange of a few prisoners in March 1953. In a last, desperate show of strength, twenty-three hundred PLA troops furiously attacked the tiny American garrison on "Pork Chop Hill" in April. During the two days of constant assault, the U.S. artillery fired more than one hundred thousand rounds, fended off the Chinese and held the hill. The attack failed and stalemate reigned. During the impasse, "too-old" Lt. Colonel Ekvall flew to Seoul, just thirty miles west of Yonan, the insignificant village where David, had been blown to oblivion in 1945.

In typical hurry-up-and-wait Army fashion, Bob got to Panmunjom about the same time as the failed attack, with truce negotiations having ground to a halt. One officer, unhappy with the arrival of an overage officer too highly-ranked to be a "mere interpreter," declared Bob "superfluous," and planned to send him elsewhere. Bob kept his powder dry and let the big guns sort things out. He went to work and caught up on what had happened before the meetings had stalled. He studied the Chinese texts of draft agreements, monitored a few meetings still held, learning the "rules of the road," the procedures and linguistic conventions agreed to by each side.

By the end of April the talks began to pick up; and on June 8, the two sides finally agreed on the terms of the contentious POW (Prisoner of War) matter. The provisions were outlined in a document call the "Terms of Reference." According to the agreement, POWs that refused to return to Communist territory were under the responsibility of a neutral commission for three months. After three months, if the POWs continued to refuse repatriation, they were set free. "With the signing of the agreement, the truce negotiation headquarters went out of existence, and the military armistice commission took its place."[242]

Now in charge of the language division, whose organigram called for 140 linguists; Bob's team had twelve, including translators, and typists for Chinese and Korean. With five or more meetings scheduled daily and having only two qualified sets of interpreters, Bob sent out an all-points alarm to the U.S. Army, Navy and Air Force. They scoured their files and "linguists" poured in. While the service records called them qualified, four out of five were sent back. The ones remaining, while not interpreters yet, showed promise. Training for these would-be workers began, and gradually they were worked into the rotation. Over time, a corps of capable interpreters came together

Panmunjom Peace Negotiation, July 28, 1953.

By October 1953, the frenetic pace of plenary meetings held every day had dropped to once a week. The competent team that Ekvall headed up had little to do. The daily joint meetings dragged along with much talk and little accomplished. During this lull, the State Department requested the "loan" of Bob from chief of the language division to personal interpreter for Ambassador Arthur H. Dean, former Deputy to Secretary of State, John Foster Dulles. A follow-up political conference was scheduled in order "to work out the basis for the unification of North and South

Korea and to take charge of the prisoners who had not as yet been ex-changed.[243] Of all the Chinese-English interpreters available to the State Department, Lt. Col. Robert Ekvall, BS in English from Wheaton and a diploma from the Nyack MTI, was chosen. With no formal training in diplomatic interpretation, he had a binary brain that maintained two lan-guage tracks, one in Chinese and one in English simultaneously, a facility that only a privileged few had.

Ambassador Dean, in his Forward to Ekvall's book, *Faithful Echo*, writes in relation to the negotiations with the Chinese communist diplomats:

> Every statement had to be carefully and precisely formulated the evening before and then translated into Chinese and Korean. Since the Chinese and English languages are in no sense similar in structure, many hours had to be spent in making sure that what we wanted to be said could be said correctly and precisely in both the Chinese and Korean languages.
>
> Dr. (sic) Ekvall's scholarly ability and his facility in turning a phrase were of inestimable value.[244]

The scene of the negotiations, located high in the mountains in the middle of the Korean peninsula, was a big army tent set crosswise, liter-ally, on the 38th parallel. On the North Korean side of the table sat the delegates from the People's Republic of China (PRC) and the People's Re-public of Korea (PRK), while on the south side, sat the delegations from the United States and the Republic of Korea. The narrow negotiating table, covered in green baize material, acted as the line of demarcation. Neither delegation had permission to cross to the other side. Since the wood stove remained on the northern side, they either left it unlit, freez-ing everyone or heated like a fiery furnace and making the windowless tent unbearable.

The preparatory political conference went on for six weeks, six-days-a week. Scheduled for only two hours daily, the talks grew longer to three hours, and one marathon session lasted five and a half hours. "Frustration lengthened the meetings: the less there is to be said the lon-ger the time to say it."[245] By December 1953, the conference had stalled due to constant verbal attacks by Chinese ambassador Huang-Hua. He and his interpreter, a PhD grad from Harvard, piled on venomous invec-tive, culminating in Huang-Hua accusing the United States of "perfidy," defined as "deceitfulness, untrustworthiness." Diplomats are trained to never "lose it," but U.S. Ambassador Dean's cup of gall had run over.

Ekvall translated Dean's curt response "'what rubbish—what garbage,' [which] had a justness of nuance in Chinese that brought a flush to the faces across the table which had not been there when they heard, with complete understanding, the original English. This final word from the American side was spoken by Ambassador Dean and interpreted by me [Ekvall] as we moved to our walkout with Huang Hua's shouted supplication 'Come back!' following us out the door."[246] The famous "walkout" occurred on December 12, 1953.

In retrospect, Ekvall believed that the clear-cut calling out of the Chinese ambassador's constant attempt at disruption had forced them to rethink their cocky attitude in future negotiations. Unfortunately, while finally resolving the prisoner repatriation problem, a final agreement of a general political settlement regarding reunification never took place because of mutually intransigent positions. Nonetheless, the horrifically pointless fighting ended. Just about that time, Ekvall's services as diplomatic translator were required at the Asian and Indochina Conference in Geneva, Switzerland. The conference, aimed at resolving pending issues resulting from the Korean War and the First Indochina War, involved several nations, and ran from April 26 to July 20, 1954 Following the conclusion of the Geneva Conference, Bob was recalled to Washington to serve as a staff officer in G-2 (Intelligence) in the Pentagon.

The modestly positive developments of the 1954 Geneva Conference led to another Sino-American Conference held again in Geneva beginning on July 18, 1955. World leaders at the conference included President Dwight Eisenhower, British Prime Minister Anthony Eden, Soviet Premier Nikolai Bulganin and French Premier Edgar Faure. They gathered to discuss world peace. The common goal of increased global security guided the proceedings. Ekvall's indispensable role as chief interpreter came into sharp focus the morning he awoke unable to talk, an occurrence which put the U.S. staff in panic:

> But why the consternation on the staff of the United States negotiator one morning in the early fall of 1955 when it seemed that I had temporarily lost my voice? I had been swimming in the evening before, too late and too long, in the cold waters of Lake Geneva and awoke with just enough laryngitis to threaten the loss of my voice. Hot coffee laced with brandy brought it back, but it still operated uncertainly on two octaves. Only after I recovered my voice, however, was there positive certainty that the meeting of the day would be held as scheduled. The United States

ambassador might have lost his voice and some member of his staff could have read his statement. But if my voice had not come back who would have mouthed Chinese across the table?[247]

By the end of the conference, it was clear that world peace was not "just around the corner." Instead, the Cold War had spawned "hot spots" around the globe. However, the Geneva Conference did help soften icy relationships between some of the leaders present. It showed the added advantage of peaceful free trade as opposed to war, whether hot or cold. Such talks gave opportunity for world leaders to begin developing better relations in order to work toward a less tense future.

Looking back, it appears that during his years "on loan" to the State Department, the established opinion of majority thinking at "Foggy Bottom" and Ekvall's did not coincide. While the officials feared a combined communist block of the USSR and PRC would compete with the US for global leadership, Bob insisted that the two so-called allies were historic enemies who feared and distrusted each other. As happened during his missionary career years before, Robert Ekvall was viewed as "thinking yellow" and being "soft on China." In addition to these ideological differences, Ekvall admitted that he was "terrible at bureaucracy politics and either wasn't able or willing to do whatever it might have taken to keep his job."[248]

Major Robert and Eva Ekvall, Reception at Elysee Palace, 1958.

Following the Geneva Conference, Lt. Colonel Ekvall was stationed in Paris as Assistant Military Attache from 1957 to 1958. Likely, he received this posting due to his reputation as interpreter and his background in intelligence. In 1958, the U.S. Army released Bob from active duty as "over-age in grade." Sixty year-old lieutenant colonels with no formal military training and an unconventional past, had little future in the U.S. military establishment. Thus, for the second and last time, Bob ended his amazing military/diplomatic career and retired with chest full of "fruit salad" as well as a Bronze Star and Purple Heart, the last two for meritorious service when he had volunteered for a military operation behind enemy lines at Liuchow, in Guangxi Province just at the close of WW 2. Ekvall left the Army aiming to reinvent himself as a writer and academic.

Chapter 14

Adventures in Academia

Now a "Lt. Col. (retd)," long on experience and short on cash, Bob Ekvall began a new period in life. During his last stint in the Army his novel, *Tents Against the Sky* had been published in 1954 with favorable reviews. Thus, he believed that writing could be part of his new career. Bob returned to Seattle with Eva, nine-year old Eric and Karin, 4 years-old, after receiving an invitation from Professor George E. Taylor, department head of Oriental Studies at the University of Washington. Professor Taylor wanted Bob to join the Inner Asia Research Project in the Far Eastern and Russian Institute. This invitation gave the Ekvall's a foundation on which to build a new life and put down some roots.

They moved into a comfortable house in the Montlake Terrace neighborhood of Seattle. Since Bob, with Betty and David, had enjoyed living in the mountains of Tibet, he took his second family camping and skiing in the nearby Cascade mountains. Eva loved having a real home of her own with room for their children and guests, a beautiful kitchen and a living room with a fire place; the new house, a dream come true for a former European refugee. She once had wandered across Europe with her parents seeking a home. Located on a quiet street with a big backyard where the kids could play, the Ekvalls had come home.

He Was Not Taken Too Seriously By the Young PhDs

Within the first few months at the University of Washinton, Bob published his first scholarly paper, "Five Universals of Tibetan Religion," which remains available online. During his years at the University of Washington, he wrote seventeen academic works covering a gamut of subjects relating to Tibetan religion and culture. His production was prolific, with a new paper being presented every few months, the fruit of years of study and experience. He spoke at the Tacoma Library on his "seven careers" and *The Seattle Times* ran an article on his serving as an interpreter at the Panmunjom negotiation.[249] Consequently, he gained some local notoriety within the Seattle community and environs. Even so, because of Bob's twenty years as a missionary, his modest educational background, not highly regarded in most academic circles, plus a fourteen year career in the military and diplomatic world, led most of the young PhDs in the department of anthropology to not take Ekvall seriously.

Due to his ability in the Tibetan language, in 1960, the University asked Bob to accompany Dr. Turrell Wylie, department head for Tibetan studies, to India. There, they would select and invite a few Tibetans exiles to become part of a research program at the university. The Indian consulate denied Bob a visa because of his earlier career in the U.S. Army as interpreter and intelligence officer, "a possible spy?" Consequently, Wylie, thirty years younger than Bob, recently granted his PhD, went alone and selected four Tibetans from south central Tibet: two sons of the Sakya royal family, their uncle, a noted lama, plus the wife of one of the royal sons. Though lacking higher academic degrees, Ekvall spoke Tibetan fluently, while Wylie lacked competence in the spoken language. One of Bob's friends who he met after retiring from the university commented on the arrival of the four Tibetan members of the research project.

> When the first group of Tibetans arrived in Seattle, according to my understanding, the Department Head stepped out to greet them, in English. They had no clue what he was saying. Ekvall stepped in and greeted them in Tibetan, and helped them adapt to that new world. I heard the account of the Professors being fairly clueless, in regard to contact with living Tibetans, instead of accounts in books.[250]

Thus, since he was the only one capable of communicating with the Tibetans, they gravitated to Bob because their English ranged from weak to non-existent. Bob led regular research discussions with them regarding the "political and economic life" of Sakya during the years 1960 to 1962. which eventually resulted in several books.[251]

About the same time, Takster Rinpoche returned to Seattle after an extended stay in Japan and India. He had come as a research associate with the Tibetan project. Once again, the Ekvall family opened their home to their Tibetan friend. For the next six months, Bob and Norbu worked together on the English translation of *The Younger Brother Don yod . . . Being the Secret Biography from the Worlds of the Glorious Lama*, a Tibetan play written by the older brother of the Dalai Lama, published in 1969 by the Indiana University Press.

Ekvall and Norbu Translating, 1962.

David Jackson, who later became a renowned Tibetologist in his own right, knew Ekvall while he studied at the University of Washington in the early 1970s. Like so many others, he "did not pay much attention to him, discounting him in my youthful zeal as an old missionary."[252] The traits which drew the Tibetans to Ekvall, i.e., his gregarious personality and his ability to relate to them led them to call him by his Tibetan name, "Sherab Tsondru" and accept him as an "honorary Tibetan." Unfortunately, those same qualities resulted in some of his academic colleagues not accepting him as a credible scholar. Despite his breadth of knowledge regarding Tibetan life and language, his lack of advanced scholarly degrees and academically-recognized expertise in a specific field of Tibetology, created a critical attitude among his younger, more erudite colleagues. This perception came to a head in 1963 "when Ekvall and another colleague, C. W. Casinelli, presented a paper at a special enlarged meeting of the the Inner Asia Colloquium, at which the director of the Far Eastern Institute, George Taylor, was to preside."[253]

Some of the conclusions of the research project developed into a book co-written by Ekvall and C. W. Casinelli, *A Tibetan Principality: The Political System of Sakya*, which resulted in an academic brouhaha. Dr. Wylie openly questioned the findings of the Sakya book. He publicly criticized Bob's "research methodology" and was joined by a twenty-five year old graduate student who questioned the accuracy of Bob's translations of Tibetan texts and other "dubious information" contained in the book. Other senior professors of anthropology agreed with his opinion that Ekvall's work was not "up to current scholarly standards," thus, putting his scholarship on trial. Several graduate students witnessing the proceedings felt that it "smacked of a kangaroo court, and they boycotted the meeting." Despite the criticism of the younger colleagues, Dr. George Taylor, department head of Oriental Studies at the university, continued to support Ekvall and his work in the Far Eastern Institute and Inner Asia Project. In addition, the four Tibetans in the research group that produced the book maintained their close relationship with him.[254]

Ekvall's son, Eric, looking back at his father's time at the university stated: "I remember some very tough years as he reinvented himself as an ethnologist and anthropologist (with a bachelors degree in English, remember) in the cutthroat world of academe, at U of Washington."[255] Around the same time of the "scholarly skirmish," his second wife, Eva, was diagnosed with aggressive breast cancer; and after a painful battle with the dread disease, she passed away on February 16, 1963 at the age of thirty nine. Apparently, she never showed interest in the Christian faith which Bob still maintained to some extent. He scattered her ashes off Orcas Island. Deeply affected by her loss, he later expressed to friends that he "wondered at the time whether by such extreme afflictions he was not being tested unfairly, like Job in the Bible."[256]

To add to Bob's trials, son Eric, a free-thinking teenager, who had already given up on God and church, followed the yellow brick road to drugs, alcohol, and the spirit of the 1960s. From his early teens, he resisted going to church with his father, pointing out that his mother had made the better choice on Sundays staying in bed with a cigarette and the newspapers. Raising teens on his own in the liberal atmosphere of Seattle proved a challenge to Bob.

Home Without a Mother Is Like a Body Without a Heart

By the end of 1964, the academic powers-that-be at the university gradually put Bob out to pasture. Now sixty-six, he no longer worked as a research instructor in the Far Eastern Department. Consequently, he left the Department of Anthropology to become the honorary curator of Asian Ethnology at the Thomas Burke Memorial Museum in Seattle. A few years after Eva's death, with Eric fifteen and Karin just eleven, their aging father sensed that a home without a mother is like a body without a heart. It so happened that while attending a social function in Seattle, Bob met a lady, Mrs. Betsey Frisbee, a well-to-do widow and accomplished yachtswoman. Bob, still a lover of the outdoors, began to see her regularly, and the relationship grew. Thinking that Karin, about to enter her teen years, would benefit from having a woman in the home, they married in 1966. The newly-weds went to Europe for an entire year to help Tibetan refugees, taking Eric and Karin with them.[257] While Bob's son and daughter studied in Paris, Bob and Betsey traveled around Europe seeking to help Tibetan refugees who had fled Tibet for India in the 1950s before being given exile in Switzerland, the United Kingdom and some of the Scandinavian countries.

From all accounts, Betsey, a "romantic," had an idealistic worldview and politics which did not match Bob's. Following their return to America, with the Vietnam war heating up, Bob marched in an anti-war protest, much to his wife's outrage and disapproval.[258] It soon became apparent that they had little in common except their love of the outdoors, which couldn't keep them together indoors. Consequently, the marriage failed, and they divorced amicably in 1969. Bob later commented to one of his former missionary associates that following the divorce, he began to draw back to God after years of indifference.[259]

As an academic, Ekvall had come under criticism for his reputation as "an old missionary;" yet on occasion, that part of his life surfaced. One day in the late 1960s, as he strode across the University of Washington campus in the company of a Tibetan Lama, he heard a loud voice calling him from across the commons, "Mr. Ekvall, Mr. Ekvall." He looked over to see a young lady; "Mr. Ekvall, it's me, Marjorie Smith!" As Bob walked over, he recognized her as one of son David's, classmates in the early 1940s. Daughter of C&MA missionaries to French Indo-China, Curwin and Sheila Smith, she first met Ekvall when he came down to visit David at Dalat and got "stuck" in Indo-China from 1941 to 1943.

For several minutes, Marjorie, now a teacher, and the "old missionary," talked together. She had heard the tragic news of David's death in South Korea; she had also known about Bob's losing his first wife, Betty, in 1940. They talked for some time remembering their internment in 1943 and the repatriation of the missionaries on the *Gripsholm*. Ekvall even told her about Eva's death and the recent divorce from Betsey Frisbee. While the conversation lasted no longer than ten or fifteen minutes, it brought back memories.[260]

That meeting, seemingly a chance encounter, reminded him of the life that he and Betty and David had led for years on the Tibetan border. David had shared stories with his Dalat classmates of exciting experiences lived with his parents. Very likely, those memories of the simple but rewarding life as a "Jesus talker" on the Kansu border contrasted sharply with the constant battle that he had fought to prove himself worthy of respect as an academic equal in Seattle.

From 1969 to 1973, Bob did occasional work as a research associate at the Burke Museum and the University of Washington. While unable to obtain grants to support his research, he maintained esteem as a senior China-watcher and expert on Tibetan ethnology and anthropology. By this time, Eric had graduated from the University of Washington, and moved to Alaska, where he received his M.A. at the University of Alaska. He later moved to Venezuela, married and had a successful career in acting and political consultation. Younger daughter, Karin, taking time after high school to decide on career and marriage, eventually married and started a family. Ekvall "expressed great respect for the strong Christian religious convictions of his daughter, Karen (sic), with whom he occasionally attended church."[261]

Bob officially retired from his academic activities as an Emeritus at seventy-five years of age, and moved about fifty miles southeast of Seattle to a cabin in Carbondale, a little town in the Cascades. Ironically, starry-eyed young college students would seek him out as an expert on Tibetan mysticism only to discover that he was not a Tibetan Buddhist guru exiled to the wilds of the Pacific Northwest. Something of a recluse, Bob enjoyed the vigorous life in the mountains and began to commit his memories to paper.

Chapter 15

Heading Home

AFTER MOVING TO CARBONDALE, Bob lived alone in a log cabin on the slopes of Mount Ranier, chopping his own firewood and delighting in the rugged lifestyle that brought back good memories of Lhamo. Still healthy at seventy six, he maintained an active daily regimen, hiking the Cascades using a unique bent-knee gait that he claimed as better on his knees. On Sundays, he attended Calvary Presbyterian Church in Enumclaw, a town about twenty-five miles from his mountain aery. Gradually, his pain-hardened heart softened, and he got serious about writing projects which he had contemplated for quite a while.

Robert Ekvall—Carbondale WA, 1981.

In early fall 1973, while visiting in Wheaton with the Fischers, Betty's family, a car accident put Bob in the hospital with a fractured pelvis and broken ribs. While recuperating, Rev. William Kerr, one of the recruits sent out by the C&MA in 1948, visited him, accompanied by Rev. John Taylor of Nyack College. This much-appreciated visit ended in prayer for his full recovery. In a letter dated October 25, 1973, Kerr wrote to an interested person who had been praying for Ekvall: "I believe that the Lord is doing a new work in [Bob's] life and he is beginning to respond to Christian friends who have shown him love and consideration over the years." This visit contributed to his rapprochement with the Lord and former colleagues.

By mid-October, back at his cabin and daily routine, Bob began pounding out hundreds of pages on his typewriter, including *Tibetan Breakthrough,* one of several unfinished manuscripts. It proposed to tell the Ekvall missionary story with the narrative opening at Bob and Betty's arrival on the field in 1922. However, after eleven fascinating chapters of life on the border with Chinese farmers and merchants, Tibetan nomads and Muslim fighters, it stopped—in the late 1920s—leaving another ten plus years of missionary life with Betty among the Tibetan nomads un-typed and untold. That is also the case with a second intriguing manu-script begun about that same time, *Attache Trek: 1947–1948.* This opus, outlined for twenty-six chapters, recounted the adventure-filled tale of Bob and Eva as they drove their U.S. Army jeep from Nanjing to Urumqi in *Xinjiang.* He finished three hundred and forty-three double-spaced pages, fifteen fascinating chapters, then stopped. The manuscript, with outlines written for the final ten chapters, remained unfinished. The brief chapter outlines provided cryptic notes on what happened and where in those missing final ten chapters.

Better Than He Deserved

In May 1975, Nyack College invited Ekvall to visit the scene of his high school studies at Wilson Academy, from 1913 to 1916, where he had be-come a star athlete and student. Following another four intensive years at Wheaton College, graduating with honors in 1920, he had returned with Betty to the Missionary Training Institute (now Alliance University) in 1921–1922 where he was elected senior class president. Accordingly, Nyack College honored him as Alumnus of the Year; on that occasion, he spoke to the students in Pardington Hall. When presented with the plaque, Bob suggested a title for the autobiography that he never wrote, *Better than He Deserved*. This humorous hint indicated his awareness of God's grace at work in his long life.

He spoke of his years of living and learning at Nyack and told them that an important part of their education consisted of "What you have received and how to use it." He opined that a major goal of education was: "(1) How to learn, (2) where to get resources to learn more and (3) how to organize in one's mind all that he/she has learned."[262]

He also spoke of the importance of his years at Wheaton College where he met his first wife, Betty, as well as his later graduate studies in anthropology at the University of Chicago. In the award speech, he synthesized one of the most important principles learned from his field experience and anthropological studies: "No culture should be carried on the back of another culture!" He said that the core of Christianity needs to be taken to other cultures without sending all of the cultural baggage and dressing of the sending culture. He stressed the definite "cleavage" between culture and the gospel of Christ.[263]

At the end of the award program, music faculty member, Marion Howell, led the students in singing the school song, "Mount of Prayer and Blessing," whose lyrics Ekvall had written as a student a half-century before. He was surprised and delighted to hear the song and recognized its place in the culture of the former Missionary Training Institute, founded by A. B. Simpson.

While at Nyack for the award presentation, the *Rockland County Sunday News* interviewed him in a full-page spread, including several pictures of Ekvall in a safari jacket outfit. He mentioned his "very strenuous exercise plan, which included swimming, tennis, hiking and cross-country skiing. He had just quit downhill skiing after breaking an arm. The wide-ranging article covered his years as a missionary on the Kansu-Tibetan border, his experiences as an Army captain in WW 2, as well as his years at the University of Washington. Interestingly, given that this interview was done in 1975 and the Vietnam War had recently ended with the fall of Saigon, he spoke of his "dovish views" regarding U.S. involvement in the long conflict in Southeast Asia and the spread of communism in the Far East. His perspective based on his years of life in Asia likely did not align with the majority view of conservative evangelicals at that time. Nevertheless, his last words in the article indicated where he stood as a follower of Christ: "I LOOK BACK on my life and ask what is the final word of what I have been and I've come to the conclusion the basic phrase is 'trying to be an interpreter—interpreting speech, interpreting language, interpreting the Word of God.'"[264]

During his time in Nyack, he visited the "Pretty Penny," the beautiful Upper Nyack home of Helen Hayes, once known as the "First Lady of American Theatre." Helen was married to Charles MacArthur, one of Bob's former classmates at the Wilson Academy, and son of "Daddy" MacArthur, one of A. B. Simpson's closest associates. Charles had gone on to become a famous and successful playwright on Broadway. After more than sixty years, Bob and Charles were reunited and had a great time recalling their years together at Wilson Academy.

Nyack College, May 1975, L. to R.) Blanche Griebenow, Marion Kerr, Cleo Evans, Carol Carlson, Robert Ekvall, Minnie Fesmire, Bonnie Carlsen.

This return and cordial reception at Nyack, gave Ekvall opportunity to reconnect with his relational and religious roots in the Alliance, the mission which had sent his parents to the West China border at the end of the 19th century. While back at the "Mount of Prayer and Blessing," he visited the C&MA's National Office recently relocated from New York City to Nyack. There, he spoke at length with C&MA mission officials about his thoughts on "missiology" and missionary preparation. While 'back east," he also met with the leadership of Christian Publications, Inc.

(CPI), the Alliance publishing house. He presented an idea for a series of books to help prepare missionaries being sent out to unreached people groups. Its purpose was to give the recruit an "in-depth, practical-yet-scholarly analysis by a veteran missionary" of the field, the people to be reached and their beliefs. While Ekvall's book proposal never saw the light of day, it apparently spurred CPI to begin the very popular *Jaffray Series* of "missionary portraits" that began coming out a few years later.

Ekvall later reiterated in a 1979 Wheaton interview this idea of a *"casebook for missions,"* which was to be his "particular contribution [regarding] the Tibetan religion as perceived by the missionary." The thirty-page unfinished manuscript, complete with scrawled-in corrections and additions, goes into great detail regarding "the gods of Tibet." The final section discusses the "Christian Religion *dKon mCHog,*" (the Rare Perfect), the Tibetan term for the "God" of the Bible, as chosen by Moravian missionary Bible translators in the 19th century. Ekvall ended the paper, apparently one section of a more extensive work, with a segment, "Interpreting Christian-Religion Doctrine in Tibetan-Religio Terminology." Even today, almost fifty years later, it has value for those called to take the Gospel to the Tibetan diaspora, or back to the Tibetan highland plateau, when God opens the door.[265]

In 1980, Bob traveled back east to meet with Christian Publications regarding his suggested series of missionary "case studies," and expressed his frustration at the lack of interest in the project. While the concept of a book for missionary preparation had merit, such a mission-focused series likely would have little commercial appeal, making it financially unfeasible. He then returned to Wheaton and was interviewed a second time at the Billy Graham Center Archive. While in town, he visited with his family and friends at Wheaton College. This was his last visit to Wheaton, although his traveling days were not over yet.

He Inadvertently Drove Off the Road

Back in Carbondale, he occasionally drove to Seattle to share tea and tsampa with his Tibetan friends. Unfortunately, due to his progressively poor eyesight, he inadvertently drove off the road destroying his car. He evidently had cataracts from years of living in high altitudes under extremely bright sunlight. After suffering a minor stroke, he moved from Carbondale to Enumclaw, a town in the foothills of Mount Rainier, where he spent most of his last years. Using a magnifying glass, he continued working on *Tibetan Breakthrough* until his sight failed. As a result, he did not finish his missionary account or *Attaché Trek*. However, Robert Carlson, son of Edwin Carlson, one of Bob's Alliance KTBM colleagues, wrote *Breakthrough: The Story of Bob and Betty Ekvall*, which provides a excellent condensed version of the Ekvall's missionary service and the conversion story of the Tebu villagers in Drangwa valley."[266]

David Jackson's chapter on "Life and Writings of Robert B. Ekvall (1898–1983)" refers to Bob's last years in Enumclaw. "Near the end of his life he worked for several years on an account of his life as a missionary, dealing in part with his own struggles of faith." He adds that some of Bob's friends believed that when he ceased to be a missionary, he "broke" with that part of his life and saw himself more as an anthropologist and ethnographer. One friend, who ran a store which sold imported Tibetan art and articles of interest to collectors, felt that Bob "appeared to be less doctrinaire and more tolerant than one would have expected from someone of his missionary background."[267] This view apparently reflected Bob's state of mind as he left the world of academics before gradually returned to his spiritual roots.

Bob had long pursued the publication of *The Lama Knows: A Tibetan Legend is Born*, printed in 1979. This novel of fact and fantasy, set in the same mountainous region where Ekvall had lived, relates the adventures of "The Earless One," a Buddhist lama, whose high spiritual achievements matched his lofty political goals. He was "as much at home on a horse with a rifle—or his girl—across the saddle, as when sitting, Buddha-like, in meditative trance."[268] While this wild "legend" was long on fiction, fact found its way into the narrative, since Ekvall had actually seen the "earless one" and heard him give a climatic speech on one occasion. Near the end of the novel, Ekvall, the "yellow head," appears: "Then the Yellow Head talked religion the way he does and preached of chosen saviors: a savior chosen by God and saviors chosen by men themselves. It was a good sermon . . ."[269]

While Bob's faith walk may have wavered during his years in the military and academia, his statements made at Nyack and Wheaton, and to his Presbyterian's pastor in Enumclaw, WA, all made in the late 1970s, point to a strong recommitment to Christ and the need to take the Gospel to all who have not heard. Just as clearly, he stressed the importance of the good news being communicated free from the cultural baggage and religious traditions of the one who carried the message to unreached and neglected peoples of this world.

In his 1979 interview made with Robert Shuster of the Billy Graham Center Archives at Wheaton College, he told of the people-movement "breakthrough" that occurred among the most violent nomad tribe in the Lhamo region after Betty's death. Years before, more than three hundred "braves" of the Drangwa Tebu tribe had attacked an Alliance station, trying to wipe out the missionary staff, but failed in their effort. Years later, in the months following Betty Ekvall's death in 1940, more than two thirds of Drangwa village came to Christ. When Bob Shuster, asked if the church survived the communist takeover of China and subjugation of Tibet, Ekvall replied that he had no knowledge about the church's survival, but remarked:

> It's . . . it's out in . . . it's in gorges and country that's terrible rough and it's out . . . out of range of current . . . of what might seep . . . seep through the border because they had no . . . They had very little contact with the border except in robbing. [Laugh] I don't know. But, the Word doesn't return void.[270]

Bob's statement revealed his belief in the staying power of the gospel that carries one through years of faith-fraying circumstances to a deeper, stronger devotion to the One who walks with us in the valley of the shadow of death.

The Tall "Long Nose" Became a Magnet

Following the gradual melting of the frigid relationship between China and the U.S. in the late 1970s, which led to the establishment of full diplomatic relations in 1979, China began to open the country for international visitors. Rev. William Kerr of the C&MA joined one of the early tour groups that same year. At Bob's request, while in Peking, Kerr obtained copies of magazine articles Bob had written years before about potential archeological sites in Tibet. On his second visit in April 1980, Bill Kerr led a missions tour and invited Bob to go with the support of the C&MA. As they visited different cities, the tall "long nose" became a magnet as soon as he spoke. People were stunned that this old-white haired American sounded like a native-born Chinese. They were more stunned when he explained that he was in fact native born! These interactions opened mouths and doors that most tour groups never accessed. Given his age, the question often came up as to why he remained so sturdy and strong. He answered by pointing upward, saying "God's good grace." The crowd reaction varied from disdain, to puzzlement, to friendly interest.[271]

Bob visited the offices of high government officials who had been his adversaries in the late 1940s and 1950s when he had been the "go-to-guy" Chinese-English interpreter for the U.S. Army and diplomatic teams in Peking, Panmunjom, Paris and Geneva. Former Chinese foes who had fought with Bob over words and nuances of meaning years before now smiled and helped clear away bureaucratic red tape so that Kerr's tour group could visit sites of interest to the members of the tour with mission backgrounds. Due to his ability to gain favor with the "minders" who accompanied the tour, he and Bill Kerr visited a house church in *Sian* of more than two hundred members. They learned much about the state of the Church in China. While not permitted to visit Kansu, his birthplace or "God's Acre," the little hillside cemetery next to the Lupa mission station and grave of Betty, his first wife, Bob considered the trip a success and thanked the C&MA for making it possible to visit China again after more than thirty years of absence.

Gradually, the "old lion" succumbed to the ravages of aging. His sight worsened, and his doctor recommended for his heart that he "have a single glass of French red wine with lunch each day . . . ."[272] Eventually, his health declined to the point that his daughter, Karin, insisted he move to a retirement home in Seattle for better care. One of his last visitors was Robert Carlson, author of *Breakthrough: The Story of Bob and Betty Ekvall*. Bob Carlson had known "Uncle Bob" as one of his heroes on the Kansu-Tibetan border. His father, Ed, had been Ekvall's closest friend on the field. The two Bobs had stayed in touch over the decades; and one last time, they fellowshipped and prayed together.

The Growing-Old Ones Generally Feel Much Better

Ekvall's last scholarly paper, "THE HIGH-PASTURAGE ONES OF TIBET ALSO GROW OLD," published in *The Briefings of the American Philosophical Society*, December 1980, contained a line which seemed to sum up his own feelings as one of the "growing-old" ones.[273] "The growing-old ones generally feel much better as they return to the tent and its routines." He described how, in later life, elderly Tibetan nomads gradually turn over the affairs of their "tent" to their sons and daughters in order to dedicate themselves more assiduously to the necessary merit-gaining practices of Tibetan Buddhism to increase their "karmic account," easing their deathly passage from this life to their next incarnation. Robert Ekvall did not base his faith nor place his eternal fate in such "works;" rather, he rested in the God of grace who was waiting to meet him as he passed from this world to the next. In a very real sense, those evocative words of the nomadic Tibetan "growing-old ones" speak to the comfort of returning to "the tent and its routines." Robert Ekvall's return to the "tent" of his Christian faith and family brought great peace and comfort to him in his final years.

After his third and final stroke at the Capitol Hill rest home, Robert Ekvall passed away on May 4, 1983, 85 years old. At the memorial service held at the Queen Ann Lutheran Church where he had become a member after returning to Seattle, Rev. James A. Davey, pastor of the North Seattle Alliance Church, representing the C&MA and Nyack College, brought a floral arrangement to the service. "Robert D. Carlson, former missionary to Hong Kong, who had grown up on the Tibetan border near the Ekvalls, gave a very moving eulogy, which for me at least set his life in proper perspective."[274]

Robert Brainard Ekvall, 1975.

In some ways, Robert B. Ekvall's life echoed the lives of some of Scripture's most outstanding figures. Like Job, he suffered deep and successive losses of loved ones, and like Job, he wondered why. What had he done wrong? What was God's purpose? And like Job, God's silence eventually led him to a deeper knowledge of His inscrutable ways. In another Bible luminary, Solomon, we see a man who experienced the manifest presence of God, a seeker of knowledge and wisdom who later wandered from close communion to years of spiritual wandering, before returning to the Lord in his last years.

Most missionary biographies have a bit of "hagiography" in them, telling the story of a hero of the faith who attempted much for God and expected great things from God, whose exemplary lives merited admiration. This is not that kind of story. Instead, *Brave Son of Tibet* tells of a man who served His Lord well, an amazingly effective missionary whose life of service was cut short by tragedy. Subsequent years in the military and diplomatic world saw him gradually "take leave" of his close walk with Christ. His latter career at the University of Washington provided ample opportunity to see the vanity and venality of the world of academic achievement and acclaim. In those last years, godly friends sought him out and retirement gave him time to reflect. Robert Ekvall not only made his peace with God, but he once again became passionate about taking the faith of Jesus Christ to the people of Tibet and the unreached worldwide. That was what really mattered for him. He likely went to his grave with many of his questions still unanswered; yet, in the end he could say with Solomon, "Let us hear the conclusion of the whole matter: Fear God and keep His commandments, for this is man's all" (Eccl 12:13 NKJV).

Endnotes

Chapter 1

1   Ekvall, *Faithful*, 24.
2   *Journal News*, D1.
3   Jones, *Cousins*, 15.
4   Ekvall, *Outposts*, 8.
5   Ekvall, *Outposts*, 213.
6   Jamieson, *Way*, 103.
7   Jamieson, *Way*, 107.
8   King, *Genuine*, 153.
9   Ekvall, *Gateway*, 62.

Chapter 2

10   Shuster, Interview, 2.
11   Willard, *Fire*, 105.
12   Ekvall, *Faithful*, 29.

Chapter 3

13   Ekvall, *Tibetan Breakthrough*, 5.
14   Ekvall, *Tibetan Breakthrough*, 4.
15   Ekvall, *Tibetan Breakthrough*, 8.
16   Ekvall, *Tibetan Breakthrough*, 9.
17   *Alliance Weekly*, "Greetings," 791.
18   Ekvall, *Tibetan Breakthrough*, 13.
19   Ekvall, *Tibetan Breakthrough*, 14.
20   Ekvall, *Tibetan Breakthrough*, 15.
21   Ekvall, *Tibetan Breakthrough*, 18.
22   https://en.wikipedia.org/wiki/Tibetan_script
23   Carlson, *Breakthrough*, 14.
24   Ekvall, *Tibetan Breakthrough*, 18.
25   Ekvall, *Gateway*, 180.
26   Ekvall, *Tibetan Breakthrough*, 19.
27   Ekvall, *Tibetan Breakthrough*, 21.
28   Ekvall, *Tibetan Breakthrough*, 24.
29   Ekvall, *Tibetan Breakthrough*, 24.

Chapter 4

30   Ekvall, *Tibetan Breakthrough*, 26.
31   Ekvall, *Tibetan Breakthrough*, 26.
32   Ekvall, *Tibetan Breakthrough*, 28.
33   Ekvall, *Tibetan Breakthrough*, 29–30.
34   Ekvall, *Tibetan Breakthrough*, 31.
35   Ekvall, *Tibetan Breakthrough*, 31.
36   Ekvall, *Tibetan Breakthrough*, 35.
37   Ekvall, *Tibetan Breakthrough*, 36.
38   Ekvall, *Tibetan Breakthrough*, 37.
39   Ekvall, *Tibetan Breakthrough*, 37.
40   Ekvall, *Tibetan Breakthrough*, 38.
41   Ekvall, *Tibetan Breakthrough*, 41.
42   Ekvall, *Tibetan Breakthrough*, 45.
43   Ekvall, *Tibetan Breakthrough*, 45.
44   Jones, *Only Thibet*, 141–42.
45   Ekvall, *Tibetan Breakthrough*, 52–53.
46   Ekvall, *Tibetan Breakthrough*, 53.
47   Ekvall, *Tibetan Breakthrough*, 47.
48   Ekvall, *Tibetan Breakthrough*, 61–62.
49   Ekvall, *Tibetan Breakthrough*, 62.
50   Ekvall, *Tibetan Breakthrough*, 62.
51   Ekvall, *Tibetan Breakthrough*, 64.
52   Ekvall, *Tibetan Breakthrough*, 65.
53   Ekvall, *Gateway*, 183.
54   Ekvall, *Tibetan Breakthrough*, 71.
55   Ekvall, *Tibetan Breakthrough*, 75.
56   Ekvall, *Tibetan Breakthrough*, 79.
57   Ekvall, *Tibetan Breakthrough*, 83.
58   Ekvall, *Tibetan Breakthrough*, 83.
59   Ekvall, *Tibetan Breakthrough*, 85.
60   Ekvall, *Tibetan Breakthrough*, 87.
61   Ekvall, *Tibetan Breakthrough*, 88.
62   Ekvall, *Tibetan Breakthrough*, 91.
63   Ekvall, *Tibetan Breakthrough*, 92.
64   Ekvall, *Tibetan Breakthrough*, 93.
65   Ekvall, *Tibetan Breakthrough*, 96–97.
66   Ekvall, *Tibetan Breakthrough*, 98.

Chapter 5

67   Ekvall, *Tibetan Breakthrough*, 99.
68   Ekvall, *Tibetan Breakthrough*, 101.
69   Ekvall, *Tibetan Breakthrough*, 102.
70   Ekvall, *Tibetan Breakthrough*, 102–3.
71   Ekvall, *Tibetan Breakthrough*, 103.
72   Ekvall, *Tibetan Breakthrough*, 104.
73   Ekvall, *Tibetan Breakthrough*, 107.

74   Ekvall, *Tibetan Breakthrough*, 105.
75   Ekvall, *Tibetan Breakthrough*, 109.
76   Ekvall, *Tibetan Breakthrough*, 109.
77   Ekvall, *Tibetan Breakthrough*, 110.
78   Ekvall, *Tibetan Breakthrough*, 110–11.
79   Ekvall, *Tibetan Breakthrough*, 113.
80   Ekvall, *Tibetan Breakthrough*, 120.
81   Ekvall, *Tibetan Breakthrough*, 122.
82   Ekvall, *Tibetan Breakthrough*, 124–25.
83   Ekvall, *Tibetan Breakthrough*, 126.
84   Jones, *Cousins*, 66–67.
85   Ekvall, *Tibetan Breakthrough*, 127.
86   Ekvall, *Tibetan Breakthrough*, 134.
87   Ekvall, *Gateway*, 79.
88   *Alliance Weekly*, "Important," 658.
89   Ekvall, *Tibetan Breakthrough*, 137–38.

Chapter 6

90   Ekvall, *Tibetan Breakthrough*, 159.
91   Ekvall, *Tibetan Breakthrough*, 160.
92   Ekvall, *Tibetan Breakthrough*, 161.
93   Ekvall, *Tibetan Breakthrough*, 161.
94   Ekvall, *Tibetan Breakthrough*, 162.
95   Ekvall, *Tibetan Breakthrough*, 163.
96   Ekvall, *Tibetan Breakthrough*, 163.
97   Ekvall, *Tibetan Breakthrough*, 164.
98   Ekvall, *Tibetan Breakthrough*, 164.
99   Ekvall, *Tibetan Breakthrough*, 165.
100   Jones, *Cousins*, 82–86.
101   Users/Owner/Dropbox/PC/Downloads/The%20Shining%20One%20HIS-
      TORY.pdf.
102   Ekvall, *Tibetan Breakthrough*, 11–14.
103   Ekvall, *Tibetan Breakthrough*, 11–16.
104   Carlson, *Breakthrough*, 44.
105   Ekvall, *God's Miracle*, 19.
106   Ekvall, *God's Miracle*, 21.
107   Jones, *Cousins*, 101–5.
108   Ekvall to Simpson, August 5, 1932.
109   Carlson, *Breakthrough*, 46.
110   *Research and Reference, C&MA in China*, 677–78.
111   *Research and Reference, C&MA in China*, 678.
112   Ekvall, *God's Miracle*, 22–23.
113   Ekvall, God's Miracle, 26–27.
114   Ekvall, God's Miracle, 29.

Chapter 7

115   Schaber to *Prairie Publications*, November 18, 2004.

116   Lary, Chinese People, 86.
117   Ekvall, *Attaché Trek*, 54.
118   Carlson, *Breakthrough,* 50.
119   Alliance Weekly, April 19, 1941, "Tibetan Voices," 250.
120   Carlson, *Breakthrough,* 51.
121   *The Alliance Weekly*, February 8, 1941, "In Memoriam," 86.
122   *The Alliance Weekly*, February 8, 1941, "In Memoriam," 86.
123   Carlsen, *In Search*, 53.
124   Rivard, *Voices*, 362.
125   Shuster 1, Interview 1, 23.
126   Carlsen, *In Search*, 53.
127   Carlson, *Breakthrough,* 55.
128   Shuster 1, Interview 1, 23.

Chapter 8

129   Ekvall, *Trail*, 3.
130   Ekvall, *Attaché Trek*, 110.
131   Ekvall, *Trail*, 5–6.
132   Ekvall, *Attaché Trek*, 54–55.
133   Ekvall, *Trail*, 6.
134   Ekvall, *Dark Camps*, 15.
135   Ekvall, *Dark Camps*, 17.
136   Philips, *Kept*, 12.
137   Ekvall, *Dark Camps*, 12.
138   Philips, *Kept*, 15.
139   Shuster, Interview 1, 35.
140   Smith, *China Experience*, 253.
141   Philips, *Kept*, 24.
142   Galt, *Journey*, 22.
143   Smith, *China Experience*, 253.
144   Ekvall, *Dark Camps*, 22.

Chapter 9

145   Ekvall, *Faithful*, 29.
146   Ekvall, *Faithful*, 29.
147   Ekvall, *Faithful*, 30.
148   Ekvall, *Faithful*, 31.
149   Ekvall, *Faithful*, 39.
150   Ekvall, *Faithful*, 39.
151   Omaha Gospel Tabernacle Bulletin, 9.
152   Kerr, Interview.
153   Ekvall, *Attaché Trek*, 1.
154   Ekvall, *Attaché Trek*, 5.
155   Ekvall, *Attaché Trek*, 6.
156   Ekvall, *Attaché Trek*, 6–7.
157   Ekvall, *Attaché Trek*, 7–8.
158   Ekvall, *Attaché Trek*, 8.

159　Ekvall, *Attaché Trek*, 12.
160　Ekvall, *Attaché Trek*, 12.
161　Ekvall, *Dark Camps*, 23.
162　Ekvall, *Attaché Trek*, 15.
163　Ekvall, *Attaché Trek*, 18.
164　Ekvall, *Attaché Trek*, 42.
165　Ekvall, *Attaché Trek*, 49.
166　Ekvall, *Attaché Trek*, 51.
167　Ekvall, *Attaché Trek*, 68.

Chapter 10

168　Ekvall *Attaché Trek*, 90.
169　Ekvall, *Attaché Trek*, 94.
170　Ekvall, *Attaché Trek*, 101.
171　Ekvall, *Attaché Trek*, 109.
172　Ekvall, *Attaché Trek*, 134.
173　Ekvall, *Attaché Trek*, 136.
174　Ekvall, *Attaché Trek*, 144.
175　Ekvall, *Attaché Trek*, 150.
176　Ekvall, *Attaché Trek*, 155.
177　Ekvall, *Attaché Trek*, 154.
178　Ekvall, *Attaché Trek*, 157.
179　Ekvall, *Attaché Trek*, 161.
180　Ekvall, *Attaché Trek*, 167.
181　Ekvall, *Attaché Trek*, 174.
182　Ekvall, *Attaché Trek*, 176.
183　Ekvall, *Attaché Trek*, 181.
184　Ekvall, *Attaché Trek*, 186.
185　Ekvall, *Attaché Trek*, 187.
186　Ekvall, *Attaché Trek*, 190.
187　Ekvall, *Attaché Trek*, 200.
188　Ekvall, *Attaché Trek*, 206.
189　Ekvall, *Attaché Trek*, 212.
190　J. Bray email to D. Jones, "Status of Tibet," January 8, 2023.
191　Ekvall, *Attaché Trek*, 223.
192　Ekvall, *Attaché Trek*, 210.

Chapter 11

193　Ekvall *Attaché Trek*, 151.
194　Ekvall, *Attaché Trek*, 236.
195　Ekvall, *Attaché Trek*, 237.
196　Ekvall, *Attaché Trek*, 255.
197　Ekvall, *Attaché Trek*, 258.
198　Ekvall, *Attaché Trek*, 261.
199　Ekvall, *Attaché Trek*, 263.
200　Ekvall, *Attaché Trek*, 265.
201　Ekvall, *Attaché Trek*, 268.

202   Ekvall, *Attaché Trek*, 278.
203   Ekvall, *Attaché Trek*, 275.
204   Ekvall, *Attaché Trek*, 278.

Chapter 12

205   Ekvall, *Attaché Trek*, 283.
206   Ekvall, *Attaché Trek*, 287.
207   Ekvall, *Attaché Trek*, 287.
208   Ekvall, *Attaché Trek*, 290.
209   Jones, *Cousins Peacemakers*, 126–34.
210   Shuster, Interview 1, 37.
211   Ekvall, *Attaché Trek*, 292.
212   Ekvall, *Attaché Trek*, 294.
213   Ekvall, *Attaché Trek*, 303.
214   Ekvall, *Attaché Trek*, 306.
215   Ekvall, *Attaché Trek*, 310.
216   Ekvall, *Attaché Trek*, 313.
217   Ekvall, *Attaché Trek*, 314.
218   Ekvall, *Attaché Trek*, 314.
219   Ekvall, *Attaché Trek*, 321.
220   Smith, *China Pilot*, 48–49.
221   Shuster, Interview 3, 18–19.
222   Ekvall, *Attaché Trek*, 324.
223   Ekvall, *Attaché Trek*, 329.
224   Ekvall, *Attaché Trek*, 332.
225   Ekvall, *Attaché Trek*, 340.
226   Ekvall, *Attaché Trek*, 7.
227   Ekvall, *Attaché Trek*, 8.
228   Laird, *Into Tibet*, 81.
229   Laird, *Into Tibet*, 81.
230   Ekvall, *Attaché Trek*, 9.
231   Ekvall, *Attaché Trek*, 10.
232   Ekvall, *Attaché Trek*, 10.

Chapter 13

233   Halberstam, *Coldest Winter*, 1.
234   Ekvall, *Faithful*, 21–22.
235   Patterson, *Patterson of Tibet*, 289.
236   Conboy, *CIA's*, 15.
237   Hino, *Three Mountains*, 614.
238   Ekvall, *Faithful*, 22.
239   Ekvall, *Faithful*, 23.
240   Ekvall, *Curriculum Vitae*.
241   Ekvall, *Faithful*, 23.
242   Ekvall, *Faithful*, 46.
243   Ekvall, *Faithful*, 7.
244   Ekvall, *Faithful*, 9–10.

245　Ekvall, *Faithful,* 47.

246　Ekvall, *Faithful,* 49.

247　Ekvall, *Faithful,* 52.

248　E. Ekvall e-mail to R. Smith, "Bob Ekvall Chronology" December 5, 2003.

Chapter 14

249　tacomalibrary.contentdm.oclc.org/digital/collection/p17061coll12/id/17493/.

250　Leeper email to Jones.

251　Hino, *Three Mountains,* 615.

252　Hino, *Three Mountains,* 609.

253　Hino, *Three Mountains,* 617–18.

254　Hino, *Three Mountains,* 617–18.

255　Ekvall e-mail to Ray Smith.

256　Hino, *Three Mountains,* 619.

257　Smith email to Jones.

258　Hino, *Three Mountains,* 619, 635.

259　Kerr, Interview Ekvall.

260　Jones, Interview with M. Smith.

261　Hino, *Three Mountains,* 620.

Chapter 15

262　Taylor, Interview with Ekvall.

263　Taylor, Interview with Ekvall.

264　*Sunday Journal News,* FAMILY 1D.

265　Shuster, Interview 1 with Ekvall, 31.

266　Carlson, *Breakthrough,* 52–55.

267　Hino, *Three Mountains,* 620.

268　Hino, *Three Mountains,* 622.

269　Ekvall, *Lama,* 94.

270　Shuster, Interview 1 with Ekvall, 25.

271　Shuster, Interview 2 with Ekvall, 17.

272　Hino, *Three Mountains,* 620.

273　Ekvall, "High-Pasturage," 436.

274　Davey to Nanfelt.

Appendix

Publications of Robert B. Ekvall

ROBERT EKVALL WROTE AND published eleven books and co-authored three more in addition to writing eight unpublished manuscripts. He published thirty-two academic articles in a variety of magazines and journals, twenty-three religious articles in missions publications, and another seventeen scholarly research papers while at the University of Washington for the Inner Asia Colloquium. While at the University, he worked as an instructor, research assistant and later curator of the Burke Museum. This list of publications is a composite made from the bibliographies of David Jackson (*Three Mountains and Seven Rivers*, "Life and Writings of Robert B. Ekvall [189801893]) and a bibliography composed by Robert Carlson, author of *Breakthrough: The Story of Bob and Betty Ekvall*.

Books

(1938) *Gateway to Tibet*. Harrisburg, PA: Christian Publications, 198 pp.

(1938) *Monologues from the Chinese*. Harrisburg, PA: Christian Publications, 38 pp.

(1939) *After Fifty Years*. Harrisburg, PA: Christian Publications, 280 pp.

(1939). *Cultural Relations on the Kansu-Tibetan Border*. Chicago: The University of Chicago Press, 87 pp.

(1946) *Tibetan Voices*. New York: Harper, 63 pp.

(1952) *Tibetan Skylines*. New York: Farrar, Straus & Young, 239 pp.

(1954) *Tents Against the Sky*. New York: Farrar, Straus & Cudahy; London: Gollancz, 264 pp. Reprint, Wheaton, IL: Good News Publishers, 1978

(1960) *Faithful Echo*. New York: Twayne, 125 pp.

(1964) *Religious Observances in Tibet: Patterns and Function*. Chicago: The University of Chicago Press, 313 pp.

(1968) *Fields on the Hoof: Nexus of Tibetan Nomadic Pastoralism*. Edited by George and Louise Spindler. Case Studies in Cultural Anthropology. New York: Holt, Rinehart & Winston, 100 pp. Reprint, Prospect Heights, IL: Waveland Press, 1983.

(1969) Cassinelli, C. W., and Robert B. Ekvall. *A Tibetan Principality: The Political System of Sa sKya*. Ithaca, NY: Cornell University Press, 423 pp.

(1969) Norbu, Thubten Jigme, and Robert B. Ekvall, trans. *The Younger Brother Don yod . . .* Bloomington, IN: Indiana University Press, 148 pp.

(1979) *The Lama Knows: A Tibetan Legend Is Born*. New Delhi: Oxford. Reprint, Novato, CA: Chandler and Sharp, 1981, 127 pp.

(1987) Downs, James F., and Robert B. Ekvall. *Tibetan Pilgrimage: Worship in Movement and Ethos in Action*. Tokyo: Institute for the Study of Languages and Cultures, Tokyo University of Foreign Studies, 155 pp.

Fields on the Hoof has been translated into Chinese and produced in mimeographed version. *Cultural Relations on the Kansu-Tibetan Border* is reported to have been translated into Japanese by the Japanese War Department during World War II, but Ekvall himself never saw a copy. *Tents Against the Sky* was translated into French and published as *Tentes Contre le Ciel* (Paris: Stock, 1959), and into Spanish and published as *Tiendas en las Cumbres* (Miami: Editorial Vida, 1982).

Unpublished Manuscripts

"Attaché Trek: China 1947–1948," n.d., 343 pp. An unfinished autobiographical account of his experiences as Assistant Military Attaché in Nanjing, China. Likely done during retiral, 1973–1983.

Dark Camps, n.d., 23 pp. Prose poems on the death of his wife up to his second marriage.

"The Star Spangled Banner and Shark Fins," n.d. An article on President Richard Nixon's visit to China; magazine editors considered it dated and irrelevant.

The Story of Ren: An Ideographic Fantasy, n.d.

The Tibetan Nomadic Pastoralist, 1964. Paper for the Wenner-Gren Foundation for Anthropological Research Symposium.

Tibetan Breakthrough, n.d., 186 pp. An unfinished autobiographical account of his years as a missionary which ends in 1929. Apparently done during retiral years, 1973 to 1983.

Tibetan Religion as Perceived by the Missionary, n.d., 30 pp. Two chapters of a monograph for a proposed but still-born series on non-Christian religions.

Universals of Tibetan Religious Observance and Their Function, 83 pp. Perhaps preliminary to *Religious Observances in Tibet*.

Magazine Articles

"Tipkah." *China Journal (of Science and Arts)* 3 (1925) 422–24.

"We Visit the King of Ngawa in Eastern Tibet." *Asia (and the Americas) Magazine* 29 (1929) 724–30; 742–45.

"Shadow of the Robber's God." *Asia (and the Americas) Magazine* 37 (1937) 439–40.

"Haunted House." *Asia (and the Americas) Magazine* 38 (1938) 112–13.

"On the SkorBa Path." *Asia (and the Americas) Magazine* 38 (1938) 491–93.

"The Pugilism of Jamtzen." *Asia (and the Americas) Magazine* 38 (1938) 440–42.

"Tam-dro Avenges His Father." *Asia (and the Americas) Magazine* 38 (1938) 551–53.

"On the Road to Tibet: When the Traveler Jumps Off into the Unknown." *The New York Times*, Sunday, October 16, 1938, 8.

"The Eared Pheasant." *Natural History* 43 (1939) 47–51.

"Tales from the Tibetan Border." *Asia (and the Americas) Magazine* 40 (1940) 478–80.

"A Tibetan Hunt." *Asia (and the Americas) Magazine* 41 (1941) 43–46.

"Tibet's Pilgrim's Progress." *Asia (and the Americas) Magazine* 42 (1942) 10–14, 111–14.

"Culture Comes to Tibetans." *Asia (and the Americas) Magazine* (1944) 110–14.

"Five Universals of Tibetan Religious Observance." *Oriens* 6-2 (1953) 334–43.

"Some Differences in Tibetan Land Tenure and Utilization." *Sinologia* 4-1 (1954/56) 39–48.

"Mis sTong: The Tibetan Custom of Life Indemnity." *Sociologus* 4-2 (1954) 136–45.

"Significance of Thirteen as a Symbolic Number in Tibetan." *Journal of the American Oriental Society* 79 (1959) 188–92.

"The Double Role of the Panchen Lama." *Western World* 12 (1959) 41–44.

"Three Categories of Inmates within Tibetan Monasteries: Status and Function." *Central Asiatic Journal* 5-3 (1959/60) 206–20.

"Tibetan Culture: in Raja Hutheesing ed., *Tibet Fights for Freedom*, Bombay, Orient Longmans. (1960) i-iv 1–1.

"The Tibetan Self-Image." *Pacific Affairs* 33.4 (1960) 375–82.

"The Nomadic Pattern of Living Among the Tibetans as Preparation for War." *American Anthropologist* (1961) 1250–63.

"Historical Sites and Cultural Relics." *Current Scene* 27 (1962) 1–11.

"Role of the Interpreter." *The Texas Quarterly* 5-3 (1962) 193–200.

"Role of the Dog in Tibetan Nomadic Society." *Central Asiatic Journal* 8-3 (1963) 163–73.

"A Note on 'Live Blood' as Food among the Tibetans." *Man* 175 (1963) 45–46.

"Some Aspects of Divination in Tibetan Society." *Ethnology* 1-1 (1963) 31–39.

"Note on Water Utilization and Rule in the Sakya Domain, Ekvall, Robert B., and James F. Downs." *Journal of Asia Studies* 22–23 (1963) 293–303.

"A Seminar on Tibetan Society and Culture." *Current Anthropology* 4-4 (1963) 368–70.

"A Tibetan Performs the Circumambulation Rite." *Sociologus* 11–11 (1964) 86–89.

"Law and the Individual among the Tibetan Nomads." *American Anthropologist* 66–65 (1964) 1110–15.

"Peace and War Among the Tibetan Nomads." *American Anthropologist* 66–65 (1964) 1119–48.

"Strangers in the Land: Chinese Colonialism in Tibet." A review of *Tibetan Sourcebook* (Ling). *Current Scene* 3.11 (1965).

"Animal and Social Types in the Exploitation of the Tibetan Plateau." By Robert B. Ekvall and James F. Downs. In *Man, Culture and Animals*, edited by Anthony Leeds and Andrew P. Vayda, 169–84. Symposium Series no. 78. Washington, DC: American Association for the Advancement of Science, 1965.

"Tibetans in Switzerland." *The Tibet Society Newsletter* 1–2 (1967) 113–17.

"P'iao Drift." *The Texas Quarterly* 12–12 (1969) 22–25.

"Demographic Aspects of Tibetan Nomadic Pastoralism." In *Population Growth: Anthropological Implications*, by Brian Spooner, 269–85. Cambridge: MIT Press, 1972.

"The Tibetan Nomad and His Horse." *Coyote Journal* 10 (1974) 66–83.

"Tibetan Nomadic Pastoralists: Environment, Personality and Ethos." *Proceedings of the American Philosophical Society* 118–16 (1974) 519–37.

"Correlation of Contradictions: A Tibetan Semantic Device." In *Language and Thought: Anthropological Issues*, edited by W. C. McCormick and S. A. Wurm, 235–36. The Hague, 1977. Reprint in J. F. Fisher, ed, *Himalayan Anthropology* (The Hague, 1978) 251–62.

"The High-Pasturage Ones of Tibet Also Grow Old." *Proceedings of the American Philosophical Society* 124–26 (1980) 429–37.

Many of the chapters of *Tibetan Skylines* appeared originally in *Asia* magazine. Some other articles which were not reprinted in *Skylines* are:

"Coins in the Crucible." November 1928.

"We Visit the King of Ngawa." September 1929.

"Revolt of the Crescent in Western China." December 1929.

"The Bombing of Chungking." August 1939.

"Ruins, Skulls and Rooftrees." February 1940.

"Culture Comes to Tibetans." March 1944.

Missions Publications

"Still Onward into Tibet." The Alliance Weekly, October 23, 1926, p. 688.

"Alliance Program of Advance in N.E. Tibet." New York: Christian and Missionary Alliance, 1926, 16 pp.

"The Opportunity in Northwest Tibet." *The Alliance Weekly*, August 27, 1927, p. 570f.

"The Next Outpost in Far Tibet." *The Alliance Weekly*, October 8, 1927, p. 666.

"Westward Into Tibet." *The Alliance Weekly*, October 15, 1927, p. 681f.

"The Call of Far Interior." *The Alliance Weekly*, October 22, 1927, p. 698f.

"Tibetan Ways." *The Alliance Weekly*, January 28, 1928, p. 58f.

"Tibetan Fires." *The Alliance Weekly*, February 18, 1928, p. 104f.

"Tibetan Prayers." *The Alliance Weekly*, March 17, 1928, p. 170f.

"Tibetan Doors." *The Alliance Weekly*, April 14, 1928, p. 232f.

These four articles were reprinted as a booklet entitled "Things Tibetan."

"How Long, Lord, How Long." *The Alliance Weekly*, May 17, 1930, p. 17.

"Getting a Foothold on the Tibetan Border." *The Alliance Weekly*, May 15, 1930, p. 168.

"Leaves from the Log of a Missionary Yak Caravan." *The Alliance Weekly*, October 10, 1931, p. 664.

"Pray for Him" *Kansu Tibetan Border News*, Vol. I #2, July 1934, pp. 2–4

"Four Years After." *The Alliance Weekly*, July 11, 1931, p. 447f.

"Program Versus Reality in Northeast Tibet." *The Alliance Weekly*, September 24, 1932, p. 616.

"An Open Door into Golok Territory." *The Alliance Weekly*, December 10, 1932, p. 798.

"The Ever Present Lord." *The Alliance Weekly*, May 6, 1933, pp. 276f. and 286.

"Conference Notes." *The Alliance Weekly,* September 23, 1933, p. 601.
"Our Foreign Mailbag, Untitled letter." *The Alliance Weekly,* December 12, 1934, p. 809.
"Behold, I Make All Things New." *The Alliance Weekly,* December 26, 1936, p. 824.
"God's Miracle in the Heart of a Tibetan." New York: The Christian and Missionary Alliance, 1936, 29 pp.
"A Missionary Statesman." *The Alliance Weekly,* in three parts: part 1, May 22, 1937; part 2, July 10, 1937; part 3, August 28, 1937.
"A Land Strange and Far." *The Regions Beyond—Newsletter of the Kansu-Tibetan Border Mission,* Vol. II, #2, 1941, pp. 6–10.

Reviews of Articles

Allen S. Whiting and Sheng Shih-ts'ai. 1958. *Sinkiang: Pawn or Pivot? Journal of Asian Studies,* 1959, vol. 18–14.
David Crockett Graham. 1959. *The Customs and Religion of the Ch'iang. Journal of the American Oriental Society,* vol. 79, pp. 58–61.
Peter Goullard. 1959. *Land of the Lamas: Adventures in Secret Tibet. Journal of Asian Studies,* vol. 19, 1960, p. 115.
Humphrey Clark, tr. 1958. *The Message of Milarepa: New Light upon the Tibetan Way. Journal of Asian Studies,* vol. 19, 1960, pp. 60–61.
Raja Hutheesing, ed. 1960. *Tibet Fights for Freedom: A White Book.* Review of Frank Moraes 1960, *The Revolt in Tibet;* and Review of George Patterson. 1960. *Tibet in Revolt. The China Quarterly,* no. 4, 1960, pp. 123–26.
Chanakya Sen (Pseud. of B. Sen Gupta). 1960. *Tibet Disappears: A Documentary History of Tibet's International Status, the Great Rebellion and its Aftermath. Journal of Asian Studies,* vol. 20, 1961, p. 534.
A. K. Gordon. 1961. *The Hundred Thousand Songs: Selections from Milarepa, Poet-Saint of Tibet. Journal of Asian Studies,* vol. 20, Nov. 1961, pp. 88–89.
Margaret W. Fisher, L. Rose, and R.A. Huttenback. 1963. *Himalayan Battleground: Sino-Indian Rivalry in Ladakh. Journal of Asian Studies,* vol. 23, 1964, pp. 313–14.
"Strangers in the Land; Chinese Colonialism in Tibet." Review of Nai-min ling, ed. 1964, *Tibetan Sourcebook. Current Scene,* vol. 3–11, Jan. 15, 1965, pp. 1–10.
W. D. Shakabpa. 1968. *Tibet: A Political History. The Asian Student,* March 30, 1968.
G. Tucci. *Tibet: Land of Snows. Journal of Asian Studies,* vol. 27–24, 1968.
Thubten Jigme Norbu and Colin M. Turnbull. 1968. *Tibet, its History, Religion and People. The Asian Student,* May 31, 1969.
Fokke Sierksma. 1966. *Tibet's Terrifying Deities: Sex and Aggression in Religious Acculturation. Indo-Iranian Journal,* vol. 11–14, 1969, pp. 318–20.
Union Research Institute. 1968. *Tibet 1950–967, The Asian Student,* September 27, 1969.
Samten G. Karmay. 1972. *The Treasury of Good Sayings: A Tibetan History of Bon. The Asian Student,* March 3, 1973, pp. 11–12.
Review of Stephen Beyer. *The Cult of Tara: Magic and Ritual in Tibet, The Asian Student,* January 4, 1975, p. 12.
Alex Wayman. 1973. *The Buddhist Tantras: Light of Indo-Tibetan Esoterism. The Asian Student,* January 4, 1975, p. 12.

Papers for University of Washington Inner Asia Colloquium

"Five Universals of Tibetan Religion." November 12, 1958.

"The Religion of the Tibetans and Their Subjective Response." April 7, 1959.

"A Tibetan Performs the Circumambulation Rite." April 18, 1959.

"Religious Background: 'Pre-Buddhist Belief and Practice.'" July 24, 1959.

"Three Categories of Inmates within Tibetan Monasteries—Status and Function." October 27, 1959.

"The Attitude of Dad Pa (Faith)." November 25, 1959.

"sKor Ba (circumambulation), February 9, 1960.

"The Tibetan Self-Image." April 5, 1960.

"The Nomadic Pattern of Living as Preparation for War." May 10, 1960.

"A Tibetan Performs the Circumambulation Rite." May 19, 1960.

"Wilderness Man: A Study of Tibetan Nomadism." July 12, 1960.

"Chap. VII of Wilderness Man." November 1, 1960.

"Note on Rus (bone): Its Relationship to Tibetan Lineages and Surnames." April 18, 1961.

"The Practice of Chos aDon (Religion Intone) I." July 18, 1961.

"The Practice of Chos aDon (Religion Intone) II." July 25, 1961.

"Religious Observances: Form and Function in Tibetan Society." October 12, 1961.

"Chap. IX: Mo (Divination)." January 11, 1962.

Biographical and Bibliographical Articles By Others

Jackson, David P. "The Life and Writings of Robert Brainerd Ekvall (1898–1983): Missionary, Soldier-Interpreter and Observer of Tibetan Nomadic Life." In *Three Mountains and Seven Rivers*, edited by Shoun Hino & Toshihiro Wada, 609–35. Delhi: Motilal Barnasidass, 2004.

Bray, John. "Sacred Words and Earthly Powers: Christian Missionary Engagement with Tibet." *The Transactions of the Asiatic Society of Japan* 3 (2011) 93–118.

Bibliography

Carlsen, William D. *Tibet: In Search of a Miracle*. Nyack, NY: Nyack College, 1985.

Carlson, Robert D. *Breakthrough: The Story of Bob and Betty Ekvall*. Unpublished manuscript, 1980.

———. *Memories of Years Past*. Unpublished manuscript, 2008.

Conboy, Kenneth, and James Morrison. *The CIA's Secret War in Tibet*. Lawrence, KA: University of Kansas, 2002.

Ekvall, David P. *Outposts or Tibetan Border Sketches*. 1907. Reprint, N.p.: Forgotten Books, 2012.

Ekvall, Robert B. *Attaché Trek: 1947–1948*. Unpublished manuscript, n.d

———. *Dark Camps*. Unpublished manuscript, n.d.

———. *Faithful Echo*. New York: Twayne, 1960.

———. *Gateway to Tibet*. Harrisburg, PA: Christian Publications, 1938.

———. *God's Miracle*. New York: The Christian and Missionary Alliance, 1936.

———. *The Lama Knows: A Tibetan Legend Is Born*. New Delhi: Oxford & IBH, 1979.

———. *Tibetan Breakthrough*. Unpublished manuscript, 1973.

Ekvall, Robert B., and James Down. *Tibetan Pilgrimage*. Tokyo: Institute for the Study of the Languages and Cultures of Asia and Africa, 1987.

Galt, Howard S. *A Journey of Repatriates: Weihsien to New York*. Unpublished manuscript, 1943. http://www.weihsien-paintings.org/DonMenzi/ScrapBook/1943–9t012-AJourneyOfRepatriates.pdf.

Halberstam, David. *The Coldest Winter: America and the Korean War*. New York: Hyperion, 2007.

Hino, Shoun, and Toshihiro Wada. *Three Mountains and Seven Rivers*. Delhi: Motilal Banarsidass, 2004.

Jamieson, Margaret H. *The Way It Really Was*. Unpublished manuscript, 1981.

Jones, David P. *Cousins: Peacemakers on the Tibetan Border*. Newark, DE: PWO, 2021.

———. *Only Thibet*. Newark, DE: PWO, 2020.

King, Paul L. *Genuine Gold: The Cautiously Charismatic Story of the Early Christian and Missionary Alliance*. Tulsa, OK: Worth and Faith, 2007.

Laird, Thomas. *Into Tibet: The CIA's First Atomic Spy and His Secret Expedition to Lhasa*. New York: Grove, 2002.

Lary, Diana. *The Chinese People at War: Human Suffering and Social Transformation, 1937–1945*. New York: Cambridge University, 2010.

Patterson, George N. *Patterson of Tibet: Death Throes of a Nation*. San Diego, CA: ProMotion, 1998.

Philips, Lillian. *Kept- Vietnam Repatriation*. Self-published, 2020.
Research and Reference Material on the History of the C&MA in China. C&MA Archives, Vol. 1, 2020.
Rivard, Gene, ed. *Voices in Worship: Hymns of the Christian Life*. Camp Hill, PA: Christian Publications, 2003.
Smith, Felix. *China Pilot*. Washington, DC: Smithsonian Institution, 1995.
Smith, Ray H. *The China Experience*. Self-published, 2013.
Willard, W. Wyeth. *Fire on the Prairie: The Story of Wheaton College*. Wheaton, IL: Van Kampen, 1950.

Ekvall C.V.

Ekvall, Robert B. *Curriculum Vitae*, n.d.

Periodicals

The Alliance Weekly, January 20, 1923, 56.45.
The Alliance Weekly, February 2, 1924, 57.49.
The Alliance Weekly, February 8, 1941, 76.6.
The Alliance Weekly, April 19, 1941, 76.16.
Ekvall, Robert B. "The High-Pasturage Ones of Tibet Also Grow Old." *Proceedings of the American Philosophical Society* 124.6 (December 1980).
Omaha Gospel Tabernacle Bulletin. 1946.
Rockland County Sunday Journal News, Family 1D, May 8, 1975.

Interviews

Jones, David P. Interview with Marjorie Smith, Seattle WA, December 15, 2022.
Kerr, William. Interview with Robert Ekvall, Carbonado, WA, October 1, 1973.
Shuster, Robert. Interview 1 with Robert Ekvall, Wheaton College, Billy Graham Center Archives, October 11, 1979.
Shuster, Robert. Interview 2 with Robert Ekvall, Wheaton College, Billy Graham Center Archives, September 18, 1980.
Shuster, Robert. Interview 3 with Malcom Maurice Sawyer, Wheaton College, Billy Graham Center Archives, September 27, 1983.
Taylor, John. Interview with Robert Ekvall, May 1975, Nyack Cassette tape

Internet

"Tibetan Alphabet." https://allabouttibetanscript.wordpress.com/tibetan-alphabet.

Correspondence

Davey, James A., to Rev. Peter Nanfelt, C&MA, Nyack, NY, 1983.
Ekvall, Robert B. Ekvall, to W. W. Simpson, Minchow, Kansu, August 5, 1932.
Schaber, Elizabeth Gunn, to *Prairie Publications*, Denton, TX, November 18, 2004.

Emails

Bray, John, email to David Jones, "Status of Tibet," January 8, 2023.
Ekvall, Eric, email to Ray Smith, "Bob Ekvall Chronology," December 5, 2003.
Leeper, Arthur, email to David Jones, "Ekvall's Years at Washington," November 7, 2021.
Smith, Ray, email to David Jones, "Dialogue with Karin," October 25, 2022.

Made in United States
Troutdale, OR
08/09/2023

11925677R00153